THE "DEMON" SPOFFORTH

In fond memory of Malcolm

Alma Jundo

May 2013

'*The Demon*', Illustrated Sporting and Dramatic News 23 August 1884, p. 613 The knowing fast bowler.

THE DEMON

THE "DEMON" SPOFFORTH

Richard Cashman
Foreword by John Arlott

NSW PRESS

Contents

Published by
NEW SOUTH WALES UNIVERSITY PRESS
PO Box 1 Kensington NSW Australia 2033
Telephone (02) 697 3403   Fax (02) 398 3408

© Richard Cashman 1990

First published in 1990

National Library of Australia.
Cataloguing-in-Publication entry:

Cashman, Richard, 1940-
  The "Demon" Spofforth.

  Includes index.
  ISBN 0 86840 004 1.

  1. Spofforth, Frederick Robert, 1853-1926.
  2. Cricket players – Australia – Biography.
  I. Title.

796.358092

Design and production: Diane Quick
Printed by Southwood Press, Marrickville, NSW.

Foreword

John Arlott

F.R. Spofforth

The problem Richard Cashman has set himself — of writing history about a legend — is a difficult one. Fred (he preferred the use of that shortened Christian name to his baptismal Frederick) Spofforth was, and is, a cricketing legend. Probably, too, as Mr Cashman suggests, he was even more admired in England than in Australia. His match results explain that.

The danger in writing about a legend lies in the temptation to write legendary material. Mr Cashman has avoided that pitfall by working strictly professionally as the historian he is.

No authoritative biography of Spofforth exists; and no one now alive can speak with authority on the man in his great cricketing days. So Mr Cashman has gone to original documentary sources: thus we have contemporary material on his family background, youth, development and maturity as a player; and his retirement to England, where he continued to play cricket for Derbyshire and then the Hampstead Club until he was fifty-two. Then came the facts about his career as managing director of the Star Tea Company and Ridgways Ltd.

It seems not unreasonable to regard Spofforth in the same light as W G Grace as respectively the outstanding bowler and batsman of the late Victorian period. Incidentally, he seemed constantly to dismiss 'The Old Man'. Grace himself said that, however well be might be set, he was not sure that 'Spoff' would not bowl him out next ball.

What kind of bowler was he — whom they called 'The Demon Bowler'? Mr Cashman — and we — are fortunate that as fine and clear an analytical critic of the game as C B Fry found him an interesting study. He described him as 'The first naturally fast bowler to discover that the subtle variations of pace and deceptive tricks by a slow medium bowler like Alfred Shaw might, with advantage, be imitated and developed in conjunction with sheer speed'. The conclusion is that 'he may have bowled at the pace of Alec Bedser, for whom keepers sometimes stood up at the wickets'.

Fortunately, too, some of the action photographs of George Beldam have been discovered; they show Spofforth's impressive leap into the delivery stride.

The man himself, in the Beldam-Fry volume on *Great Bowlers*, distinguished between finger spin and cut — he appears to have been the first man to do so in print. He added, too, 'Not even members of my own side could tell when I was bowling fast, slow, or medium and that prince of wicket-keepers (Blackham) always received a sign of what to expect'.

Here, too, we can read of the great man's foibles. Jas Scott, for instance, wrote that he was 'very prone to impulsive exaggeration; a confirmed leg-puller'. He concluded: 'He often deviated from the truth for entertainment rather than deception'. We read, too, that on the occasion of the hundredth Test he slipped into the Australian dressing room and presented each of the Australian team members with an inscribed gold medal to mark the occasion.

He was undoubtedly quick-tempered, and not beyond indulging in fisticuffs with his contemporaries. That was usually in connection with his habit of cutting up the pitch in his follow-through. Spofforth himself brought evidence to show that he only used one nail and one spike — less than any other cricketer of his time, but he certainly damaged pitches. Neither was he any respecter of persons — 'I summed up the professor as an idiot on bowling'.

'The Demon' missed the first Test match because he would not play without Murdoch as wicketkeeper, but thereafter, for many years, Australia were never at full strength without him.

Mr Cashman produces all the relevant — and highly impressive — figures of the Demon bowler's career and he has researched with quite painstaking care to write a life story that someone should have done much earlier — if only because of his importance in his time and country. The author observes 'Australia needed heroes in the 1870s because there was an emerging sense of national worth, coupled with a deeply ingrained sense of inferiority'. Trickett (the oarsman) was their first national sporting hero, being the first Australian to win a world title. Spofforth, who was often linked with Trickett, was the second.

Just how good was he, this key figure in, among others, the Test match defeat of England which gave rise to the legend of The Ashes? When he died on 4 June 1926 at the age of seventy-two, *The Times* wrote: 'He was beyond question the greatest bowler of his generation'. J W Worrall, who played with him, observed 'There is no doubt that he was the greatest bowler of all time'. Mr Cashman has produced most impressive, indeed complete, evidence in support of that claim.

Acknowledgements

G.H. Bailey.

From the outset I received active encouragement and generous support from the grandchildren of Fred Spofforth: Derek Spofforth, Anita and Pamela Spofforth, Jean Vickery and John Youle. Their collections of photographs and memorabilia were a useful starting point. One indirect result of this biography has been the return of some important Spofforth memorabilia to Australia, generously donated to the Australian Gallery of Sport, Melbourne Cricket Club.

I would also like to thank John Arlott for writing a Foreword. Visiting John Arlott at Alderney was a highlight of a research trip to England. I also appreciated the assistance of Ric Finlay who answered many research queries and contributed Spofforth's career statistics.

Others to thank include: Robert L Arrowsmith, Tom Asquith, Jim Coldham, Philip Derriman, David Frith, Stephen Gibbs, Stephen Green, Rex Harcourt, Chris Harte, H S T L Hendry, Gerald Howat, Barbara Lee, Tom McCullough, David Montefiore, Geoffrey Moorhouse, Roger Page, Frank Peach, Ross Peacock, Clive Porter, Ken Powls, Peter Reynolds, John Shawcroft, Ric Sissons, Max Solling, J Neville Turner, Robert Trumble, Cliff Winning, Peter Wynne-Thomas.

Papers on Spofforth have been read at various sports history conferences. I would like to thank my colleagues of the Australian, British and North American societies for their comments.

Material on Fred Spofforth was collected from a wide range of insitutions including Archives of Sydney Grammar School, Australian Gallery of Sport, Battye Library of Western Australia, Borthwick Institute of Historical Research, Derbyshire Cricket Club, Guildhall Library, Hampstead Cricket Club, Humberside County Council, Lord's Cricket Library, Mitchell Library, National Australia Bank, National Library of New Zealand, New South Wales Cricket Association Library, Melbourne Cricket Club Library, New Zealand Society of Genealogists, University of Durham Department of Palaeography and Diplomatic, Westpac Archives.

Many illustrations were supplied by the Spofforth Family. Others are courtesy of David Frith, Melbourne Cricket Club and Jack Pollard. I would like to thank them and *The Bulletin* for permission to reproduce material.

Abbreviations

A.C.Bannerman.

HCC	Hampstead Cricket Club
JRAHS	*Journal of the Royal Australian Historical Society*
MCC	Marylebone Cricket Club
MCG	Melbourne Cricket Ground
Melbourne CC	Melbourne Cricket Club
NSWCA	New South Wales Cricket Association
SACA	South Australian Cricket Association
SCG	Sydney Cricket Ground
VCA	Victorian Cricketers' Association

A Day of Cricket Legend

H.F. Boyle

M *onday, 27 May 1878: Australia 41 and 1-12 defeated the Marylebone Cricket Club (MCC) 33 and 19 at Lord's*

As the youthful and inexperienced 1878 Australian team walked on to the hallowed turf at Lord's just after noon on Monday, 27 May, they could not have been all that confident. Conditions were decidedly in favour of the MCC, with the weather cold and showery. Dave Gregory had lost the toss and the MCC elected to bat on a wicket which was damp and heavy and unlikely to improve.

The small crowd of around 500 applauded the Australians enthusiastically as they emerged from the pavilion. Perhaps the spectators hoped to encourage the tourists, given their poor start to the tour. They had arrived in England only two weeks earlier on 13 May, and after a few days practice at Trent Bridge in what *Wisden* referred to as 'boisterous ungenial cricketing weather', had played just one match against the powerful Notts side. The Australians were easily defeated (by an innings and 14 runs) on a very sloppy wicket and in trying conditions. Fred Spofforth,[1] who found it difficult to hold a swollen and soft ball and to obtain a foothold on the slippery turf at Nottingham, was innocuous and relatively expensive (1-39) in a low-scoring game in which the English champion, medium-paced Alfred Shaw who bowled with pinpoint accuracy, returned 11-55. The Australians, inadequately clothed in light silk shirts and no undervests, shivered in the cold wind. Spofforth later wrote that after this match 'our confidence in ourselves [was] rudely shaken'.[2]

Left-arm medium-paced Frank Allan, who never quite lived up to his extravagant nickname of the 'Bowler of the Century', and right-arm medium-paced Harry Boyle opened the bowling on 27 May. The match began sensationally. A confident W G Grace dispatched Allan's first ball to the square leg boundary, but the next ball he was caught by Midwinter playing what Spofforth later referred to as a 'shocking bad stroke'.[3] It was a lucky break for the tourists as Allan did not bowl impressively on this day. Boyle then bowled Hampshire amateur, Booth, reducing the MCC, to 2-5 after two overs.

The Lancastrian A N 'Monkey' Hornby, a fine attacking batsman, then attempted to retrieve the situation by playing his strokes, and with another Hampshire amateur, Ridley, staged a recovery moving the score along to 25. On a treacherous pitch and in an era of low scoring, when a total over 100 was considered good, this was a not unpromising position. When Gregory turned to his third bowler, Fred Spofforth, the match was evenly poised.

We do not know what thoughts raced through Spofforth's mind when Gregory threw him the ball but Spofforth would have been well aware that this contest was significant for the 1878 Australians, a match of far greater importance than what are now recognised as the first two Tests, played in Melbourne in March 1877. Australia had the distinction of winning the very first Test by 45 runs (although it lost the second) but the victory, while very significant to the Australians, did not loom as large in the eyes of informed English opinion. The Australian success was achieved against a second-string English team of professionals which did not include many of the leading amateur batsmen, such as W G Grace and A N Hornby.

When the MCC picked a side which included most of the leading amateurs and professionals and, in the opinion of one English paper, *The Globe*, 'was as good a one as could be found to represent London and England, and probably nearly as good as the Club has ever turned out',[4] it was assumed as a matter of course that they would win. *Wisden* shared this view, describing the side as one of the strongest elevens ever to represent the MCC. Their attack was shouldered by Shaw and Morley, who had bested the Australian batsmen at Nottingham just seven days before, and most commentators believed that the English batsmen were a class above their colonial counterparts. The *Illustrated Sporting and Dramatic News*, commenting on 1 June 1878, after the game was played and lost, thought that the MCC XI 'had a blemish or two in strength' but had to admit that the side was 'a decidedly good one'.

Spofforth would also have realised that the future of the tour was very much in the balance on 27 May. A poor result at Lord's might prove disastrous.The tour started inauspiciously. There was not much enthusiasm in cricket circles for what Spofforth later referred to as 'our somewhat experimental tour', nor was there much press coverage when the team left Australia.

English officialdom, too, was rather dubious about the colonials: influential Surrey Secretary, Charles Alcock, commented later that:

the idea of a visit from an Australian team ... was at first treated as something of a joke by our English cricketers ... we were slow to accredit the Colonials with the extraordinary advance they had in reality made in the development of the sport which they had learned from English professors.[5]

There was no certainty that the tour would be a financial success.

Maybe Spofforth also sensed that his own bowling future was very much on the line. His pen portrait, published in the *Sydney Morning Herald*, hinted at great promise yet to be realised: 'F Spofforth — The fastest bowler in the world, perhaps; varies his pace with great success; pretty fair batsman and excellent field'.

On this occasion, as on so many others when the stakes were high, he moved quickly into gear. In just his second four-ball over Spofforth uprooted the leg stump of Hornby, who had batted attractively for 19 and was threatening to restore the MCC innings. He then disposed of the ungainly and stubborn Middlesex batsman, A J Webbe and W. Flowers in quick succession. The tail then collapsed like a house of cards with bowlers G G Hearne, Shaw and, the attacking amateur batsman, G F Vernon falling to Spofforth off successive balls to a great ovation. It was an unusual hat-trick, and the first of three he took in first-class cricket,[6] as Shaw and Vernon were both stumped by Murdoch. This suggests that the young tearaway bowler had the sense to reduce his pace and adapt his technique to the prevailing conditions. The MCC side was all out for just 33 runs, with six of the side failing to score. Spofforth returned the memorable figures of 23 balls, 3 maidens, 4 runs and 6 wickets. He was ably supported by Boyle, who bowled unchanged throughout the innings: 56 balls, 7 maidens, 14 runs, 3 wickets.

Although they must have been buoyed up by their

AUSTRALIA v MCC 1878
Lord's 27 May

MCC

First Innings		Second Innings	
*W G Grace c Midwinter b Allan	4	b Spofforth	0
A N Hornby b Spofforth	19	b Boyle	1
A Booth b Boyle	0	b Boyle	0
A Ridley c A Bannerman b Boyle	7	b Boyle	0
A J Webbe b Spofforth	1	b Spofforth	0
Wild† b Boyle	0	b Boyle	5
Flowers c and b Spofforth	0	b Boyle	11
G G Hearne b Spofforth	0	b Spofforth	0
Shaw st Murdoch b Spofforth	0	not out	2
G F Vernon st Murdoch b Spofforth	0	b Spofforth	0
Morley not out	1	c Horan b Boyle	0
Leg bye	1		
Total	**33**	Total	**19**

AUSTRALIA

First Innings		Second Innings	
C Bannerman c Hearne by Morley	0	b Shaw	1
W Midwinter c Wild b Shaw	10	not out	4
T Horan c Grace b Morley	4	not out	7
A Bannerman c Booth b Morley	0		
T Garrett c Ridley b Morley	6		
F Spofforth b Shaw	1		
D Gregory* b Shaw	0		
H Boyle c Wild b Morley	2		
W Murdoch† b Shaw	9		
F Allan c and b Shaw	6		
G Bailey not out	3		
Total	**41**	Total for 1 wicket	**12**

	O	M	R	W	O	M	R	W
AUSTRALIA								
F E Allan	9	4	14	1				
H F Boyle	14	7	14	3	8.1	6	3	6
F R Spofforth	5.3	3	4	6	9	2	16	4
ENGLAND								
Shaw	33.2	25	10	5	8	6	4	1
Morley	33	19	31	5	8	4	8	0

FALL OF WICKETS

Wkt	MCC	Aust	MCC	Aust
1st	4	0	0	1
2nd	5	11	0	
3rd	27	11	1	
4th	29	19	1	
5th	30	20	16	
6th	31	20	17	
7th	31	23	17	
8th	31	23	17	
9th	31	34	17	
10th	33	41	19	

* captain
† wicketkeeper

performance on the field, the match was far from over and the Australians struggled against the nagging accuracy of the English masters, Shaw and Morley. At one stage, when the Australians were 8-23, it looked unlikely that they would reach the MCC total, but some later order resistance built up the total to 41, a first-innings lead of just 8 runs.

News of the astonishing MCC collapse spread rapidly around the city and by the time W G Grace and Hornby appeared at the wickets for a second time, the crowd had built up considerably. By 4 p.m. there were 4,742 paying spectators, plus members. Many, who were stunned by the MCC first-innings collapse, believed that the home batsmen, and Grace in particular, would make amends the second time round.

Gregory opened the second-innings bowling with the wrecker of the first innings, Spofforth. With the very first ball of the innings he should have dismissed Grace, who was dropped behind by Murdoch. Grace had no time to savour this reprieve because he was bowled by the following ball, a 'beautiful breakback'.[7] The next ball also produced a wicket when Webbe was also bowled. Spofforth was bowling for a hat-trick for the second time in a day, but Booth managed to negotiate the last ball of the over and prevent any further disaster.

Boyle's first over was equally sensational: he bowled Booth on the second ball and Ridley on the fourth. When

Spofforth hit Hornby in the following over, and the batsman was forced to retire for one, five of the MCC batsmen were back in the pavilion (four out, one retired), with only one run on the board. The innings was clearly in tatters and the MCC never recovered from such a disastrous beginning. Hornby returned later in the innings, with W G as a runner, but he was barely able to stand and soon fell to Boyle. The MCC were dismissed for a paltry 19 runs, with seven batsmen recording ducks. The Australians hit off the 12 runs required for the loss of only one wicket for a commanding victory.

It was Boyle who took the bowling honours in the second innings, returning the impressive figures of 6-3 off 33 balls. Although Spofforth's figures in this innings were less impressive (he took 4-16 off 36 balls),[8] he made the initial critical breakthrough in that he accounted for Grace and softened up the strokeplayer, Hornby. More than forty years later Spofforth still savoured the second innings dismissal of Grace, though it is likely that the distance travelled by the bail and the extent of his reaction had increased as the years rolled by:

I began bowling to 'W G' (in the second innings) and Mr Murdoch, behind the wickets missed him off my first ball, much to my sorrow; but the next ball knocked his leg bail thirty yards, and I screamed out 'Bowled'.[9]

The match was all over in four and a half hours. 'The news spread like wildfire and created a sensation in London and throughout England.' *Punch* acclaimed the victory with a poem which included a celebrated pun:

The Australians came down like a wolf on the fold,
The Mary'bone Cracks for a trifle were bowled;
Our Grace before dinner was very soon done,
And our Grace after dinner did not get a run.[10]

Chastened by the experience, the MCC challenged the Australians to a return fixture on the following day but the visitors declined on the grounds that a rest day would be welcome, given the arduous tour timetable. Perhaps, too, they sensed that they had nothing to gain from a second encounter with the MCC.

The English press was at a loss to explain the defeat. The Australians, claimed the *Pall Mall Gazette*, had no 'consummate an all-rounder' of the stature of Grace, nor did they have 'such [a] master of the [bowling] craft' as Alfred Shaw. This is an interesting comment, which appeared the day after the match, the writer being unable to come to terms with the Australian victory because he believed the MCC was superior in batting and bowling. So explanations of defeat drew on the element of luck, the strangeness of the Australian bowling and the contemptible batting of the MCC. The *Pall Mall Gazette* scathingly said that batsmen 'who are so nervous or so out of practice that they cannot keep half-volleys out of their wickets have no right to appear in a first-class match'.[11] It took the English officials and the press a little time to realise that a charismatic champion, who was to help transform international cricket, had arrived.

If some English critics were uncertain about the interpretation of the MCC defeat, the tourists were well aware of the importance of their success. Spofforth later reflected on the significance of this victory:

I well remember that, when we left Lord's and returned to our hotel, we could scarcely realise our victory, and all the evening callers kept pouring in with congratulations. It is impossible to over-estimate the importance of this victory in its effect on the future matches and the destiny of Australian cricket, for another defeat like that at Nottingham might have made us lose heart, besides giving the English public a far lower idea of our merits than we deserved.[12]

The importance of the victory cannot be overestimated because it proved that the Australians could be worthy opposition to the leading English teams and, as *Sporting Life* correctly predicted on 29 May, 'the Australians are sure to draw wherever they go'. The victory assured that the 1878 tour would be a profitable venture and helped establish tours as an attractive and money-generating proposition. The victory also created the suspicion, which was proven to be a reality as the tour progressed, that while England might still have an edge in batting, the tourists' bowling and fielding were superior. Writing more than four decades later, no less an authority than Lord Hawke suggested that this was 'the game that marked the commencement of the modern era of cricket'.[13]

While Spofforth and Boyle both contributed to the

destruction of the MCC (Spofforth took 10-20 and Boyle 9-17), it was Spofforth who dominated the media limelight. Tom Horan later recalled that whenever their train stopped on the way to future engagements a crowd would gather round the carriage enquiring: 'which be Spoffen?'[14] Spofforth and Boyle are not remembered as a pair in the same way that Turner and Ferris, Gregory and McDonald and Lindwall and Miller were.

There were a number of reasons for this. Spofforth followed up his outstanding bowling of 27 May with many other fine performances and it soon became obvious that he was the spearhead of the 1878 tourists and the architect of their success. Medium-paced Boyle, whose outstanding feature was his 'unerring accuracy', was a useful foil who could tie up one end while the strike bowler operated from the other. It was Spofforth who created uncertainty in the mind of England's star batsman, W G Grace. Over the entire tour which took in North America and Australasia in addition to England, Spofforth took 764 wickets at 6.08 compared with Boyle who returned 331 wickets at 6.99.

Equally significant was the much-admired Spofforth spirit — he was a truly combative and colourful personality who always performed better the bigger and more difficult the occasion. There was also the Spofforth physical presence. Tall, gaunt, a wiry athlete who stood 6' 3" (190.5 cm) and seldom weighed much over 11 stone (70 kg), eminently recognisable, with a prominent nose, Spofforth seemed to reflect the popular physical notions of what the Devil looked like — hence the nickname 'The Demon'. Physically he was the perfect foil for his ebullient, overpowering and, in today's terms, overweight arch rival. W G Grace was the archetypal John Bull, whose ever-expanding girth and luxuriant facial growth reflected the expansionary mood of the Victorian era, a time when a thickening girth and a spreading empire were not frowned upon.

Spofforth represented the antithesis of this image. Writing in 1933, 'Country Vicar' (Rev. R L Hodgson) attested to the striking presence of Spofforth:

I met him (Spofforth) in after years, and he had rather the type of countenance which one associates with the Spirit of Evil in *Faust*. A long face, somewhat sardonic; piercing eyes; a hooked nose; and his hair, parted in the middle, giving the impression of horns. He was also immensely tall — lean, sinewy and loose-limbed — with long, thin arms; he would have looked the part of the stage-demon.[15]

The image of 'The Demon' was not, however, quite complete in 1878, because what Sir Compton Mackenzie later described as his 'heavy drooping moustache' had yet to establish itself. When Spofforth first played for his colony he had no moustache and no sidelevers but by the 1878 tour there were the beginnings of long sideburns and a thin

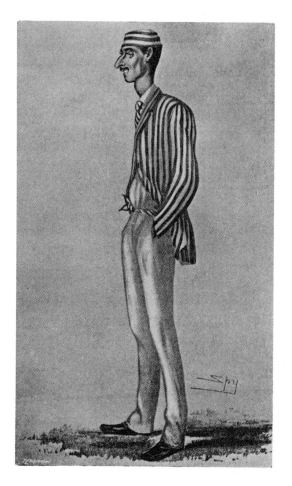

A famous Spy caricature (Vanity Fair *13 July 1878*)

moustache which did not protrude beyond his mouth. By 1882, at least, his moustache had thickened and widened, drooping below the mouth. In an era of remarkably impressive hirsute growths, 'his celebrated moustache ... stood out as a unique appendage'.[16] Later in life Spofforth was fond of boasting that his moustache measured a foot from tip to tip.[17]

Monday, 27 May 1878, was also noteworthy for Spofforth because 'it was then that I first earned my popular *sobriquet* — "the Demon"'. While there is evidence that the demon association was around before this date,[18] it is true that from this day on 'The Demon' became more widely, even universally, recognised simply because it was on this day that Spofforth's claim to international stardom was established. 'The Demon' superseded all other nicknames including 'The Windjammer', a Sydney term for a yorker given to him by a colonial journalist on the Australian preliminary section of the 1878 tour, and 'Loup',[19] which may have been Dave Gregory's contribution, but which had wide enough currency to appear in the Australian press in the 1870s. In fact 'The Demon' became so well known to the English public that his. nickname was still familiar decades after his death.[20] Spofforth's claim about the origin of his celebrated name, while not true in the literal sense, is not that wide of the mark.

Spofforth also won many accolades outside cricket circles. He quickly became England's favourite cricketer and was only the second cricketer to appear in a 'Spy' cartoon in the *Vanity Fair* series. W G Grace was the first, and his caricature, which appeared on 9 June 1877, was simply captioned 'Cricket'. Spofforth's caricature appeared on 13 July 1878; it was labelled 'The Demon' and became one of the most famous and much reproduced of the series.[21] The original sold for £2,200 in 1985.

The 'Spy' cartoon and the text demonstrated that English observers had been captivated sufficiently by the new cricket hero to want to claim him as one of their own. As a middle-class Australian who believed earnestly in Anglo-Australian ideals, Spofforth proved to be a convenient imperial symbol, who helped launch international cricket. Alongside the cartoon 'Jehu Junior' wrote that:

*The return of the conquering
heroes, Circular Quay, 1878.*
(Sydney Mail 30 November 1878)

*The adulation of the Sydney
crowd, November 1878.* (Sydney
Mail 30 November 1878)

Mr Spofforth is Australian by origin and breeding, yet like all the better kind of Australians, he is not distinguishable from an English gentleman. He comes, indeed, of a good English family . . . He is withal of excellent manners, modest and diffident, and has become a favourite with all who have known him in England.'[22]

Similar views appeared elsewhere after Spofforth's impressive bowling performance against the MCC. 'Spofforth is a Yorkshireman by extraction' whose 'father rode as straight as the best with the York and Ainsty [*sic*, Ainstey] and other hounds,' observed *Home News*, adding that it welcomed 'cheerfully' the 'prowess' of Spofforth and his colleagues because their success was proof that our 'flesh and blood' was 'not degenerating in those far-off lands.'[23]

When the Australian team steamed into Sydney on 25 November 1878 it was met by an enormous flotilla on the harbour and a crowd of 20,000 gathered at Circular Quay, about one-tenth of the city population, to greet the conquering heroes:

Every straight stick in the town, big enough to hold a flag, was elevated in some conspicuous position, and a flag of some sort was displayed therefrom. Nearly all the banks and mercantile establishments in the city were thus decorated. Besides these, in many places in Pitt and George streets, strings of flags and banners were extended from one side of the street to the other.[24]

Many other buildings were suitably decorated: the Glasgow Arms Hotel was covered with green boughs, as at Christmas time, and Punch's Hotel displayed a sign: 'Welcome home, our hero Cricketers'. The team was driven up George Street for a 'grand ceremony' at the Town Hall and the following day the *Sydney Morning Herald* devoted a long leader to the heroes, praising their campaign which had been 'a brilliant one, and their cricket, as a whole, has been of the highest order'. The result had been particularly satisfying because, prior to departure, 'it was predicted by some that although they were a strong team on an Australian ground, they would find themselves nowhere in England'. 'Others,' it added, 'reckoned' that the tourists would be 'quite unable to cope with' the strongest English elevens: Gloucestershire, Yorkshire, Surrey and Marylebone.

They were, as Fred Spofforth later recalled, the 'heroes of the hour':

I shall never forget the reception — an immense contrast to our cool 'send off'. Innumerable steamers and rowing boats came down to Port Jackson to meet us, and all the principal streets of the city were decorated with flags and flowers, while the old motto, 'Advance Australia!' seemed to span every corner. We were driven through the town by Mr Want, in a four-horse coach, and at the Town Hall the Mayor met us and presented an address of congratulation. At Melbourne and Adelaide the same thing was repeated.[25]

Spofforth never forgot the memorable day when he first startled the international cricket community. He made a reference to it on his deathbed when he commented to Lord Harris that 'I made my reputation in May'.

The Spofforths: Colonial Adventurers and Buccaneers

D. Gregory

N ot many Australian cricketers can trace their family back to 1066, nor can many point to an English village which bears the family name. Fred Spofforth's autobiographical essay began with the following comments:

My father came from a very old Yorkshire family, who fought for their country in 1066, and suffered defeat at the hands of William the Conqueror, and in consequence lost all their property, it being given to one William de Perci, to whom, I believe, one of the present dukes owes his inheritance.[1]

While the Spofforth family, including Fred, appear in Burke's *Family Records*, qualifying as a noble family with former claims to titles and lands, there are no direct links between them and the Saxon nobleman, Gamelbar, who fought against William the Conqueror. Nor is there any direct association between the Spofforth family and the Yorkshire village of Spofforth, which once was a focal point for a Saxon parish. All that can be said for certain is that Fred Spofforth's ancestors, like most other branches of the Spofforths, came from Yorkshire and may have had some indirect link with Gamelbar and the village of Spofforth.[2]

Fred Spofforth's father, Edward, was born in the market-town of Howden on 28 November 1805, in what used to be the south-eastern corner of Yorkshire but is now in Humberside County. Standing on a level plain in the midst of reclaimed marsh and fenland, Howden was a town with strong sporting traditions. It was most famous for its annual horse fair which, in 1807, was the largest in England and attracted the principal dealers from London and Edinburgh. During the week-long fair some 4,000 horses were put up for sale each day. Howden also had its three-day race meetings and agricultural shows which attracted crowds as large as 10,000 in the nineteenth century.[3]

Edward Spofforth was a keen horseman and not many years before he left for Australia in 1836, the artist W. Moore painted his portrait, revealing a young gentleman with top hat and a riding crop in a rustic setting.

The Spofforths were one of the established leading families of Howden. They had been in the town for a century at least and before that they had lived for at least another two centuries at East Thorpe, Malton, thirty miles to the north.[4] Rev. Ralph Spofforth, MA (Oxon.) was the Vicar of Howden (1798-1824) and he and a number of the Spofforth family were buried in a prominent chapel of the minster. Edward's father, Robert Spofforth Junior (1768-1830), and his grandfather Robert Spofforth Senior (1740-1827) were both attorneys at law. Robert, the second name of the Demon, was a favourite Spofforth name and for five generations the eldest son was named Robert. Both Roberts held important civil posts.[5] The Spofforth family, in addition, were substantial landowners in Howden and involved in land speculation in neighbouring areas of Yorkshire.[6]

It is puzzling why a second son from a privileged rural family chose to migrate to the infant penal colony of Western Australia, probably in 1836, when Edward Spofforth had just turned thirty. It is also curious as to why he should take up a chequered career as a traveller and businessman. There is a family story that Edward Spofforth was sent to the colonies to forget about his love for a first cousin. If it is true, the family action was successful because he did not marry until 1846 when he was past forty.

Undoubtedly Edward Spofforth must have had a great thirst for adventure; a cautious person would not have travelled to so many outposts of empire so frequently. Fred Spofforth as a youth read the popular adventure stories written by Captain Mayne Reid and James Fenimore Cooper, but his father's exploits and those of his mother's New Zealand ancestors were just as colourful and often as hair-raising as any of the fictional characters. In later years Fred Spofforth provided the following account of his father's eventful first years in Australia:

In 1829 my father went out to Australia with Captain Sterling (*sic*) (afterwards Sir James), and a second time with Sir George Grey (then Captain Grey) in 1836. This expedition lost nearly all their provisions, and over half the party died from thirst. Captain Grey was wounded, my father saving his life by shooting two blacks with a shot-gun.

Whether Edward Spofforth loved to garnish a good tale or family recollections became garbled over time, his first years in Australia, while eventful, were not quite as colourful as his son recounted. There is no record of his arriving with Sir James Stirling, founder of Western Australia, on the storeship *Parmelia* on 18 June 1829. Nor did he travel to Western Australia with Sir George Grey who did not arrive in the colony until 1837. Edward Spofforth's first arrival was on the *Addingham* on 31 July 1836.[7] Within two months he was on the move again, a passenger on the *True Love*, which set sail for Sydney on 4 September and arrived on 8 October. This set a pattern of extensive travel, presumably in the interests of new business opportunities, which he maintained throughout most of his life. During the three years when he was based in Western Australia, 1836-39, Edward Spofforth made 'several journeys' between Western Australia, New South Wales and England.[8]

The most likely explanation of the inconsistencies in his son's account is that Edward Spofforth did not travel to Perth with Captain Stirling but was present there during the second phase of his administration. The Stirling administration dated from June 1829–August 1832 and August 1834–December 1838.

Edward Spofforth did play a role in the rescue of Sir George Grey's party, but it was rather different from that recounted by his son. A party, led by Grey, left Fremantle on 17 February 1839 to explore the coast beyond Shark Bay but abandoned the mission after their whaleboats were wrecked. The strongest, including Grey, walked back to Perth leaving six debilitated men to head towards Moore River to wait for help. Two days after Grey reached Perth on 21 April a rescue party set out for Moore River: it was led by Lieutenant Mortimer of the 21st Regiment and included four soldiers and a civilian volunteer, Edward Spofforth. They arrived at Moore River two days later but none of Grey's party were there. For more than a week the rescue party split up and scoured the neighbourhood and finally Spofforth discovered the seaman, Charles Woods, 'lying on the beach, wrapped in his blanket, and fast asleep'. When he woke up, he was 'not a little delighted to recognise Mr Spofforth, whom he had seen before at Freemantle [sic]'. Owing to a shortage of provisions the rescue party had to return to Perth on 6 May.

Early the next morning, according to Grey, but possibly on 8 May,[9] another party set out headed by the Surveyor-

General, John Septimus Roe, four men, two native youths, five horses and Edward Spofforth 'who again volunteered his services'. After just one or two nights rest in Perth after a fortnight in the bush, Spofforth, 'my indefatigable companion', as Roe described him, was ready to again be in the forefront of the search. And he was with Roe when they discovered the remaining three survivors on 16 May.[10]

While Spofforth was involved in this rescue mission, he almost certainly was not a member of the expedition when Grey was wounded, nor did he save Grey's life by 'shooting two blacks with a shot-gun'. The ambush, which is described in detail in Grey's *Journals*, occurred on 11 February 1838, when Grey was exploring the Hanover Bay area in the north-west of Australia. The situation was particularly grim as Grey, separated from his main party, was ambushed by a large group of Aborigines. One of the two men with him was 'paralysed with fear'. When three spears struck him Grey felt 'giddy and faint' but did not lose his nerve and, after removing the spear from his wound, he collected himself and fired a volley which felled one of the Aborigines. The 'effect was electrical' and the Aborigines fled in panic.[11] Spofforth must have heard all the details of Grey's narrow escape when the party returned to Perth.

Somehow this story seems to have got woven into the already exotic tapestry of Spofforth family history. The most likely reason was that both father and son were fond of embellishing a good story. Jas Scott, a perceptive observer of Fred Spofforth, wrote that he was 'very prone to impulsive exaggeration' and 'a confirmed leg puller' who 'often deviated from the truth for entertainment, rather than deception'.[12] He became a polished raconteur in later life.

Not long after the rescue missions Edward Spofforth, forever it seems on the move, placed the following tantalisingly brief advertisement in the *Perth Gazette* of 28 September 1839:

ABOUT TO LEAVE THE COLONY
MR SPOFFORTH hereby gives notice, that he intends to leave the Colony by the first opportunity.

His movements from this point on are somewhat obscure. Fred Spofforth later recounted that 'some ten years later' (possibly 1845) his father 'visited New Zealand, and remained there till 1848, when he returned to England, having married in the meantime'. Edward Spofforth went there 'again with Captain Grey', who was Governor of New Zealand from November 1845 until 1854. Edward Spofforth married Anna McDonnell — he was 42[13] and she just 19 — on 23 April 1846 in the home of Anna's father at the Narrows (Rangiora) in the Hokianga area. He appears, however, to have settled in Australia a year earlier than the date nominated by his son: a Mr and Mrs Spofforth left Hokianga, New Zealand, on 15 December 1846 and arrived in Hobart on 6 January 1847. After spending fifteen days in Hobart, the couple left for Port Jackson on the barque *William Hyde*, arriving on 27 January in time for the birth of their first child, Anna Elizabeth, on 27 February. The couple's first son, Edward Arthur, was also born in Sydney on 26 October 1848.

From 1847 to 1851, and possibly later, Edward and Anna Spofforth and their young family lived at Broomoo House, on land on the sharp junction of Broadstairs Street (now Colgate Avenue) and St John Street, Balmain, a Sydney harbourside suburb. The building, which was built by John Gray in 1842–44, and still stands, was a nine-room cottage with a view over the bay and a 'large garden attached, well stocked with fruit trees, flowers and vegetables'.[14] Spofforth, who rented the cottage, was a model tenant and in 1848 Alexander Gray wrote to his brother, John, that Spofforth was the 'best tenant you have got — he keeps the place in good order, gives no trouble and pays the rent when due'. While John Gray was overseas Alexander approved structural changes for which Edward Spofforth provided the materials. Spofforth's 'labours' added to the value of the house.

The Spofforths, their two children and a servant, were passengers on the *Charlotte Jane* which left Sydney on 16 April 1851 bound for London. They returned to Sydney some time before 9 September 1853 when their second son, Frederick Robert, was born. They subsequently had two more daughters: Mary Beatrice was born in 1855, probably in New Zealand, and Adelaide Constance was born at Leichhardt, Sydney, on 6 February 1858.[15]

Just where the Spofforth family was living on 9 September 1853, is unknown but it was almost certainly in Balmain. Quite possibly they returned to Broomoo House and Fred Spofforth was born there. This was later suggested by S N Hogg, manager of the Bank of New South Wales at Balmain when Fred Spofforth worked there, but he was not always a reliable source.[16]

PR 222

Application   159725/85 A.

NEW SOUTH WALES

Registration of Births, Deaths and Marriages Act, 1973

BAPTISMS

Number	454 Vol. 39
CHILD	
Christian name	Frederick Robert
When born	9th September, 1853
Date of ceremony	28th December, 1853
Where ceremony performed	Parish of Balmain, in the County of Cumberland, New South Wales
Where registered	
PARENTS	
Father	Edward Spofforth
Mother	Anna Spofforth
Abode	Balmain
Quality or profession	Gentleman
Sponsors	
By whom the ceremony was performed	B. Lucas Watson

I,   Vernon Mark Bennett
hereby certify that the above is a true copy of particulars recorded in a register of
                                    Church of England   Baptisms kept by me

Issued at Sydney,
on   27th December, 1985

Principal Registrar

Since some authors have claimed a New Zealand birth and childhood for Fred Spofforth it is important to set the record straight and establish the extent of the New Zealand connection. Fred Spofforth's 'birth' certificate is actually a certificate of baptism, but it establishes clearly that he was born on 9 September 1853 and baptised on 28 December. Fred and his elder sister, Anna, and brother, Edward, were all baptised at St Mary's Church of England, Balmain. The abode of his father, who is listed as a gentleman, is given as Balmain so it seems almost certain that Fred was born there. So the claim, made by T W Reese, historian of New Zealand cricket, that 'the champion bowler was born close to Opononi, Hokianga Harbour, in North Auckland, and old residents still point out the house in which the future bowler was born' is not correct — a fact which Reese admitted in a later edition when J C Davis, editor of the Sydney *Referee*, established the Balmain birth of Fred Spofforth. But the myth of a New Zealand birth was a popular one, and after the first publication of the New Zealand claim Reese received 'letters from the Hokianga district' which 'confirmed the statement made, but claimed that the old home was in the Rawene parish and not in Opononi nearby'.[17]

The reason for the confusion is that the Spofforths moved back to New Zealand shortly after Fred Spofforth's birth and he later recorded that 'my first recollections are of New Zealand, when living at Hokianga'. While living there he 'received a good flogging at the hands of the parents of a boy I had been fighting', an experience 'I never forgot'. He also remembered that in those days 'the Maoris were always fighting the settlers, and we had to take great care and not wander too far from the homestead; but, this did not prevent me, at the instigation of my uncles, from stealing water-melons from the darkies underneath the leaves without being seen'.

Almost certainly the Spofforths spent less than five years in Hokianga because they were back in Sydney for the birth of Adelaide Constance on 6 February 1858. Never one to let the grass grow under his feet, Edward Spofforth was reported in the northern Queensland coastal town of Rockhampton in the spring of 1858. He was sent there by the Bank of New South Wales to open up a gold agency when several thousand diggers from Sydney and Melbourne sailed north on hearing the news of a possible new goldfield at nearby Canoona. He was dispatched to be the agent at a handsome salary of £400 per annum plus a commission of sixpence per ounce on gold purchases. Unfortunately the promise of gold was never realised and 'the agency was withdrawn before it started'.[18]

Spofforth received a posting to the New South Wales country town of Deniliquin on 14 February 1860 before returning to Head Office by 1863, if not before, when the family settled at 104 Derwent Street, Glebe, another Sydney harbourside suburb close to Balmain. During this period his salary was raised progressively from £300 to £350 per annum on 13 December 1861, when he was listed as 'Note signed & cancellation Clerk', and to £400 on 25 July 1862. On 2 June 1863 the Board resolved that 'Mr Edward Spofforth should sign the new Note Issue with his signature in full, and that the issue be now put in circulation'. As the Head of the Note Department Edward signed bank notes aggregating millions of pounds.

So Fred Spofforth almost certainly returned to the land of his birth by the age of five and remained there throughout his boyhood and adolescent years: he attended a cricket match at the Sydney Domain at the age of eight and was living in Glebe certainly by age ten if not before.

However, this was not the extent of the New Zealand connection. Edward Spofforth married into a prominent pioneering family, Anna McDonnell being the eldest child of Thomas McDonnell (1788-1864), timber trader, Additional British Resident in New Zealand and colourful and controversial character. Born in County Antrim, Ireland, McDonnell joined the Royal Navy in 1804 and then entered the East India Company in 1815 and commanded one of the Company's ships in the Red Sea: he travelled extensively in Siam, India, Egypt, China and the Islands — his daughter, Anna, was born 'at sea' during this period. In January 1831 he purchased the *Sir George Murray* and the Hokianga property and set sail for New Zealand. As a timber trader, shipyard owner and land speculator, he had a great capacity 'for keeping Hokianga on the boil' for the next few decades entering into disputes with his fellow settlers (who christened him 'McDiddle') and 'furious dissensions' with the Maori tribes. He was, according to another source, 'irascible and intolerant' and 'gross and autocratic' but became one of the most powerful Europeans in New Zealand in the 1830s. 'Through gross misrepresentation', he arranged to be appointed Additional British Resident while in England in 1834 and this 'greatly enhanced his muscle on the harbour' for the year he held this position.[19]. His 'conspicuous achievement' during this 'short and stormy' period was when he 'captured the crew of the schooner *Industry* and sent them in irons to Hobart to stand trial for the murder of their captain at sea'.

During the early 1830s 'his house and gardens were large and impressive, well fortified and protected with cannon, on the small flat-topped hill overlooking Horeke (harbour)'. But his expectations of vast profits collapsed when the New Zealand Company decided that Hokianga was unsuitable for settlement. 'After his house burnt down in 1842 in a suspicious fire, he gradually declined in power and wealth.' He died, at age 75, from the effects of a fall off a horse, in relative poverty and obscurity.[20]

Thomas' eldest son, Thomas the younger (1832–99), was 'a soldier of outstanding courage and intrepidity' who was awarded the New Zealand Cross, one of the rarest British decorations, for his outstanding gallantry in the Maori Wars at the Ngutu-o-te-Manu in Taranaki in 1868. After a serious reverse at Turuturumokai, McDonnell made plans for retaliation against the Maori stronghold at Te Ngutu-o-te-Manu and, in thick fog, he approached the position with a force of 350. After he forced the defenders to flee, 'McDonnell brilliantly extricated his men'.[21] Characters and adventurers abounded on both sides of the Spofforth family tree.

Marriage into the McDonnells may have also enhanced Fred Spofforth's cricketing genes because the McDonnells were related to the prominent cricketing family of Lord Lyttelton.[22] Just what the connection was is unclear. During the 1878 tour there was certainly no love lost between Spofforth and his relations as the Lytteltons were among his most doughty opponents. The Hon. Edward Lyttelton was the only Englishman to score a century against the Australians (113 for Middlesex) and the Hon. Alfred Lyttelton top-scored for Cambridge University (72) who easily beat the Australians.

There are only occasional glimpses into the Glebe life of Edward Spofforth. From 1863 he leased a cottage in the 48 acre (19.4 ha) Bishopthorpe Estate, Glebe. The house at 104 Derwent Street, set in a spacious street, was almost certainly designed by the prominent colonial architect, Edmund Blacket. 104 Derwent Street was typical of houses in the estate: it was a brick post-Gorgian cottage, double fronted with rectangular windows and squared veranda posts. The Spofforths lived at this address from 1863 to 1877.

A picture of Edward Spofforth which dates from his maturity contrasts with the 1828 Moore painting. The former hints at a relatively carefree, fresh-faced young gentleman from a protected and privileged environment. The latter suggests a more worldly-wise and quietly determined individual.

Spofforth apparently kept a revolver close to his bed because when his sleep was interrupted by the barking of dogs between 1 and 2 a.m. on 25 January 1864 he proceeded to his front door with a revolver in hand. What happened after that was recorded in the *Sydney Mail* of 30 January:

[He] went to the front door, on opening of which he saw a man crouching under his window in the yard which faces the house. The fellow slunk away towards the fence and though called on to stand was hurrying off when he found that he was discovered. When the young man was getting over the fence, Mr Spofforth pulled the trigger of his pistol, the contents of which lodged in the leg of the supposed burglar. Two constables were near on the spot, and the man was easily captured.

The burglar, it later transpired, was a known criminal who had been discharged only recently from Darlinghurst Gaol, after having served a five month sentence for felony.

The Spofforth home in Derwent Street was right opposite the Blacket-designed Church of St John the Evangelist (Church of England), Bishopthorpe. Edward Spofforth was a member of the St John's Church Building Fund Committee in 1868. His eldest daughter Anna Elizabeth married Charles Farquhar Clive at this church on 25 June 1874.

Fred Spofforth himself does not appear to have been a

particularly religious person though he was baptised, married and buried according to the rites of the Church of England. Fred Spofforth, according to his grand-daughter, Pamela, had psychic powers and sensed the death of a close relation even though physically far removed well before he actually knew of the event. Whether or not this power contributed to Spofforth's psychological domination of batsmen some cricket writers have suggested that this man of exceptional mental energy had some secret inner power.

It is not known whether Edward Spofforth was more than formally religious but he did believe in propriety and discipline and provided his son with the following advice, 'which I have never forgotten nor neglected', added Fred, when he took up his first job. The advice was:

1 Don't go into public houses and play billiards.
2 Always aim at something higher.
3 When placed in a responsible position, don't trust your fellow-creatures. (By this, he explained, if I was told to do anything, do it — don't get anyone else to do it for you; and if I was asked to report on anything, take no one's word things were correct — see yourself.)

Whether it was due to his father's advice or for other reasons, Fred Spofforth always had great self-discipline and inner direction. When it came to alcohol or pipe-smoking he was no abstainer, but the evidence available suggests that he drank in a moderate and disciplined fashion. His grand-daughters recall that he would pour a single peg of whisky and sit on it for a considerable time. Spofforth, from an early age it seems, had too many important things to do in life to succumb to the lures of alcohol or gamble away his money, though both were occupational hazards of star cricketers.

Edward Spofforth died at his Derwent Street home on 12 June 1875, living just long enough (presuming he was well enough) to see his son bowl against W G Grace in January 1874 and his Sydney intercolonial debut in March 1875. Compared to his grandfather, Robert Spofforth Senior, Edward Spofforth's probate — 'goods sworn at £1,000', which were left to his wife Anna — was comparatively modest. He was buried at Balmain Cemetery.

Many years later, in 1942, when what is now known as the Leichhardt Cemetery 'was about to be grassed over and turned into the present War Memorial Park', it was suggested, noted Philip Derriman, that the New South Wales Cricket Association, 'should erect a memorial to Spofforth there on the site of his father's grave'. 'It is odd,' added Derriman, 'that Australian cricket authorities never erected any kind of memorial to Spofforth, nor named anything after him.'[23] The suggestion was possibly not taken up because the association was short of funds during the war.

Fred Spofforth's mother also died in Australia, at the New South Wales country town of Molong on 28 October 1891 and was buried in the Church of England Cemetery there. His elder brother, Edward, and his three sisters lived out the rest of their lives in Australia. Fred Spofforth, then, was the only member of the family to make his way back to England and to reclaim his English inheritance.

The
Education of
a Fast Bowler

W. L. Murdoch

By early 1858 the Spofforths had moved back to Sydney, taking up residence 'on the outskirts of a large forest or bush' at Elswick (now Leichhardt), which was where they were living when Adelaide Constance was born on 6 February. 'Whenever a chance occurred,' Fred Spofforth recalled later, 'we used to wander in the bush, killing snakes and birds, of which there were plenty.' Inspired by adventure books, Fred Spofforth and his friends tried 'to emulate the chief characters, and so snakes when killed were always called scalps, and carefully recorded by us'.

Fred Spofforth did not go to school until approximately age eleven. Receiving instruction from his mother must have provided plenty of time for him to indulge in his passion for cricket, which began at a very early age: he later wrote that 'I don't remember quite when I first played cricket, but I cannot remember when I did not, so I suppose a bat and ball must have been put in my cradle'. Edward Spofforth encouraged his son, taking him to the Domain to see H H Stephenson's XI defeat the XXII of NSW on 29 January–1 February 1862. Fred Spofforth, who was only eight, later recalled that while 'almost all the Australian bowlers ... bowled underhand, a style generally prevalent in Sydney at the time', the 'chief feature of the game was that (Englishman) J Conway bowled G Wells with a round-arm delivery, the general impression being that the visitors were quite at home with that form of bowling'.[1]

Two years later Edward Spofforth again took his son to the Domain to watch George Parr's team and the young Spofforth later recalled seeing the two English bats, Carpenter and Hayward, occupy the crease for almost an entire day.[2] The bowling of the home side 'was still almost entirely under-hand'. Fred Spofforth was particularly impressed by the bowling of the roundarm bowler, the professional Tarrant of Cambridge:

It was a perfect treat to me to see him. His tremendous pace on the hard wickets positively scared the batsmen. When he hit the wicket, time after time the stumps were knocked completely out of the ground, and it was no uncommon thing for them to be split in pieces.

George Tarrant (1838–70) was known as 'Tear'em' because

he bowled at what contemporaries regarded as tremendous pace and seemed even faster because he tore into the wicket from a very long and lively run. 'Bowling round the wicket,' noted historian H S Altham, 'he worked in a good deal from the leg, and very often when he did not frighten a batsman out, he would bowl him off his legs.'[3] Short in stature (5' 7",170 cm) and slight in build (9 stone, 57.3 kg), his life was probably shortened by the great amount of work he did on the cricket field.[4]

From that point on Spofforth's 'great ambition was to bowl fast like Tarrant'. 'I myself,' he later recalled, 'never failed in my allegiance to Tarrant, and continued to bowl as fast as I knew how. People expostulated, and prophesied that I should overbowl myself; but, with the admiration of Tarrant before my eyes, I could not change my plan of campaign.' At school his 'great endeavour was to try to bowl faster'. When Spofforth entered the club cricket scene some years later he was known as a tearaway fast bowler, he bowled off an uncommonly long run for the time of sixteen paces. It was not a long run by modern standards though some fast bowlers, such as Alan Davidson (who ran fifteen paces) have generated pace off similar runs. While at school Spofforth acquired the nickname, 'Legs-and-Wings', due to the vigour and flurry of the final act of delivery of his 'catherine wheel' action which various commentators noted seemed all legs, arms and nose.

English cricket was far more advanced than colonial cricket in 1863–64. Parr's team did not lose a game on the entire tour of Australia and New Zealand (winning ten games and drawing six), even though the English XI was always pitched against sides of twice their number (XXIIs). The visit of Parr's team helped popularise roundarm bowling. Although roundarm had been tried in Sydney from the 1830s, many of the leading bowlers still bowled underhand. Spofforth later recalled that it took some time for some of the locals to 'discriminate between over-hand (roundarm) bowling and throwing' and 'it was no uncommon thing to find a bowler sending down under-hand and round-arm deliveries, impartially, in the same over'.

Spofforth grew up in a unique era in the evolution of bowling: at various stages of his career he bowled underhand, roundarm and overarm and at one stage he, unwittingly, was a thrower. As a young boy he first bowled underhand: 'When I was a boy at school — at the Glebe, near Sydney — I used to bowl underhand, as nearly everybody did at the time in Australia. It was very fast — almost as fast as my round — and generally a good length.' When the English team came over in 1862 Spofforth watched their bowlers 'very carefully' and came to the conclusion 'that the way to bowl like the Englishmen (roundarm) was to throw':

So I diligently practised, until I became quite an expert at this, and very fast. I met with considerable success too, for although it was explained to me that I had missed the idea, I felt sure I was right, and the umpires contented themselves with hinting a doubt.

He changed to a more correct roundarm action when 'two gentlemen, named Kelly and Read, were not satisfied with merely telling me that I was not doing the proper thing, but showed me what to do, and I at once set to work to bowl round'.[5] It was not an easy transition: 'I know that I myself had formed the habit of throwing and found much difficulty in breaking myself in to legitimate bowling'. Then some time after 1864 Spofforth again changed his style to overarm — or, maybe he gradually raised his arm from a position horizontal to one vertical to the body — for as an intercolonial and international player he was always noted for his very high and very straight, vertical to the body, arm action.

On 10 June 1864 the Marylebone Cricket Club made its celebrated decision to legalise overarm bowling. It is not known how long it took for the news to reach the colony, but normally there was a significant time lag, a matter of years, for some new technique to reach Australia and gain acceptance.

The initial colonial reaction to roundarm bowling illustrates both this time lag and a conservatism of colonial cricketers at this time. Although the laws of cricket were not altered until 1835, roundarm had been popular in England for a few years before this date. This technique was almost certainly introduced to the colony shortly after the Hardy brothers arrived in October 1832. Cambridge-educated J R Hardy, who joined the Australian Cricket Club, must have been puzzled by the hostile response, from within his own club, to roundarm. Club member, Thomas Stubbs, later complained that 'the novelty of straight-arm (roundarm) bowling and its 'atrocious' impertinence disunited, in one fell swoop, the whole group (club)'.[6] It was not until a decade later, in 1843, that the heresy of roundarm began to become the new orthodoxy when colonial-born Robert S Still reintroduced this technique to Sydney cricket.

One intriguing puzzle is why colonial bowling not only caught up with English practice in the 1870s, but actually seemed to steal a march on English fast bowling technique. The English cricketing public was quite startled by Spofforth's high overarm action in 1878.[7] The need to adapt bowling to Australian conditions was one possible reason for this innovation:

Hard, dry, unresponsive wickets and air lacking the humidity that caused the ball to move disconcertingly once it was propelled from about or above shoulder-height, forced Australian bowlers to bring their arms over higher and higher. Wills startled Australians in the 1860s, but in 1878 Spofforth in turn startled the English, the height of his arm being regarded as remarkable.[8]

An article, which appeared in the *Australasian* of 4 February 1871, suggested that colonial innovation had occurred over an extended period. The article, 'By an old member of the M.C.C.', began with a lament that 'the fair honest delivery of the olden time has vanished' and 'during the last half dozen years' almost every bowler has followed the 'pernicious example' of Wills and thrown the ball, with the 'windmill-throwing style' being prominent. He then added:

For all young bowlers now attempt one thing before others. That one thing is to get the arm up as high as possible, to 'bowl', in fact, over their heads. Pace and a high delivery is all that is sought after. As to variation of pace and length, and the attainment of precision, how many bowlers give such things a thought now? Given a hard, uneven ground, pace and bumpiness, and the thrower of the modern school argues thus of the batsman: 'If I cannot hit your wicket or make you give a chance soon, I'll hit you and hurt you if I can. I'll frighten you out.'

Because of the hardness of the pitch and the nature of the atmosphere, many colonial bowlers had forsaken line and length medium-pace bowling, teasing the batsmen out, for a new concept of bowling. Experimentation, including the high overarm action, was not a new development in 1878. Many Australian fast bowlers, like Spofforth, had long rejected the orthodoxy of the English masters, like Alfred Shaw, who bowled with the steadiness and guile of the slow bowler.

There are several other possible explanations why Australian bowling proceeded along different lines during the 1860s and 1870s. There had been so many changes in the craft of English bowling in previous decades, with the legalisation of roundarm in 1835 and overarm bowling in 1864, that English bowlers may have been content to rest on their laurels and to master the craft of accurate roundarm, or just above the shoulder, bowling. R L Arrowsmith has argued persuasively that 'for some years after 1864 most [English] bowling continued to be round-arm in type' though with the arm raised a little above the shoulder. Fred Morley bowled with a 'low action' and it seems that Alfred Shaw raised his arm 'very little above the shoulder'. It was probably significant, too, that it was not until the 1890s that the phrase 'over-arm' ousted 'round-arm'. Arrowsmith noted that Spofforth 'had an arm so high that it attracted considerable comment and this was no doubt partly responsible for the terror he inspired'.[9]

While colonial cricketers mostly followed and adapted English practice to suit Australian conditions, some innovations in colonial cricket began to emerge in the 1860s and 1870s. Perhaps the beginning of English tours to Australia provided greater incentive to improve and to attempt to match English cricketers. Changes occurred in the 1870s in colonial bowling, wicket-keeping and fielding techniques which cannot quite be explained in terms of adapting English practice to colonial conditions. One likely reason for innovation was that one colonial son had an exceptionally restless and enquiring mind which caused him to explore some of the possibilities of the law changes rather sooner than others.

Spofforth must have also drawn some inspiration from T W Wills (1835–80), a canny all-rounder who represented Victoria from 1857 to 1876. Wills, who introduced roundarm and overarm bowling into Victoria, was a heady bowler, with a great variety of pace and an ability to probe the weaknesses of batsmen. Perhaps he experimented too much because he was regularly accused of throwing the faster ball. Wills was involved in an incident in a Melbourne game which Spofforth would have appreciated since he too had some celebrated exchanges with umpires:

At a crucial stage of a Melbourne game Wills deliberately overstepped the crease when he bowled. He then made a mark with his foot to which he called the umpire's attention. The umpire, who had already no-balled Wills twice for throwing, fixed his eyes on the mark. The cunning Wills then scattered the stumps with a deliberate throw without being called.[10]

Spofforth was almost nine when a momentous event took place at the Oval on 27 August 1862 which was to alter significantly his future career as a cricketer. During the third over bowled by the Kent professional Edgar Willsher in the match Surrey versus England, the fastish left-armer was no-balled six times by umpire John Lillywhite, whereupon all the nine professionals walked off the ground and the game was not resumed until the following day when Lillywhite was replaced. The incident brought to a head a constitutional crisis — which was the point of the Lillywhite action — about the height of the bowling arm, which had been creeping up above shoulder height and led to the historic 1864 rule change. Law 10 was pruned substantially: it now declared that 'The ball must be bowled'. Overarm bowling was thus legalised.

By the time Fred Spofforth began attending Eglinton College, Glebe Point, he was already a mad-keen cricketer. Between the Spofforth house and the next house

was a grassy piece of level ground, part of Mother Martin's farm, and on that piece of ground Fred would practise bowling hour after hour. He would provide himself with as many balls as his pocket money would run to, and after he had bowled all of them at a single stump he would cross over and bowl them back again. He spent his holidays and spare time bowling — alone for the most part.[11]

There were other occasions when some of the neighbourhood boys joined him in practice. One of them recalled, many years later, playing 'so close' to the Spofforth family residence that 'sometimes the ball was driven into their yard, and dangerously near the windows of the house.'[12] Plenty of attention was lavished on providing good facilities on this field: 'we had no nets,' Spofforth later recalled, 'so when practising, placed a huge tree that took us days to remove behind our wicket, at a distance that would just make the ball rebound back close to us'.

From the early 1860s Spofforth attended a grammar school, Eglinton College, run by Anglican Rev. John Pendrill, MA, which operated at his residence, Eglinton House, Glebe Point. The college, opened in July 1858 and had an enrolment of seventy students by 1872.[13]

There is no record of whether Spofforth was a good student but 'at the various schools', he later recalled, 'I had a fairly good time, but regret to say I was the most mischievous boy in every school I went to, and if anything happened I was certain to be in it'. There was, however, one very revealing incident which occurred probably at Eglinton College:

Not far from one of the schools I went to there was a Roman Catholic College (probably Lyndhurst College), and every year a fight took place between us, one boy being chosen on each side. Much against my will I was the one selected, and although I tried hard to make the selectors alter their decision, they would not, and said I must fight. When the time came a spot was carefully selected, and I found my opponent quite two stone heavier. No sooner had we started than he rushed me, and landed a 'round-armer' on my nasal organ, completely breaking it, and the fight seemed all over; but I kept pegging away, and finally knocked him senseless. I had much the worst of it even then, as I carry the marks to this day.

Spofforth, even as a youth, refused to accept impending defeat.

For some reason which will forever remain obscure, Spofforth attended the Sydney Grammar School for just three months, from July to October 1869. The most likely reason for his short stay was that he turned sixteen in September 1869 and was old enough to emulate his father and brother and to join a bank. Spofforth first joined the England, Scotland and Australia Bank at a salary of £40 per year but later transferred to the Bank of New South Wales: he was 'probationer in 1875 at the age of 21 on a salary of

£150 per annum', at the head office, and 'spent most of his brief service in the note department until his resignation on 3 January 1880, when he was receiving £200'.

Even in his short time at Sydney Grammar, Spofforth made an impact on the cricket scene. His involvement was recorded in the *Sydneian* of August 1907:

As the organization (of cricket) was primitive much good material was overlooked in about 1870, a section became disgusted with the selection of the first and second teams and formed an XI from boys outside the pale, and handsomely defeated the first. F R Spofforth's bowling was the main cause of the defeat. This seems to prove that the best bowler the world has ever seen could not secure a place in the School XI.

When Spofforth achieved fame on the 1878 tour, Sydney Grammar, one of the great cricketing schools of Sydney,[14] acclaimed its uncapped old boy. The *Sydneian* published a poem, written by 'Our Special Cricketomaniac', on 'The Australian Cricketers in England', which included one verse dedicated to Spofforth:

And now let me tell
Of Spofforth as well —
The demon of bowlers they style him,
Took wickets just seven,
For runs but eleven —
After which, no one cared to revile him.[15]

Spofforth later recalled another event, which happened while he was at college in 1869,[16] when 'my drawing master, who was a keen cricketer, persuaded me to play with the eleven of the Newtown C C, one of the best clubs in Sydney, and one which contained some of the leading cricketers'. Spofforth was recognised initially as a batsman rather than a bowler:

I was asked to go in first, and carried my bat for 50. I continued with this club, and played successfully as a batsman, but was never asked to bowl until one day when, playing against the premier club (Alberts), our side had made only 65, whilst they had scored 60 for five wickets. S Jones, our captain, then gave me the ball, saying, 'Here, youngster, you have a try'... I had been gazing at him match after match, hoping to be asked. Success followed my efforts, and I clean bowled all five batsmen, the match ending in a tie.

My name was in everyone's mouth, and I read next day in the papers that a wonderful boy bowler had been discovered. At the end of the season I had secured both the batting and bowling averages.

The match in question took place on 11 November 1871 (and not 1869) when Newtown did in fact play a tie with the Albert club on the Newtown ground, each side scoring 65 runs. Spofforth performed well with the ball but the score-card, listed in the *Sydney Mail*, establishes clearly that Spofforth took only three wickets (two were bowled and one lbw), another two were run out and the other five wickets were taken by another bowler. It was yet another case of improving a good story. But there is no doubt that Spofforth came into cricket as a respected batsman and he did receive a badge at a Newtown picnic, held in October 1873, for heading the batting averages in the Newtown team for 1871–72. The Albert total of 65 included thirteen wides which, in all likelihood, was another contribution of this fast bowler.

It is the opinion of Jas Scott that Spofforth's performance as a batsman has been underestimated in that most of the critics have ventured to assert that he was 'of no great worth as a batsman'. Scott disagrees arguing that 'his worth in that respect merits some recognition' though he does admit Spofforth was 'undoubtedly a trifle inconsistent' and his motto seemed to be 'a short life and a merry one'.[17] There were occasional reminders that he could do better. Apart from his good season with Newtown there was an impressive performance for Albert Club against University on 1 and 8 November 1873, when he followed a 'clever' innings of 49 with a total of 93 in the second innings. 'Square Leg', the *Sydney Mail* cricket writer, noted that 'his batting has, I think, improved upon last season: he hits very freely, but not too recklessly, and his long reach gives him a great advantage in dealing with loose bowling'. As his bowling career blossomed outstanding performances with the bat became rarer though he did score 95 not out against East Sydney in April 1877, he batted well on the 1878 tour, and at times in later tours; he scored a Test 50 in 1885 and an astonishing 155 for Hampstead Cricket Club in 1893 suggested that he always had ability with the bat.

Spofforth could possibly have been a good all-rounder but it is difficult to avoid the conclusion that he did not develop his early batting talent. It was probably a calculated and shrewd decision, given that he was soon to carry so many responsibilities on his bowling shoulders, and a practice recommended by Alfred Shaw who advised that 'it is better not to bat too long when one soon has to bowl'.[18]

During his first season with the Newtown Club, Spofforth performed well with both bat and ball, frequently opening the bowling and batting. Intent on generating great pace he may well have been the bowler responsible for most of the fifteen wides in the match against the Warwick team at the Domain on 16 December 1871. Up until the 1878 tour there are a number of newspaper references to Spofforth as an erratic bowler. His brother, Edward, also played in the Newtown first team and joined Fred Spofforth subsequently in the Albert Club. Edward Spofforth, unlike his brother, was an ordinary cricketer who played the occasional game in the senior side for Newtown in 1871-72 and the Albert Club, 1872-74. During 1873-74 Edward Spofforth accumulated only fifteen runs in three innings though he won the badge for the highest batting average in the second eleven in 1872-73. He was, however, 'a keen gymnast and rugby footballer'.[19]

Newtown was Fred Spofforth's first senior club but before that the brothers had represented the Toxteth Second XI in 1869-70. Fred Spofforth performed well for the club both with the bat and the ball: against the Albert 3rd XI on 12 February 1870 at Toxteth Park he top scored (36 out of 107) and took six wickets. The Toxteth Cricket Club had been formed in 1863 and a ground had been turfed and levelled in May 1864 directly in front of Toxteth House, in the area now bounded by Glebe Point Road, Mansfield Street, Toxteth Road and Boyce Street. The inspiration for a private cricket ground came mainly from the Allen family, Sir George Wigram Allen, owner of Toxteth House, and his son, Reginald Charles Allen, who played one Test for Australia and who was the uncle of the English Test captain Gubby Allen. Fred Spofforth played cricket frequently on the Toxteth ground.

Cricket was taken very seriously in Glebe in the 1860s. Although it did not rank with the leading clubs of Sydney, the Toxteth Cricket Club published its own 'Rules and Bye-

Laws' in 1865. The 2nd Bye-Law related to 'practice days' which were 'Saturdays at Two, P.M., and every other afternoon at Four, P.M., shall be the regular Club Practice days. There shall be Morning Practice on Monday and Friday in each week, commencing at half-past Six, A.M.' Rule XXI directed that members playing for the Club 'shall appear in such uniform as may be selected by the Committee from time to time — any member transgressing this rule shall be subject to a fine of Two Shillings and Sixpence for each offence'.[20]

Before that Fred Spofforth played for Glebe Club. William Lloyd Murdoch (1854–1911), premier Australian bat and Test captain during much of the 1880s, whose cricket career was to become closely intertwined with Spofforth's, later recalled an early encounter with Spofforth, who had a fearsome bowling reputation even as a youngster. After the Balmain Club sent a challenge to play the Glebe Club, Murdoch could not sleep for nights before the match as 'he went to bed wondering whether he could possibly get any runs against this bowler Spofforth of whom the other side were boasting'.[21]

Fred and Edward Spofforth joined one of the premier clubs in Sydney, Albert, in the 1872–73 season. Fred Spofforth, who at this age had a mind of his own and never left anything to chance, later described the circumstances which took him from Newtown and how he convinced his father to support this move:

In Sydney at this time there were only two real cricket grounds — the 'Domain' and the 'Albert' — and the pitches on these two were really good. But it was while playing on the former (for Newtown) that I received my first reverse. I tried all day, meeting with little success, and, in spite of what my friends said, I knew the wickets were *too* good for me. Later, while playing on the latter ground, I again met with little success. I then consulted my father, and told him I could never learn to bowl properly without being a member of the club that had the best ground; so he got me elected, and paid my subscription, and I spent all my spare time practising, finally being chosen to play with the second eleven.

Formed in 1852, the Albert Club had become one of the most powerful clubs in Sydney by the 1870s, along with Warwick, University and East Sydney. The Albert Ground, in the heart of Redfern, on the eastern side of Elizabeth Street, was opened on 29 October 1864. The first enclosed ground in Sydney, it had a 'big grandstand and a pavilion with a veranda running around three sides of it' and a row of trees planted by the English cricketers touring under George Parr in 1863–64.[22] For a brief period in the 1870s the Albert Ground was the site for intercolonial and international matches until it was superseded by the Sydney Cricket Ground in 1878. The matted couch grass in the square, which favoured bowlers rather than batsmen, was criticised frequently by Victorians who preferred the fast wicket of the MCG to the notorious Albert turf which was described variously as 'treacherous', 'slow hanging', 'soft' and 'dead'. Cricketers of the Albert Club wore a white cap and trousers and a blue shirt. The Albert Club, when Spofforth joined it, organised three elevens and had a membership of over a hundred players and supporters.

Club cricket, like so much else in the cricket world, was becoming more organised and more standardised in this era. Regular competition and team championships emerged slowly. From the 1850s, the Albert Cricket Club replaced the Australian Cricket Club as the pace-setter in Sydney club cricket. Australian represented the older prototype of the pub-based club which played an occasional game for a stake. The most important change in Sydney club cricket — the introduction of electorate-based (suburban) clubs in 1891 — was a long way off.

Spofforth achieved immediate success with the Albert Club and recalled that after beginning the season with the seconds he was promoted to the seniors 'after half the season was over' and had the 'great satisfaction of securing the best batting and bowling averages in both elevens and receiving gold medals for the senior'. Spofforth's recollection is again a little faulty. He did win both the batting (23.7) and bowling averages (8.29) in 1873–74 but in the previous season he only achieved the bowling average; the batting average in the firsts was won by C N J Oliver. Edward Spofforth won the second eleven batting average.

Fred Spofforth's most outstanding performance of the year was when he wreaked havoc against the Sydney University side, clean bowling seven batsmen and finishing with 9 wickets for 10 runs (62 balls, 5 maiden overs). 'Such a performance,' commented the *Sydney Mail* on 8 February, 'is not often equalled, but the panic caused by Spofforth's success at the outset doubtless had something to do with it.' The University side included Joseph Coates, captain of New South Wales in Spofforth's first intercolonial, on 1 February 1873. The one University player whom Spofforth did not dismiss in that performance was Edmund Barton, a future Prime Minister of Australia. When New South Wales again lost to Victoria in February 1873, the sixth straight loss in seven years, Spofforth was not present although many thought he should have been in the team: the *Sydney Mail* noted that 'some people wanted an explanation' why Spofforth and A Docker had not been selected.[23]

In the 1873-74 season Spofforth had another outstanding year with the ball, taking 91 wickets at an average of 8.75 and scoring well with the bat. His performances are included in the following table:

	Balls	Maidens	Runs	Wickets	Batting
vs University (November)					49 and 93 not out
vs Warwick (November)	90	3	34	6	52
	75	3	30	5	
vs E. Sydney (February)	114	3	54	6	
	77	4	15	6	
vs Warwick (March)	107	2	48	7	
	183	3	73	8	

With Spofforth at the helm the Albert Club proved virtually unbeatable and won the cup in three consecutive seasons from 1871.

During 1873-74 the third English team, captained by W G Grace, arrived in Australia. It was the first English tour for ten years and provided Spofforth with his first opportunity to play for his colony. He was selected to play for the New South Wales XVIII against the tourists on 24-27 January 1874.

Spofforth was fortunate to arrive at a very significant stage in the history of New South Wales and Australian cricket and a formative phase in the formation of Australian sport. After winning the first two intercolonial contests against Victoria in 1856 and 1857, New South Wales had had a poor record, winning only two games to Victoria's twelve. When Spofforth made his intercolonial debut in December 1874 his colony had suffered six straight losses and a losing streak which stretched back to 1866. In 1874–75, competition between New South Wales and Victoria was expanded to two matches per season, thus assuring an annual match in each city.

Intercolonial games had become major social and sporting events which drew very large crowds of up to 15,000 spectators per day. With little competition from international matches, intercolonials created an enormous amount of interest and everyone of note attended from the Governor down. Businesses closed early on the day of the match. When a match was played in Melbourne crowds gathered outside the *Herald* office and Punch's Hotel to read the scores on telegrams posted; during a Sydney match in March 1876 'there were well-got-up lists of players' in shop-front windows 'with the odds against each one given, with the backer of the top score winning'.[24] 'Square Leg' of the *Sydney Mail* noted on 26 December 1875 that 'the excitement in Sydney during the progress of the Intercolonial match was intense, and even the international matches must dwindle into insignificance beside the interest which was centered in the contest (NSW vs Vic.)'. At this time intercolonial rivalry was stronger than international rivalry and intercolonials attracted bigger crowds than the internationals until the 1890s.

The first cricket club in Sydney, the Australian, had been formed in 1826. However, inter-club matches in the 1830s were played on an occasional basis, to settle a wager, and were not part of some ongoing competition. It was not until the 1840s and 1850s that clubs began to play in more regular competitions. Intercolonial competition, dating from 1856 in New South Wales, was a great boost for cricket.

Australian cricket, Spofforth later recalled, was both crude and primitive until the 1860s:

In those days there was no such thing as a professional cricketer in Australia. Artisans and gentlemen played together in all the clubs, and if the ordinary boots got slippery, off they came; even socks were discarded by the artisan, if it was thought to add to the comfort. Matches were only arranged for on Saturdays and public holidays, the game usually beginning at half-past two. Very few players possessed bats of their own; a stock of materials was kept in a huge canvas bag at the house of the secretary of the club, or at some member's house near the ground.

Spofforth also came to the fore at a crucial era in Australian sport. The transition was not a sudden one and the apparatus of modern sport emerged progressively from the 1820s: more regular club competition; an organising bureaucracy; enclosed grounds which permitted gate-money and the emergence of the professional cricketer; the development of rules; technological improvements and the rise of the sporting press.

Cricket in particular, and sport in general, achieved very little press coverage until the 1830s. The first newspapers in the colony were small in size and print run and expensive to purchase. Some of the editors did not consider cricket worth reporting. With the growth of a freer press by the 1830s there was a much wider range of newspapers which were larger in size and in the variety of subjects covered. From this time there were regular match advertisements, scores and lengthy reports of cricket matches. It did not take long for the potential appeal of sport to be recognised and the colony's first sporting paper, *Bell's Life in Sydney and Sporting Chronicle*, began in 1845. With each subsequent decade the public appetite was whetted still further with more and more press coverage including regular gossip columns, lithographs and eventually actual photographs. The cheaper press of the second half of the nineteenth century helped create an expanding audience for sport, and the rise of mass-circulation newspapers in the 1870s and 1880s tapped a wider working-class readership and made sport an even more saleable commodity.

There was, in addition, a demand for heroes to express a growing sense of national purpose in the 1870s. If the experience of plucky sculler Dick Green was any guide this was a relatively new phenomenon. Green was a three-times unlucky loser in world championship contests on the Thames and his losses could have provided the stuff of sporting legends; on two occasions there was considerable evidence that he had been poisoned when he threw up his hands and collapsed during the race and on the third occasion the opposition support boat ran into him. *Bell's Life in Sydney* 'regularly did its best to stir up the "natives" ' but 'the spirit of the times was not with' this proto-nationalism. Very few people turned up to honour Green for a Sydney banquet held on 11 January 1864 when he returned.[25]

By the 1870s, however, professional sculling had become the first great spectator sport. It had been big business from the 1850s, when large crowds lined Parramatta River or crowded on ferries to follow races. Much money changed hands and promoters vied with each other to put up large stakes. The press enhanced the scullers' status as popular idols, reporting races at great length, delving into training schedules and feeding the latest waterways gossip to an eager public. The occupations of scullers, who were blacksmiths, quarrymen and timber-fellers, added to their almost superhuman image. They were depicted in the press as fine specimens of Australian manhood, full of manly power and vigour. They were news wherever they went and they were frequently pestered by persons hanging round their training camps.

Poet 'Banjo' Paterson later captured some of the public adulation for these sporting demigods:

Stalking with their trainers through the little town of Gladesville, they were like Kingsley's Gladiators stalking through the degenerate Romans. Elias Laycock could eat a dozen eggs for breakfast; Maclean, an axe-man from the northern rivers, could take an axe in either hand, and fell any tree without stopping for rest; Searle had an extra rib on either side of his body, or so his opponents implicitly believed.[26]

A Sydney-born quarryman, the sculler Ned Trickett (1851–1916), was Australia's first sporting hero. When he won the world championship on the Thames on 27 June 1876, beating Englishman James Sadler, the 'excitement in Sydney was intense' and on his return to Sydney in November an estimated crowd of 20,000 greeted him at Circular Quay: 'bands and bigwigs were in abundance, and eager hands pushed horses aside so as to pull the hero's carriage through Sydney streets to Punch's Hotel, where he addressed the multitude and was "cheered to the echo" '. The result 'staggered and exhilarated Australians' and 'when the news reached Sydney the city exploded into celebration, and a purse of £850 was quickly collected for the hero's return'.[27]

Improved communication between the colonies and with England was another factor in the elevation of heroes. When Trickett rowed against Canadian Ned Hanlan on the Thames in 1880, and lost his title, 'Sydney kept awake all night awaiting the arrival of a certain telegram, which, coming, sent a sigh and a shudder through the city'.[28] It became common in this period for large crowds to not only attend sculling matches in Australia to fete the heroes, but also to inundate telegraph offices whenever overseas matches were held.

Spofforth, who was often linked with Trickett, was Australia's second national sporting hero, and both men achieved their fame in the lion's den itself, which added to their importance in the colonial mind.

Australia needed heroes in the 1870s because the emerging sense of national worth was coupled with a deeply ingrained sense of inferiority. This stemmed partly from a sense of shame for a convict past and partly from ideas, emanating from Social Darwinism, that British 'blood' may have deteriorated in an alien environment of the Antipodes.[29] Sporting heroes were important to colonial society because there were few alternative hero figures. English society, on the other hand, had a much larger pool of heroes: military figures (General Gordon); missionary-explorers (David Livingstone); nurses (Florence Nightingale); music-hall stars (Marie Lloyd); and Queen Victoria herself. Much then was demanded of Australian sporting heroes and they were often placed high on the pedestal by an adoring sporting public. Heroes, and later heroines, also helped to sell ever-increasing numbers of mass-circulation and specialist sporting newspapers which were appearing in increasing numbers at this time.

When Trickett again set off to battle the Canadian, Ned Hanlan, for the 'championship of the world' on the Thames

in 1880, *The Bulletin* of 29 May 1880 dwelt on the reasons
why sporting heroes were so important to colonial society:

The big nuggets of Ballarat and the Turon, the golden days of
Tambaroora, the fascinating tales of the native wealth possessed by
this sunny land, did much for Australia; but TRICKETT'S second victory
of the Thames would — we hope we may say will — put the names of
TRICKETT and of N.S. Wales into every British mouth and prove a
grander national advertisment than all the lectures of immigration-
agents and agents-general, from Mrs CHISHOLM down to Mr FORSTER
and SIR ARCHIBALD MICHIE But we do regard the contest for the
championship in a merely material light, for we all feel that British
pride in the physical powers of our race which has prompted many a
glorious martial deed.

Spofforth then emerged on the cricket scene at a
particularly propitious time. But it took a shrewd and
determined individual to make the most of his opportunities
and unique talents. There were others, such as Charles
Bannerman and Edwin Evans, who failed to grab the main
chance as Fred Spofforth did.

Intercolonial
and
International
Cricketer

T.W. Garrett

The visit of the English team in 1873-74, the first for a decade, created great public interest particularly because the team included W G Grace. Spofforth later recalled that 'it was this experience that raised Australian cricket for the first time to a first-class level'. Grace's team, Spofforth added, was a 'strong combination' but 'during the ten years that had elapsed since Parr's team was over, Australian cricket had sufficiently developed to be able to show good fight to their powerful opponents'. One reason for the improvement in colonial cricket was that the English professionals, Charles Lawrence and William Caffyn, tourists in the early 1860s, had remained in Australia to coach the local players. No one, however, watched the tourists more intently than Spofforth, who had just turned twenty, and was on the threshold of his first-class career.

Spofforth was able to study the tourists at first hand, for he played for the New South Wales XVIII against the visitors on 24-27 January 1874 and was greatly intrigued by the accurate medium-paced roundarm bowling of James South-erton and James Lillywhite. 'Square Leg', of the *Sydney Mail*, was also impressed by the performance of the English bowlers:

The advantage of medium pace bowling was proved in a marked manner in each International match. Constant practice and experience enabled Southerton and Lillywhite to place a ball exactly where they pleased, and the field was posted to suit them. There was no loose bowling, and the men appeared to keep going for a week. Most of our fast bowlers become knocked up in half an hour.[1]

This English style of bowling was brought to its peak by the master craftsman Alfred Shaw, who toured Australia in 1876-77 and whose bowling, along with that of Lillywhite and Southerton, was a 'revelation' to the youthful Spofforth. According to W G Grace, Shaw had

an easy round-arm action, kept an astonishing good length, varied his pace from slow to medium and made the ball break slightly in both directions. He seldom bowled two similar balls in an over, and he worked with his head as much as his body.[2]

Spofforth was so impressed by the nagging accuracy and impeccable control of the Englishmen that he 'wavered between the two styles' — the pace of Tarrant and the control of Southerton, Lillywhite and Shaw — but soon realised that 'I didn't see any reason why I shouldn't copy them as well as Tarrant, and try and combine all three (Tarrant, Southerton and Shaw)':

I very soon found that variation of pace was the most important thing of all, and with the object of disguising it I tried various experiments until I gradually found what seemed to me a style which was best for disguise as well as for ease.[3]

While Spofforth may have recognised the advantage of blending pace and guile in 1874, he did not achieve his ambition overnight. It was not until the 1878 tour, when he bowled day in and day out for fifteen months, that he mastered his craft. 'Square Leg' noted in the *Sydney Mail* of 4 April 1874 that, while Spofforth bowled quicker than most other bowlers, he bowled his share of loose deliveries:

It requires a quick eye and smart play to meet Spofforth's bowling, and, to my mind, Sheridan is one of the few men who really judge the ball. He comes down on it like lightning at the proper time, but, as a rule, the players opposed to the 'redoubtable' play at a ball a second or two too late, and that way allow the loose ones (and Spofforth bowls a good many) to go unpunished, while the well-pitched straight balls scatter the timbers ... With the ordinary medium-pace bowling they (the batsmen) are pretty well at home, but the play must necessarily be very smart in order to get a bat in front of Spofforth's 'eye-openers' in the nick of time.

While Spofforth was keen to learn from the best English bowlers of the day and to adapt and develop their various styles, he did more than imitate English practice. His keen mind led him to reflect deeply on the movement of a cricket ball in the air. At the time this was referred to as 'curl', 'swerve' and 'air break' rather than 'swing'. Spofforth analysed the bowling of Frank Allan, who was 'the greatest swerver I ever saw', and he also studied closely the baseball swerve. During these experiments Spofforth even wrote to a 'very learned University Professor' asking him for an explanation of swerving and was not impressed when the Professor stated that 'it was impossible'. Spofforth's reference to a subsequent meeting, written many years later, suggests that this seventeen-year-old was not overawed by a professor:

I consulted him … and wanted him to witness what he called an optical illusion, but although seemingly interested, he told me it was impossible. However (being only seventeen at this time), I summed up the Professor as an idiot on bowling, and persevered, and discovered that there were three ways of swerving — right, left and vertical.[4]

Because a cricket ball then was very different from the modern ball — it was larger, less glossy and the seam was not raised as much — it swung far less than the modern ball. Spofforth found 'vertical curl' more productive than the modern practice of horizontal movement, and when the practice of swing bowling emerged in the 1900s he was sceptical of the practice. Spofforth achieved movement from left-to-right by cutting the ball off the wicket, bowling off-cutters.

While English bowling technique was analysed and copied by Australian bowlers, the high overarm action of the local bowlers does not seem to have interested the visitors. It is rather puzzling why this new action did not create any impression until 1878, as the English bowlers had many opportunities to observe it in the 1870s. There are two likely reasons. While there were many colonial high overarm bowlers in the 1870s, it was not until the 1878 tour that its potential was fully developed. English bowlers regarded their accurate, medium-paced just-above-the-shoulder bowling as the superior technique. Another reason was that English cricketers, born and bred on the superiority of English cricket, took limited notice of an evolving colonial style of bowling.

There is a delightful story of the supposed first encounter between the champion batsman, W G Grace, then at the height of his powers, and the future bowling champion, on the threshold of his career, at the nets in Melbourne. According to Spofforth this meeting occurred when he 'could not resist the temptation' of making a special trip from Tasmania to Melbourne to watch the first match of the tour, the visitors versus a Victorian XVIII (26–29 December 1873) and recounted that he was 'on the whole … disappointed with the visitors', though Grace played 'a grand innings — one's fullest expectations were realised'. The story, it should be noted, was not recounted until forty-five years after the event, so Spofforth's account, submitted for the *Memorial Biography of Dr W G Grace*, may have improved over the years:

I had a lark with the Old Man (Grace) at the nets. In those days, though I stood six feet three inches, I only weighed ten stone six. But I could bowl faster than any man in the world. W G was at the nets at Melbourne and I lolled up two or three balls in a funny slow way. Two or three of those round (me) asked: 'What's the matter with you, Spoff?' I replied: 'I am going to have a rise out of that W G' Suddenly I sent him down one of my very fastest. He lifted his bat half up in his characteristic way, but down went his off stump, and he called out in his quick fashion when not liking anything: 'Where did that come from? Who bowled that?' But I slipped away, having done my job.[5]

Tasmanian historian Ric Finlay has retraced Spofforth's trip to Tasmania and his careful research has thrown considerable doubt on whether this meeting ever took place in Melbourne. Fred and Edward Spofforth left Sydney on the SS *City of Sydney* on 15 December 1873 and arrived at Hobart on 18 December. They did not call in at Melbourne on the way. The brothers appear to have come to Tasmania on a holiday: they were described in the *Mercury* of 29 December as 'visitors from Sydney'. Both played in a match on 27 December and in a single-wicket match on 30 December when they defeated two local cricketers by 11 runs to 7 with a second game unfinished. The Spofforths boarded the SS *Derwent* at Launceston on 12 January and arrived at Melbourne the next day, by which time the Englishmen had long since left. The brothers arrived back in Sydney on 17 January on the SS *City of Adelaide*. The Spofforth brothers were in Tasmania for the whole period from 18 December 1873 to 12 January 1874.

Given that Spofforth's version of the supposed first encounter did not appear until 1919, it is not surprising that some dates and places may have been confused. Perhaps the young fast bowler and the Grand Old Man had this encounter just prior to the match between the tourists and the New South Wales XVIII.

Spofforth did not have to wait long to meet Grace on the field of play as he was selected for the New South Wales XVIII, along with another promising colt, Charles Bannerman, to play the Englishmen at the Albert Ground on 24-27

January 1874. Spofforth was in good form with both bat and ball: in November he had recorded scores of 49 and 93 against University and 52 against Warwick, and in the latter game he took 11 wickets for 64 runs.

With government offices closed on Saturday, 24 January, a large crowd of 10-12,000 turned up. It must have been an intense disappointment to Spofforth not to get a bowl in the English first innings: Coates, Tindall and Faithfull dismissed the visitors for 92 in the first innings. Spofforth failed with the bat in both innings, scoring 5 and 1, but he had the consolation of taking 2-16 off 52 balls in the second innings, coming on as the fifth bowler. New South Wales, thanks to an innings of 32 by Dave Gregory, won the match by 8 wickets. W G Grace commented later that Spofforth was a 'promising youngster' and a 'very fair bowler' but he remembered Spofforth more as a 'long, thin fellow standing in the deep field and throwing in so terribly hard'. Grace added that 'I had little thought that he was to stir the whole cricket world some four years later'.[6]

Not yet a member of the New South Wales XI, Spofforth was not selected in the combined New South Wales-Victorian XV which were beaten comfortably by the visitors by 218 runs. Charles Bannerman, who first played for New South Wales in March 1871, was picked for this match but scored only 9 and 0. Bannerman, who had scored a useful 32 runs, with five fours, on his intercolonial debut, had failed in his next five innings for his colony.

The following season did not start well for Spofforth. He had a series of low scores with the bat, including a pair against University, where he returned only 1-44 off 108 balls and 0-18 off 66 balls though he did have the satisfaction of taking a 'great left-hand catch' near the pavilion fence 'just as the ball passed over his head'. However, as the season progressed his bowling form improved: he took 5-43 against Newtown on 28 November and promised enough to be selected for the intercolonial trial on 12 December — the Intercolonial XI versus XV. Watched by the selection committee, Spofforth had a fine match with the ball taking 10-63 off 132 deliveries but he had to share some of the limelight with another promising newcomer, Edwin Evans. While wickets fell all around him Evans held the innings of the XV together and remained 51 not out, a 'chanceless' and 'splendid' innings out of the total of 122.

Penrith all-rounder Edwin Evans, three years older than Spofforth, made an immediate impact on the Sydney competition when he played for the Warwick Club in 1874-75. 'Square Leg' of the *Sydney Mail* noted that Evans was a 'likely man' and wrote on 5 December 1874:

Last season I attended a match on the Albert Ground between Newington students and ex-students — if I mistake not — and was, with several others, impressed with the bowling of a player named Evans, who obtained wickets wonderfully fast.

A medium-pacer who bowled 'a little over the shoulder', Evans could break the ball from the off, work it from the leg and 'also sends a rather fast one now and then'.[7] As a batsman he was renowned for his infinite patience. Evans, who stood over six feet (183 cm) and weighed around 13 stone (87 kg), of which every ounce was 'muscle and bone', was 'considerably broader and thicker about the shoulders than most Australians' but also had a 'combination of looseness of limb and great muscular power possessed by a few ... really fine athletes'.[8] After his excellent batting in the selection trial there were strenuous efforts to recruit Evans for the first of the two intercolonials of the 1874–75 season, which was set down for Melbourne in December.

Evans, however, was a quiet and unassuming man — 'one of nature's gentlemen' as one commentator called him — and was reticent to thrust himself into the limelight. His behaviour was in 'strong contrast', the *Sydney Mail* noted in December 1876, 'to one or two other shining cricket lights who are not overburdened by modesty'. It seems clear that Bannerman and Spofforth were the two in question: the colonial press more than once accused them of big-headedness. Evans was, as Philip Derriman put it, 'surely the most reluctant champion Australian cricket has known' who repeatedly turned down opportunities, often at the last moment, to play intercolonial and international cricket.[9] He provided any number of excuses ranging from injury and ill health, family problems, pressure of business[10] and even seasickness. The correspondent of the *Sydney Mail* became quite irked when Evans seemed unable to decide whether to tour in 1882 and wrote that 'it is a pity, however, that he (Evans) cannot let the public know what his intention really is'. When Evans finally withdrew from this tour the same writer added that 'Evans found it impossible to screw his courage up to the sticking point'.[11] It took Evans almost a decade to make the decision to tour England but by 1886 it was too late; his talent was very much on the wane.

It is not clear why Evans pulled out of the Melbourne game. Possibly Spofforth may have contributed as it was reported in the *Sydney Mail* of 19 December 1874 that 'some time ago Evans injured his foot, and on Saturday (12 December) a ball from Spofforth touched him upon the tender spot, and not only crippled him, during his innings, but for several days after'. Spofforth may well have bowled just a little faster to Evans because he was envious of him. The new star soon became the darling of the press and the public and rapidly established an enormous reputation both in Australia and England. Spofforth's rise to fame was much slower and, in some respects, more difficult. Spofforth in 1874 was not without his critics. He later wrote that 'my selection' to play for New South Wales 'did not give universal satisfaction. Both sides went to extremes, my friends declaring I was the best bowler in the world, and my opponents that I was absolutely useless, and could not last three overs.' Being an ambitious individual, he must have resented the seeming ease with which Evans glided to the top of the cricket tree and equally he must have been quite puzzled by the extreme reticence of this very talented individual to grab his main chance. Perhaps it was a combination of these factors which led Spofforth to back himself to take 100 more wickets than Evans on the 1886 tour,[12] an astonishing action if true, which was not inclined to add to team harmony or morale. Certainly the boast indicates a long-standing rivalry.

With the last-minute withdrawal of Evans, along with the unavailability of Dave Gregory, Faithfull and Massie, the Sydney press was despondent about their team's prospects. When the match began on Boxing Day, 1874, each of the four innings was on a separate area within the square, a not uncommon practice at this time. Having insisted that they had the right, as visitors, to chose to bat or bowl and then sent the Victorians in, the New South Welshmen took the field attired in blue and white caps. The field set for the young Sydney speedster, Spofforth, underlines how different fast bowling and the game of cricket were in the 1870s. The slip cordon consisted simply of a short slip and a point. Three men were placed behind the wicket in what would now be regarded as defensive positions: at third man, long leg and long-stop. Only one of the remaining four fieldsmen stood in an attacking position, at short leg: the other three were at cover, mid-off and mid-on.

Spofforth opened the bowling from the western end and had immediate success, producing a 'fast home-pitch' (probably a yorker) of 'lightning velocity' which shifted the leg stump of opener James Slight off the fourth ball. After such an auspicious beginning New South Wales went on to a surprisingly easy seven-wicket win with Spofforth taking three wickets in each innings and scoring a useful 21 runs in his only time at bat. According to the report in the *Sydney Morning Herald* of 31 December, 'Spofforth's varieties of pitch, pace and work created quite a sensation', though his second innings figures indicate that he was far less economical than Coates. Whereas Spofforth took 3-67 off 97 balls, his captain Coates took 5-46 off 189 balls. The other star of the match was Charles Bannerman who scored 81 runs in 150 minutes in the first innings, which 'Our Special Correspondent' of the *Sydney Morning Herald* described as 'one of the finest innings I ever saw' and distinguished especially by his 'marvellous defensive powers'. Bannerman was 32 not out in the second innings.

The news of the New South Wales success created immense public enthusiasm and large crowds followed the results on the telegram board outside the *Herald* office. When the team returned they were 'enthusiastically received' after their 'unexpected victory' and were 'picnicked and feted to their hearts' content'. The Sydney papers, noted the Melbourne *Australasian* on 23 January 1875, 'gushed somewhat, as might have been expected'. To honour the success the *Sydney Mail* also published a lithograph of the team which provides the first known picture of Spofforth: at age twenty-one he had yet to grow a moustache or sideburns, his hair was brushed back and rather longer than was later the case and his face was not as sharply etched as it later became.

It was Bannerman who was 'hailed as the man of the hour' by the media and the public, while Spofforth 'did not receive as much acclaim as some of the others' even though he too had played a decisive role. The *Sydney Mail* announced that it would present Bannerman with a silver cup. Born in Woolwich, Kent, Bannerman was brought to Australia as an infant. After joining the Warwick Club in 1868–69, he blossomed as the outstanding Australian batsman, far superior to any other and famous for his nimble footwork and fluent driving. Bannerman challenged batting orthodoxy, which was to play the medium pacers from the crease: he danced down the wickets and attacked them as if they were slow bowlers. From 1875 to 1878 he became what the *Sydney Mail* referred to as 'a star of the first magnitude'.[13] Bannerman, however, never quite sustained his lofty status and his time at the top was all too brief. Nor was he able to prove himself where it really counted, against the very best English side in England itself. Drinking and gambling appear to have played a significant role in his rapid loss of form after 1878.

The return intercolonial at Sydney in March 1875 stirred much local interest because there were many who believed that New South Wales' victory in December 1874 had been a fluke. Victoria were installed the favourites at 5-4 on, even though the home side were bolstered by Evans, Faithfull and Gregory.

The match proved a triumph for the home side and for Evans in his debut match for the colony. New South Wales (116 and 102) beat Victoria (71 and 70) by 77 runs. Evans proved to be a man of enormous patience with the bat, lending good support to top-scorer Edward Gregory (65) in the first innings and grafting 31 runs in the second innings in 330 minutes on a spongy and slow Albert wicket which clearly favoured the bowlers and made strokeplay difficult. Evans did not bowl in the first innings but he took 6-25 off 120 balls in the second.

Spofforth had a useful though not spectacular match. He did not bowl all that well on the first day but bowled better on the second morning to finish with 2-25 off 108 balls.

However, he did perform well with the bat in the second innings, scoring 13 in 70 minutes: 'Spofforth,' noted the *Australasian* of 27 March, 'gave an example of imperturbable patience, which no one would have expected from so very young a player.'

However, for the second intercolonial in a row it was another young player who stole the limelight. When the match was all over and an exuberant public ignored all the rules and posters of the Albert Ground and swarmed all over the field and threatened to force their way through the gate and over the fence to carry the players round in triumph to celebrate the first home win since 1866, it was Evans whom they cheered most. Within minutes £60 had been subscribed to purchase a trophy for Evans and he received rave notices when the press filed their stories. 'He is all they painted with both bat and ball,' noted the *Sydney Mail*, 'and Coates must feel proud of his pupil.' The following week the same paper added that Evans is 'the best player we have in Sydney ... He is the most patient batsman I have seen, and with a little practice (a thing he seldom gets) has all the material for as fine a player as has ever stripped.'

The second New South Wales victory in a season also proved an enormous boost for local cricket for 'hundreds of people who knew nothing about cricket, and cared as much, are now to be heard babbling, with infantile assumption of wisdom, the names and doings of the doughty ones of Sydney.'[14] Spofforth finished off a very good season, in which he had consolidated his position in the colonial side, with an outstanding all round performance for his club against University in April; in fact he 'pulled the match out of the fire when the state of the game was very critical'. He scored 19 and 45 with the bat and took 5-35 off 108 balls and 7-28 off 90 balls.

Just three months after Spofforth played his first home intercolonial his father, Edward, died on 12 June 1875. Fred Spofforth seems to have felt the loss keenly because he wrote that 'I had the great misfortune to lose my father, and whenever I met with success afterwards in any kind of sport I always regretted he was not present to see it'. Edward Spofforth left goods to the value of £1,000 and a few months later, on 7 December, his widow wrote to the Board of the

Bank of New South Wales, 'appealing . . . for some consideration of her late husband's lengthened service in the Bank'. The result of this appeal is not known. However, bank records indicate that on 6 April 1877 an advance of £200 was granted to Mrs Anna Spofforth upon security of 163 acres (66 ha) of land at Whangarei in the Province of Auckland, New Zealand.

Spofforth was in good form early in the following season, but he could not prevent Evans' Warwick Club dominating the Sydney competition. The November game between the Alberts and the Warwicks was virtually a tussle between Evans and Spofforth. Spofforth won easily in the first innings, scoring 28 and taking 5-43 off 79 balls with Evans scoring only 3 and taking 3-48. But in the second innings, when it really counted, Evans returned 6-21 off 78 balls and scored 54 while Spofforth was out for a duck and returned 2-65 off 145 balls. The Warwicks (64 and 154) beat the Alberts (136 and 56) by 26 runs. The Albert score in the first innings was boosted by 29 runs from William Murdoch.

If the Albert Club could not get the better of the Warwicks, they had the satisfaction of comfortably beating Tasmania at the Albert Ground, scoring 140 and 179 and dismissing the opposition for 87 and 106. Spofforth had an outstanding return of 8-43 and 6-37.

The Victorians no longer underestimated the New South Wales side, particularly as it was strengthened by the inclusion of Evans for the December intercolonial at Melbourne. On arrival in Melbourne, these 'two crack trundlers of the eleven' were among the 'bad sailors' in the team who 'suffered very much' and they 'presented a very pale and subdued appearance as they stepped from the deck of the ship to the pier'.[15] If Spofforth was a regular sufferer from seasickness, it did not stop him undertaking five major cricket tours to the Northern Hemisphere and numerous other sea voyages.

When the match began the young New South Wales bowlers, dressed in a dark blue uniform, immediately made an impact on the Victorian batsmen, outfitted in light blue. Spofforth bowled Campbell with his very first ball and Evans, not to be outdone, trapped Frank Allan with his initial ball. When Spofforth bowled Tommy Horan Victoria were three wickets for one run. After Victoria recovered to score 136 (with Evans taking four wickets and Spofforth and Coates three each), they appeared to be back in the game when they dismissed New South Wales for 171 with Bannerman scoring 83. But the Victorians suffered what the Melbourne papers referred to as a 'disgraceful defeat' scoring just 34 runs in the second innings to lose by an innings and one run. Spofforth, the strike bowler of the first innings, did not bowl in the second: Evans once again stole the show with 7-16 off 71 balls; he was supported by Coates who took 3-16 off 68 balls.

During the match the New South Wales keeper, Nat Thompson, injured his hands when he dropped a chance and a twenty-one-year-old batsman who had batted very low in the order at number nine, scoring just 6 runs, took over from him and kept very neatly. William Murdoch, playing in his first intercolonial, was familiar with the bowling of Spofforth as he kept wickets for the Alberts after transferring there from the Warwick Club in 1874-75.

Born in Sandhurst, Victoria, on 18 October 1854, but brought up as a New South Welshman, Murdoch's career paralleled and was closely intertwined with Spofforth's. Murdoch, 5' 10" (178 cm), a stylish and correct bat with a great penchant for cutting and driving on the off side and with keen eyes (he was an excellent rifle shot) and great powers of concentration which enabled him to hit up mammoth scores, became Australia's premier bat after the 1878 tour and was thought by many to be one of the best batsmen in the world, if not the best, in the early 1880s. Murdoch was a very talented and well-rounded individual physically, intellectually and socially. A Sydney University-educated solicitor, he had a buoyant personality, relaxed air and sense of humour and was a natural and astute leader.

The continuing success of the youthful New South Wales side created enormous enthusiasm in Sydney and when the final telegram was posted on the *Herald* board, announcing the result, there were 'enthusiastic cheers'. When the return match began at the Albert Ground on 3 March 1876 there was a crowd of 10,000 on the Friday and 15,000 on the Saturday. The home side were clearly installed as the favourites with the betting wavering from 3-1 to 6-4 on.

Despite the attempt of the Albert Ground authorities to crack down on gambling during the 1870s, there were clearly many at the ground and outside interested in taking a punt on the result or even on the top-scorer. Shop-front windows in various streets of the city featured 'well-got-up lists of the players, with the odds against each one given, the backer of the top score winning'.[16]

The match did not begin all that well for the New South Wales team, which was dismissed for just 99. Frank Allan, who was generally regarded as one of the best bowlers in the country for much of the 1870s, took 5-23 off 87 balls. But New South Wales, spearheaded by Spofforth and Evans, hit back and routed the visitors for just 37, the second innings in a row the Victorians had failed to reach 40. By all accounts Spofforth bowled very fast in this match. He broke the bat of opener B B Cooper and then bowled him for no score; shortly after he broke a stump in bowling Horan for one. During this match Murdoch was retained as the keeper — Thompson was in the side as opening batsman — and impressed the *Sydney Mail* correspondent of 4 March with 'how he managed to take some of Spofforth's "wind-jammers" '.

The wrecker of stumps and batsmen was suitably rewarded at the conclusion of the match when 'Sir Hercules Robinson, the Governor, presented me with the broken stumps mounted in silver'. Anita and Pamela Spofforth inherited one such stump which was inscribed: 'Mr E [sic] Spofforth from Mr Chas Thorne, Momento, Intercolonial Match, Vic vs NSWales, Syd 1876'. In 1988 the Spofforths returned the stump to Australia, along with some other memorabilia, donating it to the Australian Gallery of Sport, Melbourne.

New South Wales batted much better in the second innings, scoring 228, and then dismissed Victoria for 95, winning by what was in those days the huge margin of 195. For once Spofforth shared the bowling limelight with Evans, both bowling unchanged throughout the match: Spofforth took 9-72 off 148 balls and Evans returned 10-52 off 140 balls. However, the versatile Evans also performed well with the bat, scoring 10 and 46 while Spofforth bagged a pair, dismissed in both innings by Allan.

Spofforth did not play a lot more cricket in this season as he injured an arm and was again on the sick list at the beginning of the 1876–77 season, which heralded the arrival of the fourth English team of twelve professionals captained by James Lillywhite. It was a side which was rather stronger in bowling than batting. The attack was spearheaded by Alfred Shaw, whom English critics rated as the best bowler in the world and whom *Conway's Australian Cricketers' Annual* referred to as 'that world-renowned bowler'.

Late in October the *Sydney Mail* fretted as to whether New South Wales could mount a worthwhile attack with Spofforth sick, Evans in Bathurst and Coates about to leave for England. But by 7 December, the start of 'one of the most exciting and interesting matches ever played' on the Albert Ground between the New South Wales XV and the English XI, Spofforth had recovered, Evans had obtained leave and Coates was still in Sydney (though he missed the next two international contests). The home side (81 and 12-151) defeated the visitors (122 and 106) by just two wickets. Spofforth had a very good match: batting at number 12 he top-scored for New South Wales with 19 runs in the first innings. He took 7-73 off 169 balls (in two innings). But as usual Evans did just a little more: he took 9-85 off 313 balls and scored 38 runs in the second innings. He was singled out by *Conway's Annual* for special praise: 'Well might the New South Wales cricket-loving public sing the praises of their Evans, for he well deserved special honour for his spirited play in every branch of the game'.[17] Spofforth's achievement was only marginally inferior but was overlooked in this report.

After the English colours were again lowered by the Victorian XV, who beat them by 35 runs, the tourists returned to Sydney on 12 January somewhat worse for wear owing to the rough passage from Melbourne and some self-inflicted handicaps and suffered an ignominious defeat at the hands of the New South Wales XV by 13 wickets. Spofforth for once shared the limelight with Evans. When the tourists crashed to 5 wickets for just 8 runs, Spofforth had taken three wickets and Evans one. Spofforth finished the innings with 5-20 off 64 balls and match figures of 8-78 off 164 balls, while Evans took 8-64 off 170 balls.

Chastened by this humiliating defeat, the Englishmen prepared themselves for the next encounter against New South Wales on 15 January, a match played on even terms (eleven-a-side). They spent a quiet day before the match which did wonders for their form. Although the match was drawn, the Englishmen had much the better of the game, hitting up a very large total of 271, against which New South Wales could only manage 82 and 5-140. For the visitors Ulyett starred with the bat, scoring 95, and Shaw lived up to his reputation with 9-54 off 386 balls in the two innings. Evans also put in a marathon performance, taking 5-94 off 212 balls, but Spofforth for once was collared and took only 1-80 off 140 balls. Despite this setback Spofforth could be well satisfied with his performance in the three internationals and in February he was presented with a very fine cup with very delicate silverwork.[18] The inscription read: 'Presented to Mr F R Spofforth by a few friends for his grand display of All-Round Cricket in the International Matches Season 1876-77 Sydney February 1877'.

By the 1876-77 tour colonial cricket had improved sufficiently to compete on even terms with the tourists. Two matches organised at Melbourne in March 1877 are recognised as the first and second Test matches. Now hallowed as the beginning of a great institution, the First Test almost took on farcical proportions before a ball was bowled. The New South Wales Cricket Association was unhappy that the team was selected by a Victorian agent and issued a resolution complaining that the game had been 'arranged without any reference to the Association or in any way under its auspices; and that the match cannot be regarded as a match in which the chosen representatives of New South Wales take part'.[19] Evans declined to make the trip for business reasons and, according to the *Sydney Mail*, was also banking on the possibility of a return match in Sydney. There was no such match in Sydney that season and the Test debut of this reluctant traveller did not occur until 31 December 1881.

Worse was to follow for the organisers when Spofforth announced that he would not play because the New South Wales keeper, Murdoch, had not been selected. The Melbourne press had a field day with this sensational news: *The*

Argus 'severely censured, and in some degree held (him) up to ridicule as a bowler with a private wicket-keep',[20] while the *Australasian* of 17 March 1877 accused Fred Spofforth of big-headedness:

Spofforth . . . apparently considering his success was due to his wicket-keeper and not his own merit, and fearing he would be shorn of lustre if another 'who knew not Joseph' were behind the sticks, declined to play unless his own special wicket-keeper was selected. As this could not be arranged, this modest gentleman had to remain behind.

It was, on the face of it, an arrogant and astounding demand made by a twenty-three-year-old yet to establish his international reputation.

While not condoning such an impetuous action of an overconfident young man, the *Sydney Mail* was the one paper which placed Spofforth's action in some broader perspective and suggested that there were some reasonable grounds for his withdrawal. There was 'strong feeling here' that Murdoch deserved a place in the side as a batsman in his own right, even if not selected as a keeper, and that had the local association played a role in the selection there was little doubt that he would have been selected. Murdoch was not only the New South Wales keeper, he was also a club-mate of Spofforth and, more than probably, the action reflected an expression of loyalty to Murdoch.[21] Even as a young man Spofforth was prepared to stick his neck out for a principle without heed for the consequences.

So Spofforth missed out in playing in a match which long after came to be regarded with great reverence. One suspects that had he had any inkling of the long-term significance of this match he might well have played with or without Murdoch, for when the hundredth Test was played at Nottingham in 1921 Spofforth presented the entire Australian team with gold medals.

The man chosen to replace him, Frank Allan, offered a flimsy excuse for not playing. Allan informed the cricket officials that he preferred to mingle with friends at the Warrnambool Agricultural Show.

Without the three leading Australian bowlers, Evans, Spofforth and Allan, the *Sydney Mail* believed that the combined eleven did not have much chance against the tourists and commented that 'the agent who so mismanaged matters in reference to the selection of our contingent (N.S.W.) as to lose Spofforth as well as Evans cannot be surprised if little interest is exhibited in the contest'.[22] The Melbourne public showed only limited interest in the game with crowds of around 4,000 on the three weekdays with approximately 10,000 on the Saturday.[23] Intercolonials often drew much larger crowds.

Fortunately for Australia the Englishmen, who had arrived only the day before from New Zealand, were still overcoming the effects of seasickness and were handicapped by the absence of their keeper, Pooley, and Bannerman chose to play one of the great innings of Test cricket, 165 retired hurt. This memorable innings rescued the game from historical oblivion and paved the way for its later canonisation as the First Test. The innings was impressive because it was made on a rough track and represented two-thirds of the Australian total. It also represents an astonishing record — the highest score on debut, which had not been equalled more than a century later. In an era of low scoring, when centuries were few and far between, it was a mammoth score. Spectators at the ground raised £83 7s. 6d. and a committee was formed to collect subscriptions for a testimonial. With the depleted bowling resources the performance of slow left-arm bowler Tom Kendall was also crucial to Australian success by 45 runs. Kendall took 7-55 in the second innings off 33.1 overs.

Neither Kendall nor Bannerman was able to sustain his star performance. Overindulgence rapidly eclipsed their brief stardom. Spofforth later reflected on Kendall:

For one season, indeed, Kendall was as fine an example of a break-bowler as the world has ever seen. He was left-handed, with a very easy delivery, and it was almost impossible to judge from which side the ball would break in. Unfortunately, he put on flesh very rapidly; and so lost his energy and elasticity early.

Kendall was an 1878 tourist, but after completing the Australian and New Zealand legs of the tour, he did not proceed further for reasons of indiscipline.

With such an unexpected victory and the heroic deeds during the 'Test', the colonial press quickly changed its tune to celebrate the event and began the process, which has continued ever since, of mythicising victory. It was, *The Age* suggested to its readers, something more than a victory over a second-string English side but 'a crushing reminder to those unpatriotic theorists who would have us believe that the Australian race is deteriorating from the imperial type, or that the lengthened residence under the Australian sun must kill the Briton in the blood'. 'Corn Cob' of the *Australasian* published a poem suggesting that while Australians might well have a passion for 'blowing' they at least had something worth 'blowing' about:

> Anthony Trollope
> Says we can wallop
> The whole of creation at 'blowing'
> It's well in a way
> But then he don't say
> We blow about nothing worth showing.
>
> We grow bone and muscle,
> To stand a stout tussle;
> We've licked 'All England' at cricket;
> How well we can row
> 'Twere needless to show,
> Since Britain knocked under to Trickett.[24]

Spofforth later wrote that 'it was an all-round triumph: a red-letter day in cricket history':

Not only had the colony at last defeated the mother country, but Charles Bannerman had defied the best bowling that England could produce . . . The Englishmen themselves assured me that it was one of the finest exhibitions of batting they had ever seen; and from this day there was no longer any question but that Australia could hold their own against the world. Nor was the triumph entirely Bannerman's. It was achieved by good all-round cricket; and one of the chief constituents of success was the admirable bowling of Tom Kendall.

Spofforth played in the second Test in Melbourne a little over a fortnight later. Blackham was retained as the Australian keeper but Murdoch was included as the batsman. With the addition of Spofforth the Australian team was expected to win.

Despite the Australian victory in the earlier match there were only 5,000 spectators in attendance on the opening day — a very moderate crowd for a Saturday — to see Australia dismissed for just 122 with Spofforth being bowled for a duck in his first Test innings.

The Australian bowling was opened by the slow bowler Kendall at one end and he bowled Jupp with his fourth ball. Spofforth opened at the other and, not surprisingly, appeared breathtakingly fast in comparison. *The Argus* reporter filed a vivid account of his first overs:

He took a run of 10 or 12 yards, and amidst a somewhat bewildering movement of legs and arms, hurled the ball forwards with a velocity and recklessness as to the consequences enough to make all timid people tremble for the safety of the batsman, the wicketkeeper and even the longstop. The action which preceded the delivery of the ball, carefully looked into, turned out to be not at all complicated, but the legs strode so rapidly over the ground, and the arm swept through the air in such a magnificent curve, that one felt greater surprise at seeing the bowler pull himself up so suddenly as he did than perhaps one might feel if he followed after the ball in a succession of somersaults. Shaw manifestly did not like to have so hot a fire opened upon him, and the only person perfectly cool was the wicketkeeper — Blackham.[25]

It was Blackham, ironically, who stumped Shaw for one in Spofforth's fourth over. England were two wickets for just four runs.

The match, from this point on, did not proceed so favourably for the home side and England went on to build up a commanding first innings of 261. The Australians batted much better in the second innings to score 259 (Spofforth scored 17), but it was not enough to prevent an English victory by 4 wickets. Kendall bowled economically to return match figures of 6-106 off 69.2 (four-ball) overs. Spofforth was more expensive with 4-111 off 44 overs. While Spofforth bowled well in his opening spell, he was not nearly as effective on the subsequent days.

The Melbourne *Argus* of 5 April 1877, perhaps disappointed by an Australian defeat and mindful of the reluctance of Spofforth to play in the previous Test, took great pleasure in cutting the young Sydney upstart down to size. 'The feeble bowling of Spofforth' was the factor that most spectators would 'consider the proximate cause of defeat'. The newspaper analysed the failure of Spofforth at length:

But it needed no great insight to discover the cause of failure of Spofforth as a medium-paced bowler. As a fast bowler we do not criticise him; fast bowlers are always uncertainties. They have their days out and their days in, and in this match it was not Spofforth's day. The reason why he was not effective when he bowled at moderate speed was that he had an inadequate command over the ball, as was shown by the number of times he pitched it ludicrously short — about the worst thing he could have done. So long as he takes a run of 12 yards to deliver a slow ball, the same uncertainty of results may be expected.

The Age of 5 April endorsed this viewpoint and blamed the captain, Gregory, for his 'undisguised partiality for the deliveries of Spofforth' which had a 'good deal to do with losing the match'. The *Sydney Mail* of 14 April saw some humour in the situation and suggested that the 'redoubtable Spofforth' was placed in an 'unenviable position' by being blamed for defeat and that it was 'a rather good joke that Spofforth, after disappointing those in Victoria who wished to have him in the first team, should consent to play in the second, and become instrumental in the downfall of those whom he was expected materially to assist'. However, while the *Sydney Mail* was generally sympathetic to Spofforth, it had to admit that he 'fluctuates considerably, and that he tries too many experiments to make him as trustworthy a bowler as Evans or Garrett; but it is very easy to put him on when he is in form and take him off when he is otherwise'.

The howls of the Victorian press provided a salutary lesson for Spofforth. The colonial press, demanding much from prominent sportsmen, was notoriously fickle. One week a sportsman might be placed high on the pedestal of public respect, but just a week later he might be the object of ridicule and savage criticism.

Spofforth finished the season with an impressive 95 not out, including 10 fours, for the Alberts against East Sydney in April 1877. He had consolidated his reputation as one of the leading Australian bowlers, but Evans and Allan were still regarded as superior. At the outset of the 1878 tour the cricket correspondent of the *Sydney Mail* declared that 'there is no doubt that Allan is the best bowler in Victoria and Evans the best in NSW'.[26] Evans was also, as the *Australasian* put it on 16 December 1876, the 'great popular cricket idol'. Spofforth had to bide his time.

The Technique of a Fast Bowler

The beginning of Spofforth's intercolonial career is an appropriate point to consider a series of technical problems about the nature of bowling and the game in the 1870s. What was Spofforth's bowling action? How fast did he bowl? What was his field? What did he do with the ball? What was the state of the ball and the wicket? All these questions are relevant to an assessment of Spofforth as a fast bowler.

There are no easy answers as Spofforth bowled in an era before the movie camera came into existence. We can only see Spofforth's run to the wicket through the eyes of others, though there are photos of the final act of delivery.

Another significant problem was that cricket changed significantly from decade to decade and from 1850 to 1914 it altered far more than it has changed since. It was during this period that cricket emerged from an amateur club game to a commercialised mass spectator sport. Colonial, and later national bureaucracies were set up to run wider competition between colonies and later countries. Commercialism and professionalism emerged as powerful forces in their own right in the 1870s and 1880s, creating new tensions between officials and players. Many important rules, techniques and orthodoxies were defined and developed after 1850. Technology drastically altered the face of cricket. Improved communications, cheaper press and larger stadiums all helped develop cricket's expanding audience. Technology also played a role in improved equipment — bats, balls and pads — and wickets.

Wickets changed more during this period than any other facet of the game. When Spofforth began playing wickets consisted of natural surface soil and were, in today's terms, grossly underprepared and usually prepared on the morning of the match. It was not until later in the century that the invention of improved rollers and mowers and the use of clay and marl enabled groundsmen to produce fine manicured and true surfaces.

Wickets in the 1860s and 1870s were frequently described as uneven, bumpy and treacherous, and unplayable when wet. The scoring totals in the sixteen New South Wales versus Victoria intercolonials before Spofforth made his debut, attest to the batsman's struggle to make runs. New

South Wales did not reach 100 until the seventh intercolonial, having been all out twelve times before this. From 1856 to 1865 New South Wales averaged 80.4 runs per innings, improving to 110 from 1865 to 1874. Victoria had a stronger batting side and achieved equivalent averages of 96.4 and 147.8. It was not uncommon for matches to be over in one or two days. During Spofforth's career only three days were allocated for Test matches in England. Wicket preparation did not become a science until the end of Spofforth's international career, when higher scores became more frequent. With more reliable and even bounce, bowlers had to refine and improve their techniques to dismiss batsmen.

The problems of evaluating the Spofforth technique were brought home during a 1986 interview with ninety-one-year-old H S T L 'Stork' Hendry. Although he did not play first-class cricket until the 1920s, he was born in 1895 and must have heard many stories about the Demon. But Hendry admitted candidly he had no idea of how fast or what the Demon bowled. The answers to the above questions can only be inferred second-hand, from the written word.

One general description of his action was published in the London *Times* of 5 June 1926, that is after Spofforth's death:

He took a rather long run up to the crease, crossed his feet at the moment of delivery, and almost brushed his right ear with his biceps. His long, skinny arm cut through the air like a whip-lash, and the sharpest sight was needed to detect the pace at which it was moving.

Another account came from the pen of C B Fry:

He took a long run, came up to the crease with long, vigorous strides, and delivered the ball with all the speed he could muster. He appeared to throw the whole swing of his long arm and his long body into his effort, and after he delivered the ball his body and arm followed right over until his hand almost touched the ground.[1]

Also worth noting is the comment of Lord Hawke that 'his delivery was terrifying, for he came to the wicket, a long lean man, all arms and legs, and all apparently making amazing evolutions'.[2]

Spofforth's action can be divided into three segments: the run to the wicket, the moment of delivery and the follow-through. His run-up was an oblique one: Spofforth, noted

Grace, started 'some yards to the off-side of the batsman, and giving the impression that he is aiming at a point nearer short-leg than the wicket'.[3] The run to the wicket was not particularly rhythmic or graceful. Murdoch hinted that this was the case when he wrote that both 'Spofforth and Ferris have very peculiar actions, and were always difficult to watch'.[4] 'Peg Leg' Ferris was known to have an ungainly run to the wicket. The absence of any testimony about the Spofforth run to the wicket, as distinct from his high leap, delivery and follow-through, also suggests that there was nothing particularly memorable about it. Many writers attested that Spofforth rushed in to the wickets but one of his fellow-tourists, S P Jones, stated that though he took 'a very long run' it 'was more of the nature of a fast walk sometimes, before the actual delivery' when 'he would bound in the air'.[5] Undoubtedly Spofforth charged in to the wicket much more quickly as a young man when his run was of sixteen paces. In the early 1880s he reduced his run-up and pace, bowling off nine paces in the 1882 Test.

Spofforth's 'extravagant action' at the point of delivery, as Tom Garrett put it, was what impressed most commentators. It included a high leap, 'a final bound at the wicket' according to the Earl of Darnley, with his 'long lean arms through the air from a commanding height'. He came at the batsman, as Home Gordon put it, 'like a human octopus' or as Sammy Woods stated, 'all legs, arms and nose'; others have referred to his 'catherine wheel' style of bowling. Fortunately Spofforth's club career extended long enough for him to be photographed by George Beldam, one of the pioneers of action photography of sport. Beldam travelled to the Hampstead Cricket Ground in September 1904 to take a series of action shots, many of which were printed in *Great Bowlers*, of an elderly Demon who was then aged fifty-one. Given the age of the bowler and the experimental state of sport photography, one photo, which features the Spofforth high leap, was a classic and has been much admired ever since. The photo captures the celebrated leap — astonishingly high, possibly half-stump high, for a man of his age — at which point his body is perfectly balanced with the left arm extended high in front of the face and the right arm extended downwards before the final high overarm action.

Some cricket writers have assumed, erroneously, that this is a photo of Spofforth at the peak of his career.

A cartoon painted by *The Bulletin* artist, W. McLeod, dating from the early 1880s,[6] captured the vigour and vitality of the Spofforth action a moment later: Spofforth had completed his high leap, had planted his right foot by the wickets and was in the process of raising his right arm to the high overarm position. In addition to conveying a sense of speed, the cartoon suggests vividly how the Demon's legs, arms and back were extended to their very maximum as the ball was about to be catapulted at the batsman.

Bulletin *cartoonist McLeod was clearly impressed by the vitality of the Spofforth delivery.*

The cartoon in question has quite a romantic history. It and another were originally painted on the panels of a door in an old New South Wales station homestead often visited by cricketers. When the building was pulled down the panels were passed on to the New South Wales Cricket Association where they languished in a cellar for many decades. After they were rediscovered they were presented to the Museum at the Sydney Cricket Ground.

Equally impressive was what Sammy Woods referred to as his 'perfect follow through', when he bent his back to such an extent that his hand almost touched the ground.

When questioned in 1892 about the extent to which he bent down after delivery, Spofforth argued that it was the bend 'which was just the thing which prevented any strain'.[7] Spofforth followed on 'straight down the wicket': according to Lord Harris he placed 'the left foot on or about the popping crease, right foot well on to the half volley pitch, and then both feet plump on the awkward pitch; and when wickets were soft, he undoubtedly made a mess of the pitch'. The Earl of Darnley also referred to his 'long stride coming down with great force and damaging effect on a very awkward spot for a breaking-back ball bowled from the other end'.[8] The damage caused by Spofforth's action was to involve him in future controversy.

One of the questions debated at length in cricket literature, and the one most frequently asked of Spofforth, is the pace at which he bowled. It is an important one because it relates to the central question as to whether Spofforth can be referred to as the first of the tribe of fast bowlers.

This is a tricky question because there is no way that his pace can be established objectively. The first 'scientific' measurement of pace occurred during the career of C T B 'The Terror' Turner, who came to the fore as Spofforth bowed out of Test cricket. Turner, who is said by some to have bowled as fast or a little faster than Spofforth (but were they comparing Turner with the younger or more mature Spofforth?) was tested through a screen at Woolwich Observatory, near London, where chronographs established that he bowled at 85 feet (25.9 m) per second — 55 miles (88.5 km) per hour — which would make him very much the tortoise amongst the modern fast bowling hares: modern fast bowlers have been measured at 85-90 miles plus (136.8-144.8 km-plus) per hour.

Pace is a relative concept: a bowler who is much faster than the others of his generation will appear fast. Spofforth certainly was. He bowled, for instance, faster than the batsmen anticipated on 28 March 1874 because the batsmen of the day were as a rule playing him a second or two too late. Opening the bowling with medium and even slow bowlers also added to the aura, even the illusion, of speed. The slow left-arm spinner, Kendall, opened the bowling in Spofforth's first Test and it was not surprising that spectators were impressed with the Demon's speed at the other end.

A more important consideration is that Spofforth bowled fast enough to intimidate opposition batsmen. There are numerous references which suggest that the young Spofforth created panic in the opposition. Spofforth was perhaps at his fastest when

I bowled unchanged against Victoria (at Sydney in March 1876) taking in all eleven wickets (actually nine) and breaking two stumps — B B Cooper's and T. Horan's (Felix). In addition to this B B Cooper's bat was broken three times and at the conclusion of the match Sir Hercules Robinson, the Governor, presented me with the broken stumps mounted in silver.

Whether Spofforth wreaked quite as much havoc as he claimed in 1903 is open to doubt but newspaper reports establish that he broke Cooper's bat at least once, and Horan's stump.

By the end of the next season Cooper had decided to retire and S P Jones, an 1882 tourist, believed that the bowling of Spofforth was the prime reason: 'I had heard that B B Cooper relished Spofforth so little that, after his leg as well as the stumps had received rough treatment, he thought discretion the better part of valour, and retired from Intercolonial games'. Jones added that he had been present on one occasion when Charles Bannerman had requested Spofforth 'not to bowl too fast' at practice.

Another problem which has clouded the issue is that Spofforth bowled much faster and ran back further in the earlier part of his career than in his mature phase in the early 1880s, when he confused batsmen by bowling a mixture of fast, medium and even slow-medium deliveries with the same action. The change was a gradual one. He was already known for his varieties of pace in the mid-1870s. During much of the 1880s he retained the ability to bowl fast, but he increasingly reserved the fast ball, which Lord Harris referred to as his 'judgment ball', as an unexpected shock delivery. There were occasional times when he bowled flat out. Robin H. Legge wrote to the London *Daily Telegraph* on 5 June 1926, the day after Spofforth died, expressing the opinion that he could not understand 'the present depreciation of the pace of Spofforth's bowling' which 'was terrific at times'. Legge recalled the day when Spofforth bowled for the Australians against Cambridge University at Fenners in 1882 and 'with each of the four balls of his first over, he beat not only the bat, but "Billy Murdoch" (the keeper) ... and each ball ran up the pavilion steps for four byes'.

Never one to hide his light under a bushel, Spofforth was wont to boast 'that he was the fastest bowler that ever was', which Lord Hawke dismissed as 'harmless delusion' because 'he never had anything like the pace of (Johannes Jacobus) Kotze (1879–1931) or (Charles Jesse) Kortright' (1871–1952)[9] or, for that matter, a number of other bowlers such as Thomas Richardson (1870–1912), who emerged in the 1880s and 1890s. At best Spofforth can probably claim to be the fastest bowler around in the 1870s and possibly the early 1880s.

In today's terms Spofforth would rank as a fast-medium bowler at the very best; that is, his fast ball might fall into that category. He was certainly not, by modern standards, fast. His first wicket in Test cricket, achieved during his opening spell (in the fourth over) was a stumping, and five of his ninety-two Test wickets were stumpings. This would suggest that he may have bowled at the pace of Alec Bedser, for whom keepers sometimes stood up at the wickets. Blackham and Murdoch stood at the stumps for the majority of Spofforth deliveries, though they retreated a few paces when Spofforth signalled that he intended to bowl a faster delivery.

What must be remembered, too, was that Spofforth played in an era when well-controlled fast-medium and medium bowling was sufficient to defeat the batsman. J W Trumble, whose first tour to England in 1886 was Spofforth's last, argued that the less prepared wickets of the 1870s and 1880s did not assist genuine fast bowlers:

These former turf wickets were not favourable for the fast bowlers, and consequently fast bowlers of class were not so much in evidence as they have been in recent years. Spofforth, the greatest bowler of all time, started his career as a fast bowler, but soon realized that fast bowling on the wickets of his day did not pay, and came down to slower bowling with a fast ball put in occasionally as a surprise delivery.[10]

It also seems clear that Spofforth had no slip cordon because the ball did not swing as much as it later did. An analysis of the thirty-eight Test catches taken off Spofforth's bowling reveal that only three were taken in slips — a very low proportion by modern standards.[11] The lack of swing was probably due to a combination of factors: the ball until 1927 was a little larger than the modern ball, it was less glossy and the seam was less raised. In addition to this the stumps were a little lower and the popping crease was narrower.[12]

Without swing, the repertoire of the fast bowler was much more limited. He had to depend more on pace and variations of pace, cut from the wicket, yorkers and bowling at the stumps. Accurate bowling was often sufficient to take wickets as the uneven bounce of many wickets caused some balls to jump and others to shoot. Catches at point — four of Spofforth's Test victims were caught there — were not due to away swing but were the result of balls which 'bumped' (jumping up off a good length) causing the batsmen to cock them up to point. One of Spofforth's great attributes, true of some of the great fast bowlers such as Lindwall, Statham, Alderman, Holding and Hadlee, was that he invariably homed in on the stumps or hovered in their close vicinity. Spofforth bowled 50 of his 94 Test victims, another 5 were caught and bowled and 3 were lbw: 58 of his Test wickets, or 61.7 per cent, were dismissed without assistance of the fieldsmen. The proportions of Spofforth's unassisted wickets are much higher than contemporary bowlers'. Melbourne sports historian J Neville Turner has calculated the equivalent rates for sixteen post-1945 fast bowlers which vary from Lindwall, 59.2 per cent, to Thomson, 32.5 per cent. The figures underline further the changing art of fast bowling. Thomson's proportion of unassisted wickets is low because he had many more wicket-taking options, such as the batsman caught off a bouncer.

All the batsmen who played against Spofforth agree on two other important attributes of his bowling. He had complete control of length and direction and could also control the amount of cut: whether the ball broke a lot, a little or not at all. It was probably not until 1878 that he had developed such pinpoint accuracy. Spofforth was also a master of disguise and almost no batsman was confident that he could pick the pace or likely movement of a delivery. As Spofforth's wicket-keeper and captain, Murdoch had plenty of opportunity to appreciate Spofforth's skills:

From that position (as wicket-keeper) I saw how he mastered and perfected his variation of pace. I have seen him take the same run, go through the same action, and to all appearances, bowl with exactly the same strength as the previous ball; but, when the batsman played forward, he was much too soon. He also bowled a fast ball very well indeed, and could do it at the very last moment, without any apparent change: the only thing he did was to change the position of his fingers, as he held the ball.[13]

Spofforth's success cannot be explained entirely in terms of technical mastery. He was, like all great bowlers, a fierce competitor who seemed to strive just a little harder than his contemporaries to defeat batsmen. His great self-confidence was also a powerful psychological weapon which was directed against batsmen even before they took block.

Country Vicar' noted that Neville Cardus even 'appears to suggest that there *was* some secret, sinister power in Spofforth'. Cardus also regarded Spofforth as 'a stark man who let in with him the coldest blast of antagonism that ever blew over a June field', and he quoted a player who recalled the impact of this antagonism:

It was at the Oval. I were in right form and not afeared of him when I goes in to bat. He'd just taken a wicket, but I walks into t' middle jaunty like, flicking my bat, makin' rare cuts through t' slips as I went over t' grass . . . as I got near Mr Spofforth he sort of fixed me. His look went through me like a red-hot poker. But I walks on past him along t' wicket to t' batting end. And half-way down something made me turn round and look at him over my shoulder. And there he was, still fixin' me with his eye.[14]

The studied glare has become so much part of the psychological armoury of a Dennis Lillee or a Merv Hughes that it no longer attracts much notice. The comment of Cardus hints at a novel practice of what may have been the first angry fast bowler.

Team-mate George Giffen supported the Cardus view that Spofforth was the master of psychological warfare:

He looked the Demon every inch of him, and I verily believe he has frightened more batsmen out than many bowlers have fairly and squarely beaten. When the Demon meant business, the batsman had to look out for squalls. His pitch would be perfect, and it would be impossible to get the ball away.[15]

Colonel Phillip Trevor also made reference to the Spofforth presence in an obituary article in the London *Daily Telegraph* of 5 June 1926:

If, as I think, he did owe much to the prepared atmosphere in which he delivered the ball, he, at any rate, created it himself . . . If I were a bowler and could create for myself the atmosphere the Great Spoff created, I would not care technically how I bowled. I should get sufficient success to satisfy my vanity if I could make my opponents afraid of me.

Spofforth also made effective use of the occasional theatrical gesture to unsettle batsmen once they had begun their innings. In a match against Surrey during the 1878 tour Spofforth bowled a loose delivery down the leg side which was hit out of the ground by the batsman to thunderous applause. Spofforth was not at all impressed by this treatment and his 'confidence and full intention for revenge was shown by deliberate preparation, the removal of his cap, and a medium-paced delivery'.[16] The batsman was made aware that the bowler was about to get serious and shortly after he was bowled by a yorker.

Even more important than body language and self-confidence was the greatest asset of any fast bowler — his fertile mind. Jas Scott wrote that Spofforth was a 'man of exceptional energy, both mental and physical'.[17] Spofforth was a deep thinker about the art of fast bowling, a shrewd tactician who would probe the physical and mental limitations of his opponents, and a man willing to risk experimentation in a difficult and challenging situation.

Spofforth thought so deeply about cricket and problems linked with the movement of the ball in the air that he invented a family trick which was to throw an egg seventy yards (64 m) without breaking or even cracking the shell. Spofforth, who had observed that an egg would not break if it landed on its end, devised a way of throwing it to achieve a perfect landing. He taught the trick to his sons who were observed to have successfully thrown an egg over a chestnut tree at the cricket ground at Weybridge.

In addition to his mental attributes, Spofforth was a superb athlete. He was fleet of foot and was awarded a handsome trophy, now in the possession of grandson John Youle, for winning a 100 yards (91.4 m) sprint in New South Wales in 1881. He also had great stamina and was relatively free from injury over five strenuous tours. He had an ideal build for a fast bowler. Some photographs suggest some striking physical resemblances to another great thinking fast bowler, Dennis Lillee.

So was Spofforth entitled to be called the founder of a 'new school of bowling' as C B Fry claimed, or a 'pioneer' who 'revolutionised' bowling as E H D Sewell suggested, or as the first great fast bowler who helped establish the art of fast bowling? The case against this proposition rests on three unconvincing premises. Spofforth was not a fast bowler in the modern sense, some may suggest, because he did not swing the ball. This criticism is unfair simply because he performed in the era before swing bowling. Another criticism, that he moved the ball mostly one way, bowling off-cutters with the occasional small amount of drift in from the leg, is not a significant one because there was great variety in his bowling. Finally, he did not bowl at the speed of the modern fast bowler but, in terms of his era and particularly in the 1870s, he was regarded as quick. He also bowled as fast as was necessary to dismiss batsmen.

Spofforth, more than any other bowler, was the father of modern fast bowling simply because he elevated it to an art. It was he who first combined successfully the speed of a Tarrant with the subtle skills of a Shaw, or as C B Fry wrote:

he appears to have been the first naturally fast bowler to discover that the subtle variations of pace and deceptive tricks practised by a slow-medium bowler like Alfred Shaw might with advantage be imitated and developed in conjunction with sheer speed.

Put in another way, Spofforth realised that the speed merchant should do something more than blaze away at the batsman. Rather, he should think and plan the batsman's dismissal just as much as the slow bowler. The fast bowler needed to develop control, cunning and variety as much as the slow bowler; each ball bowled should be different to keep the batsman guessing. Spofforth was the first thinking fast bowler.

The Making of a Hero

F.R.Spofforth

*I*t will never be known just what went through Spofforth's mind as he sailed out of Sydney Harbour on the RMS *City of Sydney* on the afternoon of 29 March 1878. Embarking on the northern hemisphere leg of the 1878 cricket tour, Spofforth and his team-mates could not have been certain that the trip would be highly profitable, that his share of £50 would return a substantial dividend of £700–750 at the end of the tour — four times Spofforth's annual salary at the bank. More probably, Spofforth and the other tourists thought simply of making ends meet, using cricket as a means of financing a voyage of discovery. Unlike the English professionals who were lured to Australia by the prospect of making money — they were guaranteed fixed sums, varying from £150–250 on the first four tours, plus all travelling and living expenses — the Australian tourists were rather more inspired by the notion of a cultural pilgrimage to the home of cricket. England at this time was still regarded by many middle-class Australians, including Spofforth, as 'home' and *The Argus'* account of the 1878 tour referred to the voyage as 'the trip home'.

Spofforth must also have looked forward keenly to discovering some of his roots and meeting relations in England. Although most of the Spofforths had moved away from Howden by this time, his uncle Robert had retired to the resort of Gristhorpe, just south of Scarborough. Fred Spofforth probably met this branch of the family when the Australians played a Scarborough and District XVIII in August. Fred Spofforth, also, must have met his second cousin, Markham Spofforth (1825–1907), who had been a prominent figure in the Conservative Party and had become Senior Taxing Master in the Chancery in 1876. Markham was featured in a *Vanity Fair* cartoon in 1880: it was an unusual honour for one family to produce two Spy cartoons in two years.[1] Fred Spofforth's first son, christened Reginald Markham, provides further suggestion of some link.

Perhaps, as the boat steamed out of the Heads, Spofforth also sensed that the extended fifteen-month tour might provide him with the opportunity of proving himself as a fast bowler in the toughest league of all, English cricket. The decision to resign from the bank for an extended period would not have been taken lightly as Spofforth always set

The young tourist, 1878.
(*Reynolds* The Australian
Cricketers Tour . . . 1878).

great store on pursuing a career beyond cricket. S N Hogg, manager of the Balmain branch of the Bank of New South Wales, later recalled that Fred Spofforth's father, Edward, was 'averse to his son Frederick's desire to give up his secured position' and the general manager of the Bank (for the colony), Shepherd Smith, 'pointed out to the young man, whose services he valued, the risk he was running in following the bent of his inclination'. When Fred Spofforth chose 'to take the chance', Edward Spofforth 'secretly admiring his independence, gave way'.[2] In order to join the tour he had been granted twelve months' leave without pay from the Bank of New South Wales on 4 November 1877. In fact Spofforth did not rejoin the Bank until 1 June 1879, when he was accepted back on the same salary scale as when he left — £175 per annum.

According to Spofforth the idea of an English tour first came from the players: 'D W Gregory was the first to suggest such an experiment, in which he was supported by Charles Bannerman'. However, 'the first definite move in the matter' was made by John Conway, who was both manager and promoter of the tour, and liaised with James Lillywhite who helped to arrange the English matches. Conway, who played for a Victorian XVIII against Stephenson's XI in the first match of Stephenson's 1861–62 tour, had represented Victoria from 1861 to 1874, and was involved subsequently in cricket journalism, publishing a cricket annual. Most of the leading colonial players joined the tour. A notable exception was Edwin Evans, one of the first approached, who declined on the grounds of his 'state of health', according to the *Sydney Mail*.[3]

The players left without the blessings of the local cricket associations, who were not all pleased that the tourists would be unavailable for the intercolonials. The press, Spofforth later wrote, initially 'ignored our movements almost entirely' and when they did take notice of the tour were downright discouraging, such as the paper which dubbed the tour 'a presumptuous adventure calculated to dampen the ardour of the most enterprising speculator'. The public, too, 'seemed to regard the scheme with coolness' and when the team sailed out of Sydney for Brisbane on the *Baraclutha* on the first leg of their Australasian tour on 3 November 1877, 'there was no particular demonstration by the friends of the team' and the 'demonstration of crick-eters' on the Australian Steam Navigation Company's Wharf was of the 'mildest description'.

The side was one of the youngest ever to leave the country, with an average age of just twenty-three. Tom Garrett was the youngest at nineteen and captain Dave Gregory, at thirty-two, was the only player over thirty. There was little margin for illness and injury: the side consisted of only twelve players despite a heavy English program of thirty-seven matches, twenty against the odds, organised by James Lillywhite. Without a baggage master the team had to drag around its own equipment, as Spofforth recalled later:

Before starting on the home tour, we had an immense canvas bag made, with 'Australian Eleven', in bold letters, across it; and we used to draw lots to decide who should look after the bag from match to match. I remember that at one place in New Zealand, Murdoch and myself had charge of the 'caravan', as it was called, and for a mile and a half we had to climb fences, and scramble over gates with the huge thing in tow. We carried it to England, and landed it safely at Nottingham; but in London it was lost, and no man knows its burying-place.

In order to raise money for the venture, the tourists travelled extensively through Australia and New Zealand from 9 November 1877 until 25 March 1878 and played twenty-three matches against the odds, against teams with fifteen, eighteen and even twenty-two players. Some of the initial matches of their tour were not well publicised and aroused limited public interest. When the match between the Australian XI and the New South Wales XV began on 23 November there were only several hundred spectators, though the crowd swelled to 6,000 on the following day, a Saturday. Evans was not much help to the XV as he could not get to the ground, because of reported family sickness, until the Australian innings was almost over. He took only 0-12 and 1-58 whereas Spofforth took 7-60 and 12-48.

Just before the touring side left for New Zealand they played an exciting tie against New South Wales–Victoria at the Melbourne Cricket Ground. The tourists, by then, had earned the respect of the cricketing public and good crowds turned up on each of the three days to see Evans take eleven wickets including the wicket which secured the tie. Spofforth took five wickets in the first innings but this time Harry Boyle starred for the tourists, taking 10-29 off just 96 balls in the second innings.

Officials and spectators in New Zealand were certainly enthusiastic about the first Australian tour to their country. There was a sizeable assembly at Canterbury — 18,000 over three days — where the tourists lost their only match of the preliminary tour against the local XXII. This reverse, 'Square Leg' believed, was not due to the 'superior cricket' of the Canterbury side but was more a case of 'bad wickets, bad weather and bad umpiring'. In fact the news of this defeat was received in Sydney with 'unmitigated regret', the tour had proceeded 'so well' that the tourists were looked upon with 'considerable favour'.[4]

Travelling around New Zealand was often primitive and sometimes dangerous but as the following anecdote, recalled by Spofforth, makes clear, the tourists endured their lot not without a sense of humour:

While we were coasting along New Zealand we were caught by a terrible storm; and, being in a very small steamer, we were in considerable danger. Charles Bannerman, who was an expert swimmer, was very frightened. He refused to go into his cabin, and said if he ever got on dry land again he would never leave it as long as he lived.

'Well,' I said, 'suppose we *are* wrecked. What will you do?'

'First,' he said, 'I'll save Alick (his brother), then Murdoch, then yourself.'

'Well, but what about the Victorians?' I asked.

'Let them drown,' he replied, 'let them drown. D'you think I'm going to risk my life for *them*?'

There were also some rewarding moments for Spofforth, who must have had the opportunity to renew links with the McDonnell family.

Frank Allan, whom the *Sydney Mail* believed was the best bowler of the tourists, did not go on the New Zealand leg because of injury. In his absence Spofforth took on the dual mantle of strike and stock bowler. During the preliminary Australasian tour Spofforth bowled 3,845 balls and took 281 wickets at an average of 4.3. He bowled 34 per cent of the side's total balls bowled and took 40 per cent of the wickets taken. The next leading bowlers, Tom Garrett and Tom Kendall, took only 103 and 102 wickets respectively. Spofforth thrived on the added work and responsibility and it was fortunate for the tourists that his broad shoulders could carry the weight. By the time they left Australia Kendall had been dropped from the team because of his drinking problems.

With the team performing well on its Australasian tour — fourteen games were won, seven drawn, one tied and only one lost — there was a little more public enthusiasm when the team finally left Sydney for San Francisco on 29 March 1878. After the cricketers had been entertained by a number of friends at Punch's Hotel on the previous evening, a large crowd gathered at the wharf to farewell them and their ship was accompanied down the harbour by *Bellbird*, *Britannia* and *Prince of Wales*. As RMS *City of Sydney* passed through the heads the band of the Permanent Artillery, stationed at the cliffs near South Head, played 'Auld Lang Syne' and the soldiers gave the cricketers three cheers.[5]

It took more than six weeks to travel from Sydney to Liverpool, 29 March to 13 May: a steamer to San Francisco, travel by train across the United States to New York, and another boat to Liverpool. The tourists must have been pleased with their enthusiastic welcome in England. Arriving in Nottingham on 14 May they were met by cheering crowds which crushed against their horse-drawn omnibus and some 8,000 people lined the streets. They were, to some extent, the objects of curiosity: many were surprised to discover that the tourists were not black, since a group of Aborigines had been the first Australian cricketers to tour England, in 1868. Comments made by one Nottingham spectator were to be repeated throughout the tour 'Whoy, Bill, they beant black at all; they're as white as wuz'. No doubt some spectators expected a troupe of cricket entertainers who could throw boomerangs and run backwards during breaks in play.

Although Spofforth and his fellow tourists had been brought up on a regular diet of English culture, the reality of England was unfamiliar to them. Spofforth later recalled his reactions when the Australians arrived at their first English cricket ground at Trent Bridge, Nottingham:

The ground itself was quite different from those to which we were accustomed. I remember very vividly the impression it made upon me; it seemed much smaller than any of the principal grounds in Australia, and the turf much greener, while the red roofs of the surrounding buildings gave the whole enclosure a quaint and unusual appearance to our eyes.[6]

The English public, and the press for that matter, had a hazy idea of who the Australian cricketers were. Australia was a faraway exotic and bizarre country. *Punch* published a cartoon on 10 August 1878 of the Australian team members supposedly on the back of a kangaroo but, while the creature had the body of a kangaroo, its face resembled a camel.

The Australian loss to Nottinghamshire by the wide margin of an innings and 14 runs and in the first match of the tour, was a damaging one. The crowds who flocked to watch the tourists must have been doubly disappointed: they weren't an exotic troupe who combined cricket and some elements of circus entertainment; nor, it seemed were they

ADVANCE. AUSTRALIA!"

The 1878 team on a peculiar kangaroo. (Punch 10 August 1878).

very good cricketers. It was unfortunate that the visitors were pitted against the powerful Notts XI just seven days after their arrival and before they had a real chance to acclimatise themselves or to practise after the long voyage. 'We travelled to London,' Spofforth later wrote, 'with our confidence in ourselves rudely shaken.'[7] The events of 27 May 1878 not only bolstered the spirits of the tourists but also pricked once and for all the bubble of English cricket complacency and established that the 1878 Australians were competitive on the cricket field.

When large crowds turned out to watch the Australians in subsequent matches, Spofforth and his team-mates proved that the MCC match was no flash in the pan. In the next game they beat Yorkshire by six wickets and then defeated Surrey by five wickets, with Spofforth taking nine and eleven wickets respectively. After the Notts loss the Australians won eight of their first-class games, losing four and drawing three. While they did not play a Test on this tour, five of the games were against representative elevens: two against the Gentlemen, two against the Players and one against the MCC.

Spofforth played a key role in most of the eight victories. He took twelve wickets against both the Players and Gloucestershire, eleven against Surrey, ten against the MCC and nine against Leicestershire, Sussex and Yorkshire. His achievement was particularly meritorious because the Australian batting often proved unreliable. Only Charles Bannerman had a good tour with the bat, accumulating 567 runs at an average of 21 in the fifteen first-class matches. The next best batsman was G H Bailey who scored just 254 runs at an average of 14.9.

The task of the bowlers was made even more difficult because the team lost the services of Midwinter in the ninth match of the tour. Just before the match against Middlesex, Midwinter was virtually kidnapped by W G Grace, who hustled him back to the Oval where Gloucestershire was playing against Surrey. Although contracted to play with the Australians for the entire tour, Grace claimed that the Gloucestershire-born cricketer also had an agreement to play with the county. Despite strenuous efforts by the tour management, Midwinter did not play another game with the tourists. Without him or Kendall, the tourists had to rely mainly on four bowlers — Spofforth, Boyle, Garrett and Allan — and the latter did not have a good tour. Spofforth carried the attack: he bowled more than one-third of the overs (658.1 out of 1758.3) and took close to half the first-class wickets (97 out of 223). The loss of Midwinter also meant that none of the eleven remaining players could be spelled, though manager Conway played an occasional game. Spofforth was rested for only three of the thirty-seven games.

One reason why the Australians were successful and why Spofforth developed such a reputation during the tour was that they, and to some extent he, kept the champion batsman, W G Grace, quiet. In five first-class innings against

the Australians Grace scored only 56 runs with a top score of 25. Although Spofforth only dismissed him once, Grace was never comfortable against the Demon, as suggested by the report of the first match against the Gentlemen in which Grace scored 25 (b. Boyle) and Spofforth did not bowl all that well, taking 2-53. When the innings of the Gentlemen began:

W G obtained 2 off Spofforth for a fluke, and was then missed at the wickets, a rather easy chance of catching him on the off side. The leviathan did not appear to like the bowling at either end, and was much knocked about by Spofforth on legs and body. He soon made a desperate smite at Spofforth, and only just pulled the ball beyond the bowler's reach for a single.[8]

Late in the season Spofforth played a pivotal role in the ten wicket defeat of Gloucestershire, champion county of 1877 and dominated by the Grace family: the team included W G, E M and G F Grace and their cousin W R Gilbert. Although Spofforth did not take W G's wicket in either innings, he took twelve wickets in all and scored 44, a 'fine hitting innings', and 4 not out.

There were some occasions when Spofforth did not bowl well. Against Middlesex he did not take a wicket in either innings and came in for a certain amount of punishment. However, he more than made up for his lack of bowling success with a remarkable innings of 56 in under an hour of brilliant and dashing cricket which included only one difficult chance. In an era of low scoring it must have been regarded as an orgy of spectacular hitting. It was, at the time, the highest Australian score of the tour (in the ninth match) and there were only several higher first-class innings: Alick Bannerman scored 71 not out against Thornton's XI. Spofforth not only played some useful innings but also had the second highest aggregate in the first-class matches (304 runs), though he was sixth in the averages (12.7).

In between matches against the leading sides there were jaunts against XVIIIs and XXIIs where Spofforth and Boyle, in particular, mowed down opposition of dubious quality. Wickets fell dramatically in a match against the Elland XVIII, with Boyle dismissing seven batsmen in eight balls. When someone called out 'Send a man in!', a wit replied 'Send in three or four at once: one's no use!'

Many of these games provided colourful stories which Spofforth loved to recount in later life. After the Rochdale and District XVIII[9] ran up a sizeable score Spofforth was approached at his hotel by the mayor, who boasted that his son, Willie, had made the highest score and added that 'he could easily play my bowling, but did not like Boyle's'. When asked by Blackham what he thought of that Spofforth quipped: 'Very unkind, considering I allowed him to do it. However, I will next innings bowl him for a goose's egg.' The mayor, who did not sense that Spofforth was joking, was incensed by the reply and 'offered to bet any amount that I would not do it'. He then proceeded to wager £10 that Spofforth could not remove Willie for no score. When the match resumed Spofforth was in a difficult position 'because everyone in the pavilion had heard about the matter and was anxious to see the result':

I really did not remember Master Willie, and had to keep asking; but at last he arrived, and having taken his guard, I placed all the fieldsmen as close as possible, and, taking an extra long run, bowled with all my might. Willie's leg stump turned a complete somersault.

The mayor later apologised for his behaviour and his son declared that he did not see the ball which bowled him.

Towards the end of the tour there were some shades of future controversy, in the second match against the Players, when the selected team of professionals refused to accept the match payment of £10 offered by Conway and demanded twice that amount. It was a hefty demand because the current rates were £5 and £6, respectively, for home and away county games and £10 for a representative match. Possibly the professionals believed that they should earn more because the Australian 'amateurs' were making so much out of the 1878 tour.[10] Their replacements played well and 'we had the worst of the match'. With the players needing just nineteen runs and with five wickets in hand, Gregory approached Spofforth and commented: 'Loup, we are going to be beaten by a lot of second-raters'. Spofforth volunteered to come on at one end, because 'I felt confident that any moment I might begin getting wickets myself' and suggested Garrett bowl at the other, to tie it up. Spofforth took three wickets in the next over and the Australians won by eight runs. After the match 'we ourselves', added Spofforth, paid each of the Players £20.

It was during the 1878 tour that Spofforth became a hero. It was he, more than anyone else, who carried the attack. Time and time again, whenever the situation was difficult, Gregory would throw the ball in his direction and Spofforth would produce just a little bit extra. He was the man for a crisis. As the tour progressed he must have grown both in confidence and maturity. He was also a quick learner and progressed rapidly from a person who learnt something about bowling from Alfred Shaw in 1876-77 to a tactician observing weaknesses in the English bowling. He later remarked that he was surprised that the English bowlers 'used to place the field almost entirely according to the system recognised in text-books, without regard to the character of their own bowling or the tricks of the batsmen'.

By the end of the 1878 season Spofforth was a hero both inside and outside cricket circles. The publication of the Spy cartoon on 13 July 1878 was a unique honour. Spofforth was the first Australian recognised and only another two featured in the series of forty-seven prints which appeared from 1877 to 1913: George Bonnor in 1884 and Sammy Woods, who was Australian-born but who played all his senior cricket in England, in 1892. The cartoon, which features a rather sardonic Demon, is one of the most celebrated in the *Vanity Fair* series and suggests that the artist had no trouble capturing the essence of a man who had become an interesting and compelling character.

Spofforth was as popular with the English public as he was with the Australian. Even though he was the architect of some historic English defeats he always received a very good response from the English press and public. His popularity was partly because there were so many overlapping areas between English and middle-class Australian culture. Heroes appealed to values which were appreciated in both societies.

There were, however, slightly different reasons why Spofforth was lionised in each country. To the English he was an imperial symbol whose success established the vitality of their game in exotic climes: whereas Grace epitomised English cricket, Spofforth was the symbol of the new vogue of international cricket. To the Australians he was a symbol that colonial culture, which was feared to be inferior, was worthwhile. Spofforth was also a symbol of an emerging pro-imperial nationalism.

Twentieth-century Australian heroes, from Trumper to Lillee, have been more identifiably Australian. While they have all been revered and respected by the English public, none was acclaimed and adopted in the sense that Spofforth was. Spofforth was as much an English or imperial hero as he was an Australian one.

At the end of the tour Spofforth achieved rave notices from the English press. Typical was the elaborate and highly complimentary article published in the *Daily News*:

But the name of all others that will be remembered by the English public is that of Mr Spofforth; without whom the results of Mr Conway's management and Mr Gregory's generalship would have fallen short of actual achievements. Mr Spofforth earned for himself the highest bowling renown. Not even George Freeman, or Tarrant, at his best, ever created such a panic among batsmen. Taking a long run, delivering the ball at the full extent of an unusually long reach, and so disguising his intentions that few can tell whether the coming ball will be one of the famous 'fast yorkers' or a slow break-back, Mr Spofforth is simply the most puzzling and destructive bowler that his generation has seen.

The wet summer, the same writer added, had suited Spofforth. When the wickets were 'fast and true' during July Spofforth was played 'with confidence', but 'as soon as the rain began again' in August the Demon 'had matters pretty well his own way' and 'was almost unplayable'.[11]

Many others echoed this assessment. He was, as Lord Hawke put it, the 'star turn' of 1878. The journalist 'Anglicanus', who covered a number of tours, argued that it was Spofforth who made Australian cricket what it was in England on this and subsequent tours. By the end of the tour Spofforth was acclaimed by quite a few English critics as the best bowler in the world. John Lillywhite wrote:

His bowling I consider second to none in the world, having the great gift of bowling fast or slow, with the same action, it being very difficult to judge his pace. A great many of the best batsmen in the country had a taste of his quality, and several thought he was the most difficult bowler they had ever played.[12]

The Australians proved immensely popular in England and drew well wherever they went. With so much money flowing into the cricket coffers English officials and the press were generally prepared to overlook the fact that all the tourists, with the exception of Charles Bannerman, were defined as amateurs yet they were involved in what turned out to be a highly lucrative venture. Another reason for their popularity was that the tourists were Anglo-Australians, Anglicist in culture and sympathetic to broader imperial goals. Their very success underscored popular notions, supported by Social Darwinism, that British culture was both superior and resilient. On 10 August 1878 *Punch* published an imaginary interview with the Australian cricketers in which they pointed out that Australia was something more than a land of 'gold, and Australian beef and kangaroos':

Australia also had progressed in terms of commerce, education, architecture and politics but was still British to the core. The cricketers declared:

> We love the Old Country. We know how to handle the oar — as Trickett has taught you — as well as the bat; and as for the rifle — *should* the time come — 'We don't want to fight; but, by Jingo . . .'

The Australian team played a series of matches in North America during October, and 'we were made perfect heroes of' when they arrived in Sydney Harbour on 25 November. Spofforth recalled that it was 'one of the greatest sights I have ever seen' when 'all the crowded steamers met us outside the Sydney "Heads" to welcome us back'. Manager Conway later wrote that 'the reception exceeded anything they could have anticipated, all classes doing their utmost to show how genuine was the appreciation of the fellow-colonists'. He added that on 'no previous occasion had Sydney been so moved'.[13] Presumably Conway was referring to previous cricket occasions because there was equal enthusiasm when the world champion sculler, Ned Trickett, returned two years before. Spofforth must have savoured the public adulation and regarded it as just recognition of much hard work over the past year.

The celebrations in Sydney were repeated at many other places. The journey of the team to Melbourne was 'more like a triumphal march' with 'people turning out in every town they passed through, to do them honour'. When the team arrived at Spencer Street Station, the approaches were completely blocked and the roadways to the Town Hall lined with people. 'After speeches from the Lord Mayor and the Bishop of Melbourne at the Town Hall the team was honoured on the following evening by an open air concert at the East Melbourne Cricket Club. The eleven arrived at the ground by a torch-light procession.'[14]

Subsequently the tourists were feted and banqueted around the country. Numerous editorials dwelt on the significance of the tour, reiterating a theme elaborated in *The Age* after the home team's first Test win in March 1877, which was 'a crushing reply to those unpatriotic theorists who would have us believe that the Australian race is deteriorating from the imperial type, or that lengthened residence under the Australian sun must kill the Briton in the blood'.[15] Regarding themselves as transplanted Britons the local press also dwelt on the significance of the cultural pilgrimage to the mother country, establishing their own worth in England itself.

The tourists had little time to celebrate in earnest because they were on the road again, playing another eight games in Australia before the party was disbanded on 10 January 1879. Perhaps they banqueted just a little too much because the tourists were brushed aside easily by a New South Wales XV who beat them by an innings and 12 runs. They did have some bad luck in that only nine players could bat in the second innings after Bailey fractured his arm and Spofforth was ill.

However, by the sixth match the tourists and Spofforth had recovered sufficiently to defeat the 'Gentlemen of England' comprehensively in what is now regarded as the third Test. Captained by Lord Harris, this amateur team, which was bolstered by two professionals, was the fifth English side to tour Australia.

The Test, which began at the Melbourne Cricket Ground on 2 January 1879, was a triumph for Spofforth who grasped the opportunity to demonstrate his new-found maturity. On the first morning Spofforth and Allan dismissed four visitors cheaply and then, with the score at 26, Spofforth achieved the first hat-trick in Test cricket: he bowled Royle and Mackinnon and then had Emmett caught by Tommy Horan. He was perhaps a little fortunate to secure the third wicket because the ball to Emmett was a 'loose ball ... a little to leg' and Emmett skied it into Horan's hands at long-stop. It was one of two catches taken by Horan off Spofforth at long-stop in this match. Wicket-keeping and batting technique were to change in the next decade making long-stop redundant both as backstop and catcher.

Spofforth finished the innings with impressive figures: 25 overs, 9 maidens, 48 runs, 6 wickets. England recovered from 7-26 to reach 113 and then dismissed three Australian batsmen for 37. Spofforth, batting at number five, then scored a valuable 39 in difficult conditions — in between rain interruptions and in bad light — and put on a useful partnership of 64. The Australians totalled 256. Spofforth was again the wrecker in the second innings: 35 overs, 16 maidens, 62 runs, 7 wickets. His 13 wickets and 39 runs paved the way for an easy Australian victory by 10 wickets.

After playing two more matches against Victorian country sides the 1878 Australians disbanded on 10 January 1879, fifteen months and a day after their first Australasian match and undoubtedly one of the longest and most demanding cricket tours ever. The tour bowling figures established the significance of the role played by Spofforth, who was both the strike and the stock bowler of the side. He bowled more than a third of the total overs — 35 per cent, almost twice as many as any other bowler — and took 41 per cent of the wickets.

Wickets Taken on the 1878 Tour

	Australasia	England	North America	Australia	Total (Average)
Spofforth (3, 110.2 overs)	281	326	69	88	764 6.1
Boyle (1, 658.1)	90	197	27	17	331 7.0
Garrett (1, 463.1)	103	123	29	36	291 5.7
Allan (1, 379.1)	68	88	44	17	217 8.5
Kendall (522.2)	102				102 6.3
Others (689.3)	67	U	U	U	150 6.9

The Harris tour is best remembered for the riot which occurred at the Sydney Cricket Ground on 8 February 1879. It was the worst instance of crowd violence in Australian cricket history and had a significant impact on the shape of the next tour to England. Spofforth played an unwitting role in the outbreak of the riot. The night before the first match between the tourists and the New South Wales XI, which began at the Sydney Cricket Ground on 24 January, Spofforth had sprained his wrist and withdrew from the home side. Despite the absence of the star all-rounder, the New South Wales team performed well and beat the tourists comfortably by five wickets. Murdoch was the outstanding batsman in this game, scoring 70 and 49. Although he had not played all that well on the English tour — he scored 274 runs (less than Spofforth) in first-class games at an average of 13.05 — Murdoch had clearly benefited from the experience.

With Spofforth available for the return match against the visitors, which began on 7 February, the New South Wales public installed the home side as strong favourites and a lot of money was invested. But the match did not go well for the home side from the start. The Englishmen hit up a sizeable total of 267 and Spofforth, perhaps not back to his best after his injury, was relatively expensive taking 5-93. The colony managed 177 with Murdoch scoring 82 and Spofforth 0 — he made a pair. The riot took place during the second innings when Murdoch was adjudged run out by Victorian umpire, George Coulthard, whose services had been engaged by Lord Harris. The decision angered the crowd because it occurred after several doubtful decisions and many people believed that Murdoch had made his ground. Many years later Spofforth gave his own brief version of what happened:

Then the crowd could stand it no longer and rushed on to the field, refusing to budge until the umpire was removed. I have no wish to dwell on this painful occurrence, but I should like to point out that the feeling aroused was almost entirely due to the spirit of rivalry between the Colonies . . . The umpire was a Victorian, and the party spirit in the crowd was too strong. 'Let an Englishman stand umpire,' they cried; 'we don't mind any of them. We won't have a Victorian.' There was not the slightest animosity against Lord Harris or any of his team; the whole disturbance was based on the fact that the offender was a Victorian. But Lord Harris stood by his umpire; and, as a result, the match had to be postponed till the following day.

Spofforth's account, admittedly written fifteen years after the event, is intriguing because it is so understated and because he seems quite unwilling to buy into some of the controversies generated by this event. He did not comment on the Lord Harris view that gambling, and the tolerance of gambling by the authorities, played a significant role in the riot. Spofforth may well have sympathised with the Harris perspective because he later supported another Harris moral campaign, which was to clean up cricket by eliminating throwing. Spofforth also avoided any comment on the suggestion that New South Wales captain Dave Gregory may have encouraged the rioters, an opinion aired several years later by Murdoch.

There was another painful result of the return encounter against New South Wales which was to cause Spofforth much future moral anxiety. In his report of the tour, published in the 1880 'Red' *Lillywhite*, Harris pointed out that Spofforth had damaged the pitch by his action: 'By the time 220 was up, Spofforth, owing to his action, had worked such a hole in the pitch that it was evident, if Evans went on at the other end, the innings was to all intents over'. Gregory eventually made this change and the Englishmen collapsed from 4-220 to be all out for 267. Harris made no suggestion that Spofforth's action was deliberate and constituted unfair play. But within a few seasons, there were others who were far less guarded in their comments and contended that Spofforth was spiking the pitch deliberately.

An Eccentric and Wayward Demon

J. Blackham

*E*arly in the 1879-80 season Spofforth was embroiled in a controversy that reveals a great deal both about his character and the demands placed on the local hero. Perhaps worried by the possible absence of Evans, for business reasons, and Coates, unable to get leave, 'Square Leg' of the *Sydney Mail* was decidedly uneasy about the behaviour of the 'trump card for NSW' prior to the first intercolonial. For some reason, which 'Square Leg' could not 'for the life of me comprehend', Spofforth insisted on playing for the 'fifteen all-comers' against the New South Wales XI which was the trial match for the intercolonial. Believing that Spofforth's decision was an indication of his unavailability for the intercolonial, and while freely acknowledging his excellence as a bowler, 'Square Leg', in the *Sydney Mail* of 8 November 1879, proceeded to lecture him at length on his obligations as a star player:

Spofforth, the erratic, is, I hear, coquetting with the selection committee, and I shall not be at all surprised if, at the last moment, he leaves the colony in the lurch. Should he do so, the team may manage to get on without his assistance, but it is probable that the public will express considerable disgust at the 'Demon's' waywardness ... The latest phase of eccentricity on the part of 'the demon', is a desire to play for the fifteen all-comers against the eleven.

A lengthy reply, penned by Spofforth on 10 November and published in the next issue of the paper, was quite remarkable because it was clearly a letter written in hot haste and one in which he made no effort to disguise his anger at the unreasonable demands placed on him. Point by point the letter demolished the argument of the journalist in an extremely meticulous fashion:

Sir, — My conduct has been questioned, and a good many unkind and untrue remarks have been published, both by you and your contemporaries, because I am not going to play in the forthcoming Intercolonial Cricket Match.

In the last issue of the *Mail* I am accused of 'coquetting with the selection committee', who knew before they selected the team that I was not going to play, if chosen.

In another paper paragraphs have appeared to the effect that I will not play because some bet (of which I have no knowledge) remains unpaid to me by one of the Australian Eleven; another reason given is that it is on account of some private quarrel with Mr Garrett, and I dare say a score of other assertions just as absurd will be made before the match comes off.

It seems to me very hard that, because I happen to be chosen to represent New South Wales in a cricket match, I am almost *compelled* to play to stop untruths being published which might seriously affect my future prospects.

Now the facts are these. I am not going to play cricket all my life, and I think it is about time I turned my attention to more serious pursuits; besides this, I cannot afford time to practice (sic) so as to do myself and my side justice.

I did make an attempt, but after going out three afternoons without getting an innings, I spoke to the committee. No alteration being made, I gave up after three more efforts. This has been frequently the case with all players who cannot get to the ground by four o'clock, as many can testify. The best batsmen get down early, go in first against good bowling, and before the ground is cut up; they then stand about watching the young aspirants for intercolonial fame trying to show good cricket against tired bowlers, or men who don't even profess to bowl, and on rough wickets. Then the public wonder why they don't make scores in the matches, and the papers say they are nervous (which means they never get another show). Why should the people of New South Wales grumble at me? Did I ever help to lose an intercolonial match, or disgrace them while in England?

In conclusion, I may state that, even should other things permit, my present health will not allow me taking part in this match — I am, & c.,

Fred. R. Spofforth

The letter is a revealing document of the personality of a man of high standards who could not tolerate sloppy organisation. He was quite fearless in expressing his mind and in taking on the selection committee and the press. Then there was the surprising suggestion, given that he still had four of his five English tours ahead of him, that there was a life worth pursuing beyond cricket and there was just the hint that if local cricket was not better organised he might well retire. It is unlikely that anyone, including Spofforth, took this threat too seriously, as he was an individual who was not afraid to vent his immediate feelings. However, the suggestion was an interesting one as it indicates that even at this early stage Spofforth was mindful of a career beyond sport.

Spofforth's trenchant letter put 'Square Leg' very much on the defensive who accepted the plea of ill-health and apologised. Even so, 'Square Leg' was still rather puzzled by Spofforth's behaviour:

If I have wrongfully accused Spofforth of coquetting the selection committee I must throw the blame on the committee, for if they really knew before the practice team was chosen that he was not going to take part in the match, they ought to have published the fact by striking his name out of the list. It is rather curious, though, that if Spofforth's firm intention was not to play, that he should have attended practice regularly at the Association Ground.

The journalist must also have wondered how sick the Demon was because Spofforth demolished the picked XI in the second innings, taking 5-27 off 111 balls in a match in which the All Comers XV (158) easily defeated the XI, who managed only 57 and 52.

In spite of listing a number of reasons why he could not play for his colony, Spofforth did play in the November match in Sydney. He did not bowl all that well in the first innings when he was severely handled, but when it really counted it was Spofforth who was instrumental in pulling the match out of the fire: he bowled best on the final day, when the wickets were cut up, to take 5-29 off 79 balls and secure a win for New South Wales by just 38 runs.

Although 'Square Leg' was pleased with the role Spofforth played he continued to lecture the star player on his obligations to cricket and the sporting public, advising Spofforth before the match that if he played he had 'a splendid opportunity for retaining and increasing his popularity'. Commenting on the match itself the same reporter noted: ' "The Demon" was steadily declining in popularity during the first two days of the match: but the way in which he administered the *coup de grace* to the Victorians on Monday night brought him once more to the summit of public favour'.[1]

Prior to the return intercolonial at Melbourne in December, the New South Wales selectors must have been driven to distraction about the availability of their star bowlers. It was a scenario which was to be repeated on many occasions. Spofforth was reluctant to play and decided to join the team at the very last minute, which was about the time Evans pulled out of the side. On this occasion at least, Spofforth had a good excuse: illness prevented him from joining the practice team and it was on this basis that 'Square Leg' assumed he would not play. Shortly before the match the *Sydney Mail* reported that Evans had overcome the problems of 'obtaining leave of absence' and that 'all he had to do was to start overland and join the rest of the team'. However, Evans 'seceded almost at the last minute when everything had been prepared for his departure'.[2]

There was another reason why Spofforth almost did not play in the Melbourne intercolonial. He was reluctant to request leave from his bank even though its manager, Shepherd Smith, was sympathetic to Spofforth's cricket involvement and would have granted leave. Just why Spofforth was not keen to play in this game is not known. Perhaps he was tired of travel. A more likely explanation, however, was that as a man of propriety he was aware of his obligations to the bank and intent on developing his career. Spofforth only played in Melboure after the New South Wales Cricket Association pleaded with Shepherd Smith:

If our cricketters (*sic*) manage to win the next intercolonial match (at Melbourne) we shall be level with Victoria. To win without Spofforth is impossible and as he will not apply for leave of absence though willing to play I have been requested by a large number of our association to ask you to intercede with him with a view to inducing him to play. One word from you will be quite sufficient, and the great interest you have taken in these contests induces me to hope that you will kindly come to our rescue.[3]

Spofforth had enhanced his reputation to such an extent on the 1878 tour that he was now considered indispensable.

The match at Melbourne must have been a painful one for Spofforth because he had not played in a losing side against Victoria and New South Wales had won seven intercolonials in a row (he played in five of them). New South Wales were thrashed by an innings and 96 runs, Spofforth returned the unflattering figures of 3-121 off 180 balls. The Melbourne correspondent of the *Herald* commented that 'on a sound true wicket no good batsman need fear Spofforth' and aired a theory which was echoed in many papers that Spofforth was a far better bowler on wet and difficult rather than hard and true surfaces. It was not an altogether fair contention, as Spofforth proved himself on all types of wickets, but it did contain an element of truth. The *Sydney*

Mail of 10 January 1880 believed that 'exaggerated confidence in their own powers' was one of the reasons for the New South Wales defeat.

Long before this time, moves had been afoot to organise another tour to England. Victorians Harry Boyle and David Scott planned the second tour. Boyle was captain and another Victorian, George Alexander, was manager. The tour, in terms of time, was as ambitious as the first: it began with a tour of Australia on 1 January 1880 and finished with a tour of Australia and New Zealand which continued until 21 March 1881. The touring party consisted of thirteen players, including a player-manager. This time the tourists went with the blessings of the local associations, although this amounted to little more than an expression of good wishes as the associations had no hand in the formation of the team, nor did they have any control over the finances. As in 1878, the tourists were a youthful side: there was only one player over thirty years of age (Boyle, thirty-two) and three were only nineteen (Jarvis, McDonnell and Palmer); the average age on 1 January 1880 was just 23.8 years. On this occasion Spofforth did not seek leave from the bank; he handed in his resignation on 3 January 1880.

The 1880 tour was ill-fated from the start. The composition of the side — nine Victorians, three New South Welshmen and one South Australian — drew criticism from the New South Wales press which regarded the side, without Garrett and Charles Bannerman (owing to ill health) and the Victorian Horan, as inferior to the 1878 tourists. This was not an assessment supported by Spofforth, who later argued that the 1880 team 'was much stronger than the last'.

Then there was an astonishing cricket coup at Suez, on the voyage to England, when the tour organiser, Boyle, was deposed as captain and replaced by Murdoch. Just what role Spofforth played in this decision, if any, is not known but undoubtedly Spofforth would have sided with his club and colonial colleague.

From a cricketing point of view the decision to appoint the astute and affable Murdoch in preference to the more taciturn Boyle was a wise one. However, in the minds of some English critics, Murdoch was too closely linked with the Sydney riot of 1879 which still rankled in the minds of

English officialdom. This was the primary reason why the tourists were given a decidedly frosty reception when they arrived in England and why they found it difficult to arrange matches with worthwhile opposition. There was another cloud on the horizon in 1880. The English press, players and officials were more critical of the financial basis of the Australian tour. The English press was now far less willing to accept that the Australian 'amateurs', with the exception of Alick Bannerman who received a guaranteed sum for the tour, also stood to make large profits at the end of the tour. The tourists were dubbed 'commercial cricketers' by one paper and another referred to them as a 'money-hunting crew'.

Arriving in England on 4 May 1880 it must have been a great disappointment for the Australians, and Spofforth in particular, to find that the organisers had only been able to arrange five matches against four county elevens (they were scheduled to play Yorkshire twice) in the industrial north. No matches were arranged against the MCC, the Players or the Gentlemen, nor was a Test match in the offing.

So from 13 May until 1 September the Australians played only five games against first-class opposition and another twenty-five against lesser opposition, against XVIIIs. Spofforth was in irresistible form and was the key bowler in all five games against the XIs: he took thirteen, twelve and eleven wickets respectively against Derbyshire, Gloucestershire and Yorkshire and in the single innings he bowled against Leicestershire and Yorkshire he took six and five wickets respectively. In the first match against Yorkshire Spofforth's off-cutters were working well and he made great use of his attacking fieldsman, Boyle, who fielded close to the bat at silly mid-on: five of the Yorkshire batsmen were dismissed in the second innings, caught Boyle, bowled Spofforth.

Spofforth, as usual, must have tried a little harder when he took on the Graces of Gloucestershire in early August. On this occasion some of the Graces got runs against Spofforth: E M scored 65 and 41; G F 25 and 10; and W R Gilbert 48 not out and 10; however, the champion bat, W G, again failed against the Australians scoring only 6 and 3, falling to Palmer and Spofforth. Spofforth spearheaded the Australian victory with 11-130 off 80.1 overs. The Australians did not keep W G out of the match entirely because he took 11-134 and for once turned the tables on Spofforth by taking his wicket twice.

Spofforth was in great form just before the thaw in relations between English officialdom and the Australians which provided the side with a Test and a much better program for the final seven matches in September. In six days of play against the XVIIIs of Hunslet, Bradford and Sunderland over 5 to 13 August he took fifty-six wickets which was more than half the total opposition wickets taken (102) in these games.

During this tour Spofforth added to his legendary status and English spectators invented many fanciful stories to embellish and explain his prowess. One correspondent reported remarks made by persons in the crowd:

They called Spofforth the demon emu, and said the reason he was such a good bowler was that he was an emu-hunter, and made his living by catching emus, his mode of operation being to knock them over with balls made of wood, the same size as cricket balls.[4]

However, in the next match against the Scarborough XVIII, although returning 12-98, Fred Spofforth had the great misfortune to break his finger. It occurred at the very worst time 'within half-an-hour of this memorable match (the Test match) being arranged' and 'has always been a great regret to me'.

As well as being a great personal disappointment, Spofforth's injury was a body blow to the tourists. He missed the next nine matches and while he batted in the final match he did not bowl. It was during this period that the tourists suffered their only losing streak: they lost three games when Spofforth was absent and the Scarborough match in which he was injured. It is not hard to discover why. Spofforth was the undisputed spearhead of the attack, taking far more wickets than any other bowler and at a much better average. The 1880 attack rested all too much on the shoulders of just three bowlers.

Three bowlers accounted for 87.3 per cent of the overs bowled and 93.5 per cent of the wickets while their average per wicket was less than half that of the part-time bowlers.

Australian Bowling Averages in Representative Matches, 1880 Tour

	Matches	Overs	Runs	Wickets	Average
Spofforth	28	1,559.3	2,018	391	5.6
Palmer	37	1,744.2	2,103	268	7.2
Boyle	35	1,463.3	1,850	250	7.1
Others		608	894	59	15.2

The Australians without Spofforth lost the Test by five wickets. The English win was set up in their first innings when they totalled the very large score of 420 with W G Grace, celebrating the absence of his nemesis, contributing 152. The Australians, dismissed for 149 in the first innings, fought hard in the second with Murdoch, 153 not out, surpassing Grace and promising young batsman, Percy McDonnell, contributing 43 in a total of 327. The Englishmen hit off the required 57 runs for the loss of 5 wickets. The *Australasian* expressed a popular view that had Spofforth played the result might well have been different:

I can well imagine how pleased the great W G Grace and his comrades were to have Spofforth out of the way. I feel persuaded that if Spofforth had been against him that the champion would not have made his large score of 152, for I know he has never played with confidence when playing the bowling of the renowned New South Welshman.[5]

After the English section of the tour ended Spofforth received even finer notices from the English critics than after the 1878 tour. Edgar S Pardon wrote in the 1881 'Green' *Lillywhite* that Spofforth was

doubtless the most effective of living bowlers. No need is there to enlarge upon his special gifts and peculiarities. Many of those who met him considered that he had much improved even upon his wonderful form of 1878. He again showed himself a plucky bat, and an excellent point.

This assessment was echoed in the 1881 'Red' *Lillywhite* which noted that Spofforth was 'more destructive than even in 1878'. Although he showed greater potential in 1880 and was head and shoulders above the other Australian bowlers, he was not fully tested: he did not play in the Test and the games against the Players, the Players of the North, Notts and Sussex.

The 1880 side, as Spofforth suggested, may have had more potential strength than the 1878 team. The batting was more reliable with the greater maturity of Murdoch, supported by McDonnell, the hitting of Bonnor and the stonewalling of Alick Bannerman. The youthful Palmer blended in very well with the established bowling duo of Spofforth and Boyle, but after that there were no bowling reserves, which was a critical weakness. In 1878 there were four front-line bowlers, and a fifth until Midwinter seceded.

The colonial press was generally satisfied with the record of the 1880 Australians in England: they had won twenty-one games, drawn seventeen and lost only four. The Australians, and Murdoch in particular, had worked hard and successfully to restore good relations between the authorities in the two countries. However, they had not won the crucial games and when they returned they were not acclaimed as conquering heroes. When the tourists had just about completed the Australasian leg of the tour, *The Bulletin* reported on 12 March 1881 that 'the Australians are displeased by the absence of a public reception on their arrival in Sydney', and added that the 1880 team could not expect the acclaim meted out to the 1878 tourists since tours were now becoming an ordinary occurrence.

There was also criticism for the 1880 Australians on their return because the local cricket authorities and press were anxious that they play in the 1880-81 intercolonials. Instead, there was an extended tour of Australasia to augment tour funds, which lasted from 19 November 1880 to 21 March 1881 after negotiations for the tourists to play in the intercolonials had collapsed. 'Square Leg' believed that the comment made by a London paper that the tourists were a 'money-hunting crew' had some justification and the *Australasian* complained that 'it is candidly admitted by the team that £.s.d. is the goal at which they will aim, and that, while gate-money rolls in to swell their already large credit balance, the cohesion of the team members will continue to exist'.[6] Although the English section of the tour had not been as successful as 1878, the jaunt through Australasia augmented funds so that the final dividend paid was not much less than the amount received after the previous tour.

Before the team disbanded on 21 March 1881 there was

another tour of New Zealand: the Australians played ten matches from 17 January to 23 February. Spofforth and Palmer bowled magnificently reaping rich harvests of 148 wickets at 3.7 and 141 wickets at 3.3 respectively, and 'hardly a change of bowling was made'. Few other bowlers were called upon: Boyle returned forty-eight wickets and Alexander just fourteen.[7] Spofforth's best figures were 13-13 against Oamaru.

Immediately after the New Zealand tour, the 1880 tourists played the best of the other colonial players, a combined New South Wales–Victoria XI at the Sydney Cricket Ground. Perhaps the tourists were weary after an extended tour but they suffered a humiliating loss to the Rest by 246 runs. With the Rest scoring 197 and 289, as against the tourists' 155 and 85, Spofforth came in for some harsh treatment taking 3-69 and 0-92. The comments after the match in the *Sydney Mail* of 12 March 1881 must have been particularly hurtful to Spofforth as the journalist, on the basis of one bad match, questioned his ability on a hard and true wicket, comparing him unfavourably to Evans. It must have been illuminating to Spofforth to discover that while he was acclaimed by many English critics as the best bowler in the world, Sydney writers still had their doubts and championed the cause of a player who only occasionally put his reputation on the line:

Spofforth, no doubt, bowled well thoughout the match and it was perhaps natural that such a great trundler, returning to Sydney flushed with his success in Maoriland, should have resented the punishment administered to him by Massie as a piece of extraordinary presumption on the part of the latter; but the fact remains that his bowling was knocked all to pieces, not only by Massie, but by other batsmen. This is not a very remarkable circumstance in Spofforth's career in this colony, and to my mind he cannot claim very great superiority over Evans, especially when the weather is fine and the wickets are in good order.

'Square Leg' concluded, rather unfairly, that this defeat confirmed that the Australian XI was 'not by any means the strongest team the colonies can produce'.

Some time after the end of the season, and perhaps wearied by so much cricket, Spofforth left Sydney for an up-country station, a few hundred miles north-west of Sydney, where he was engaged in squatting pursuits. He travelled to Collaroy, at Cassilis, the property owned by the family of Charles Farquhar Clive who had married Spofforth's elder sister, Anna, in 1874. Collaroy, which consisted of over 100,000 acres (40,469 ha) and was one of the largest sheep stations in New South Wales, had been in the Clive family since the 1850s. Spofforth had another incentive for travelling in this direction: on 24 November 1878 his brother Edward had been appointed manager of the Bank of New South Wales at Coonamble, which was approximately another 100 miles (160 km) further to the north.

It was while he was at Cassilis that Spofforth had a serious accident which was reported in *The Bulletin* of 13 August 1881:

Spofforth, the Demon bowler, narrowly escaped death the other day, near Cassilis. He was mounting a fresh horse, and having his gun in one hand and pipe in another, was unable to control him, when he suddenly dashed off. Spofforth was half mounted and was by degrees getting into his seat, when the horse collided violently with another throwing the Demon very heavily, severely injuring the side of his face, breaking a bone in the right jaw, and apparently a bone in the left wrist. Spoff is recovering!

Spofforth must have enjoyed life in the bush because he returned there many times later. He was also decidedly reluctant to return to the city and to pick up a bat and ball even with the incentive of playing against the sixth English team to visit Australia in 1881-82, a team of professionals captained by Alfred Shaw. 'Square Leg' reported on 29 October 1881 that while Spofforth had been selected for the intercolonials and internationals he could not be counted on to play. By mid-November the same correspondent expressed a degree of irritation at the Demon who was 'wasting his sweetness on an up-country station' and added the Demon had written that 'even if he could visit Sydney' he was 'unlikely to be in form, as he had not touched cricket material' for some time. Later in the month it was reported that Spofforth had written to the New South Wales Cricket Association that he would not be in Sydney to represent the colony against the tourists in a match which began on 9 December 1881.

Spofforth did not respond to newspaper hints that he was acting selfishly and was not a member of the New South Wales side which lost the Melbourne intercolonial by just two wickets. Nor was he a member of the Australian side which played in the First Test at Melbourne over the New Year holiday and which saw Edwin Evans, overcoming his reluctance to travel, make his Test debut. Evans bowled lengthy spells in both innings (71 and 75.2 overs) with the mediocre match figures of 3-144.

One player who was not at all reluctant to play for Australia or England was Billy Midwinter, who this time round was a member of the English Test team. But scarcely two months later he was anxious to become a member of the 1882 Australian side, which prompted *The Bulletin* to make the sarcastic comment that 'In Australia he plays as an Englishman; in England, as an Australian and he is always a credit to himself and his country, whichever that may be'.[8]

By this time the colonial press was fed up with Spofforth's reluctance to reappear on the cricket scene. The *Australasian* believed that the First Test side would have been much stronger with the addition of Allan, Jones and Spofforth. Some comments were directed at Spofforth:

By the way, what has become of our demon Freddy? We must get an influential deputation, consisting of the Governor, the Chief Justice and Dr Begg to wait on him and ask him to play in the next match, and if Freddy is asked nicely perhaps the dear fellow will condescend once more to do the demon business in the presence of a spell-bound concourse.[9]

There was considerable doubt in the press, until mid-February 1882, as to whether Spofforth would play any major cricket that season and whether he would join the 1882 tourists who sailed from Australia on 16 March 1882.

Some of the newspapers speculated as to why Australia's champion bowler was so reluctant to return to cricket in season 1881-82. There was a rumour mentioned in the *Sydney Mail* of 21 January 1882 that Spofforth had not played intercolonial and international cricket because the association had not acceded to a demand for money. The association emphatically denied such a demand and it is unlikely that Spofforth made the request.

There were probably more basic reasons why Spofforth appeared to be such a reluctant tourist waiting until the very last moment to declare himself available both in 1882 and 1884. After his second long and arduous tour, when he carried the Australian bowling, Spofforth needed an extended break from cricket to recover physically and mentally. There was also the opportunity, in the solitude of the bush, to escape from the continuing glare of publicity and from the demands of the cricket media and public. Being alone provided this intense and sometimes brooding individual with the opportunity for introspection and self-renewal.

There seems little doubt, too, that Spofforth relished life in the Australian outback. He was by all accounts an able horseman and many hours in the saddle helped him build up his stamina to such an extent that he could once again be used as a tour work-horse.

As well, there are good grounds for suspecting that Spofforth, who had a finely-honed sense of humour, greatly enjoyed the game of keeping the press and public on tenterhooks. The more frantic the press became, the more Spofforth must have been tempted to keep them guessing as long as possible to extract as much humour from the situation as possible.

During December 1881 Spofforth supposedly rode 400 miles (644 km) to a country cricket match where he bowled all twenty batsmen (20-48) and scored more than sixty runs. Knowing Spofforth's love of a good story, the distance may have been a little exaggerated. He also wrote a letter much later to W G Grace, which was auctioned in 1986, minimising this performance and suggesting that the feat was not that impressive because the opposition was not all that strong. No scorecard of this unique achievement has yet been found.

A number of researchers have made a concerted effort to discover details of this match to include in *Historic Non-First-Class Matches in Australia*. So far the search has only yielded one brief, and indirect, reference to the feat by Felix in the *Australasian* of 7 January 1882:

If what I have heard be true, Spofforth is still the 'demon' bowler. I am told that in a country match round about where he is stationed the tall

Sydneyite clean bowled the whole ten wickets in the first innings, and repeated the performance in the second.

Ernest Gross in *The Cricket Statistician* of May 1874 claimed that this match was played at Bendigo in New South Wales, but he may have confused the Victorian town of Bendigo with Bendemeer, north of Tamworth in New South Wales. Spofforth was in northern New South Wales rather than Victoria at this time.

The failure of the metropolitan press to provide many more details suggest that they shared Spofforth's assessment of the quality of his opponents.

Spofforth emerged from his cricket hibernation in February 1882, much to the relief of the Sydney press which rejoiced that the New South Wales team again had its spearhead. 'Spofforth took the ball in hand, long and lithe, and angular and flat, and demoniacal as of old, reaching almost from wicket to wicket and spreading half across the field', noted the *Sydney Mail*.[10] After New South Wales hit a mammoth 775, with Murdoch accounting for 321 runs, Spofforth helped the home colony to victory with a marathon spell in the first innings of 292 balls, 122 runs, 25 maidens and 6 wickets.

Spofforth was expected to play in the Third Test of the series which began at Sydney on 3 March 1882 and which was the first match of the 1882 tour. When the match began Spofforth could not assist the home side because he had skipped away to Melbourne, much to the puzzlement of the *Sydney Mail* which analysed his 'eccentric' behaviour at some length on 4 March:

As for the 'Demon', his nature is of so erratic a character that very few persons who know him were surprised to read in the Melbourne telegram which appeared in Thursday's *Herald* that he had suddenly and unexpectedly appeared in that city. But the question is, why did he leave so unostentatiously just on the eve of a match in which he was expected to work wonders? The rumour is in Melbourne that he did not want the Englishmen to play his bowling until he got to England, and such a report is quite foolish enough to have been circulated by Spofforth himself. In Sydney rumour has been busy in guessing at the why and wherefore; but the only matter with which the cricketing public have to deal is the fact that he has suddenly left the team to which he belongs in the lurch at the last moment, and has not vouchsafed a particle of reason for his conduct.

The *Sydney Mail* then proceeded to lecture the Demon on his responsibilities as a hero. His successes in England had given him 'a strong hold upon public admiration here', but 'I fancy this last eccentricity of his will sweep his popularity to the winds'.

The Bulletin of 11 March suggested that the Melbourne press was equally puzzled by Spofforth's behaviour:

Spofforth was in Melbourne when he ought to have been in Sydney to play in the first match of the Australian Eleven. The Melbourne sporting writers are trying to account for his actions. On this side we have given up hope long ago, and remain merely thankful for his small mercies.

Evans was also absent from the Sydney Test because he still had not made up his mind whether to tour or not. 'He dreads the sea voyage,' noted the *Sydney Mail* of 4 March, 'and apart from that, family reasons act as a bar to his joining the team.' It was 'a pity', added the same writer, 'that he cannot let the public know what his intention really is' for 'every one is anxious' to see him tour England and 'there can be no doubt that if he did, his performances with the ball would open the eyes of cricketers at home'.

Spofforth did play in the next Test, at Melbourne, which was the final match before the tourists set sail. His match figures of 1-128 off 66 overs were not flattering but were hardly surprising, given that he had had so little practice.

Just why he avoided the Sydney Test is a mystery. Perhaps he realised that he was short of match practice and that his psychological edge over the Englishmen might be diminished on the plumb Sydney wicket where New South Wales and Victoria had amassed the total of 1412 runs in three completed innings in February.

There was a simpler and more convenient explanation aired in the colonial press: the hero had become big-headed, frequently behaving in an erratic and eccentric manner. Whether this was the case, there is no doubt that Spofforth was well aware of his prima donna status. He knew that his presence in the Australian side was so vital he could enter and exit at a time of his own choosing.

Above: *Member of the successful New South Wales team. Lithograph of NSW team published in* Sydney Mail *16 January 1874.*

Above: *Fred Spofforth may have had noble ancestors.*

Above: *The Albert Ground. (Courtesy of Jack Pollard)*

Facing page,
Far left: *Another Spofforth 'Spy' caricature: cousin Markham in 1880.* Centre:
*Edward Spofforth aged twenty-two, from a painting by Moore in the possession of
Derek Spofforth.* Right: *Edward Spofforth in his maturity. (In the possession of
Derek Spofforth)*

Above: *104 Derwent Street, Glebe*

Above: *The 1878 team: (Left to right) Back: T Horan, F R Spofforth, J Conway (Sec), F E Allan. Centre: G H Bailey, T W Garrett, D W Gregory (Cpt.), A C Bannerman, H F Boyle. Front: C Bannerman, W L Murdoch, J McBlackman.*

Above: *Edwin Evans. (Courtesy Phillip Derriman)*

Above: *The Ashes*

Above: *Spofforth in 1892 (left) and 1882 (right). There is a resemblance to another great Australian 'thinking' bowler: D K Lillee.*

Above: *Australians versus Cambridge University, 1882. (Left to right)* Back: *G E Palmer, H F Boyle, W L Murdoch, P S McDonnell, F R Spofforth, T Horan, S P Jones.* Front: *C W Beal, G Giffen, A C Bannerman, T W Garrett, H H Massie, G J Bonnor.*

Above: *The Australian XI in 1884, (Left to right)* Back: *J M Blackham, H J H Scott, Umpire, W E Midwinter, P S McDonnell, W H Cooper.* Centre: *G Giffen, H F Boyle, W L Murdoch (Cpt.), G J Bonnor, G E Palmer.* Front: *A C Bannerman, F R Spofforth.*

Right: *Fred Spofforth in 1902.*

Below: *Australian XI vs
Sheffield, 1886. (Left to
right)* Back: *G Giffen, F R
Spofforth, Major B Wardill
(manager).* Centre: *F H
Farrands (umpire), Bates
(scorer), W Bruce, J
McIlwraith, T W Garrett, E
Evans, J W Trumble, Salter
(scorer), R Thoms
(umpire).* Front: *G J
Bonnor, J M Blackman, H J
H Scott (captain), S P
Jones, G E Palmer, A H
Jarvis.*

Above: *Reunion at the Sydney Cricket Ground during the 1901-02 series (Left to right) D Gregory, F R Spofforth, H Massie, A Bannerman and T Garrett.* Left: *Frontpiece of Beldam and Fry. Great Bowlers.*

A remarkable photograph of the Spofforth classic leap giving the illusion of a much younger man.

Above: *Another Beldam photograph in which the Demon's age (51) is more evident.*

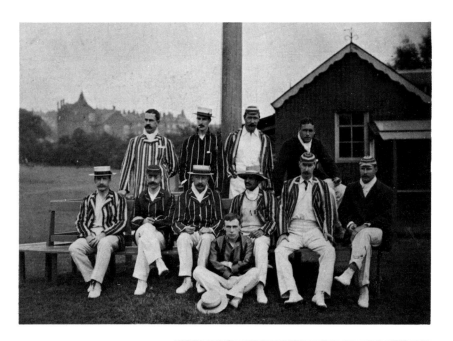

Above: *Hampstead Cricket Club.* Standing: *W R Moon, D J Crump, S S Pawling, L J Moon.* Seated: *W S Hale, T S Wheater, A E Stoddard, Ahsan-UL-Hak, F R Spofforth.* Front: *F W Orr.* Right: *111 Broadhurst Gardens, Hampstead.*

Ashley Cottage

Entertaining Anzacs during World War 1. Phillis is the second from the left.

Right: *The Spofforth children in a Victorian pose.* Above: *Buildings of the Star Tea Company, London EC1 now demolished. (Courtesy of Hackney Archives Department.)*

Above: *Formal photographs of Fred and* Facing page above: *Phillis Spofforth, 22 October 1913.* Below: *Passport for the trip to Australia, 1924–25. (Donated to the Australian Gallery of Sport)*

	Wife - Femme		
Profession / Profession	*Director*		
Place and date of birth / Lieu et date de naissance	*Sydney Australia* / *8th September 1853*	*Manchester* / *1th February 1864*	
Domicile / Domicile	*England*	*England*	
Height / Taille	*6 ft 3 in*	*5 ft 3 in*	
Colour of eyes / Couleur des yeux	*Blue*	*Blue*	
Colour of hair / Couleur de cheveux	*Grey*	*dark brown*	
Special peculiarities / Signes particuliers	/		

CHILDREN - ENFANTS

Name / Nom	Age / Age	Sex / Sexe

Above: Generation gap! Fred Spofforth (extreme left) is more formally attired than some of his children; (right) Reginald and his wife Dorothy. Below: The last reunion in Australia, 1924–25. (Left to right) T Garrett, Lord Foster, F R Spofforth and M A Noble (in the front).

Ashes Test Triumph

H. H. Massie

*T*he thirteen Australians who left Melbourne on P & O steamship *Assam* on 16 March 1882, were regarded as the pick of the colonial cricketers with only Evans declining, yet again, to tour. Despite the offer of leave with full pay from the government, Evans opted out of the tour owing to his wife's health. Cricket mercenary Midwinter would have liked to join the tour but the tourists objected to his changing loyalties. Seeing he could not play with the Australians, Midwinter travelled back to England with the English professionals and appeared in a number of games, but not in the Test match, against the Australians. His performance against the tourists suggested that his form was not good enough to make the side anyway: he scored just 68 runs in eight innings and took 11 wickets at an average of 25.5 each.

The 1882 Australians only played two games in Australia before they set sail for England, stopping at Point de Galle (Ceylon), Port Said and Malta. Before they departed twelve of the players each contributed a share of £100 entitling them to a future tour dividend. The other, Alick Bannerman, was treated as a professional and guaranteed a fixed return.

Much stronger than their predecessors, the 1882 Australians have been acclaimed as the strongest side to tour England in the nineteenth century. The bowling had greater depth: the 1880 trio of Spofforth, Boyle and Palmer was augmented by the 1878 tourist Garrett and newcomer George Giffen. For the first time, too, the tourists went to England with a strong and reliable batting side, headed by Murdoch, who was at his peak and regarded by many as the best bat in the world. Murdoch was ably supported by former tourists Horan, Alick Bannerman, Bonnor and McDonnell and the newcomers Hugh Massie and George Giffen. Only one of the batsmen, S P Jones, failed to come to terms with the English wickets. The side could also run and throw well with some of the newcomers, such as Massie, adding to their prowess. Massie, an 'athetic, spare youth' who was 'as shapely as a greyhound', was an 'excellent field'.[1]

It was fortunate that the tourists were much stronger than the previous teams, because they were confronted with a much tougher program where week after week they met competitive opposition. By this third English tour the

Australians had established a reputation as worthy opponents to the best English teams that could be assembled. By this time Australia had won four of what later became recognised as Tests (but all on home soil), England had won two and two were drawn. They were no longer underestimated or neglected as they had been in 1878 and 1880 respectively.

Gone were the games against inferior XVIIIs and XXIIs. Although the Australians played only one Test, they played numerous games against representative elevens such as the Gentlemen, the Players, the MCC, and the North and the South of England. The tourists were confronted by the leading bats and bowlers time and time again: W G Grace, who batted only five times against the 1878 and 1880 Australians, played twelve innings against the 1882 side and the leading professionals Ulyett and Emmett played twenty and sixteen innings respectively. There was little margin for injury or loss of form because the majority of thirty-eight games, played from 15 May to 26 September, were first-class fixtures.

Although the tour was much better planned than the previous two, many traditions of international cricket were still evolving. On this tour the Australians appeared in their third set of colours. The blue and white of the 1878 team had given way to faded magenta and black in 1880 and red, black and yellow, the colours of the 96th Regiment, in 1882. Australia had no cricket colours in the nineteenth century and the organisers of these private ventures chose whatever combination they thought appropriate.

Spofforth was not in good form with the ball in the first five matches of the 1882 tour: he took only eight wickets at a cost of 39 runs each. After he laboured without much success against Oxford University in the first match, a 'facetious young gentleman' predicted that 'Spoff wasn't going to be the prima donna on this tour'.[2] The press aired various theories about Spofforth's lack of form in May. One school suggested that the sound and good wickets of a dry May were not to Spofforth's liking. Another argued that with so little bowling in the 1881–82 Australian season, Spofforth needed a little longer to find his form.

The more likely reason for Spofforth's lack of form was

that, for the first time, he was the member of a very strong side and he could afford to coast in the early games to preserve his strength for the important matches. During May the Australian bats and bowlers, other than Spofforth, were in outstanding form and the side won four matches and drew the other. Massie's 206 in the first game was followed by Murdoch's 286 not out and 107 not out in the next two games. Meanwhile Palmer, Garrett and Giffen all had some excellent returns with the ball.

If there were any doubts about the Demon's form, they were dispelled in the sixth match of the tour against Lancashire, the champion county of 1881, when he took twelve wickets. In the first innings he took 6-48 off 31.1 overs and followed this with a marathon spell of 59.1 overs when he returned 6-109. From that point on, Spofforth resumed his role of spearhead of the Australian attack.

Two matches later the tourists were involved in controversy at Nottingham when the fiery and patronising secretary, Captain Holden, failed to provide the tourists with lunch. The Australians were not impressed by this pointed gesture since it was the custom to provide lunch for amateurs, leaving the professionals to jostle with spectators in the public refreshment tents. The incident led to a hostile exchange between Holden and the Australians about tour conditions. One reported exchange between Holden and George Bonnor threw some further light on Anglo-Australian ideals. After a heated debate which involved Holden, manager Beal and Bonnor amongst others, and after Bonnor became so angry that he had to be restrained, Holden declared that he had had enough. He then proceeded to take out a cigar and enquired pointedly: 'Will some *Englishman* give me a light?' This unsubtle aside was too much for Bonnor who retorted instantly: 'I can tell you, sir, I am as much an *Englishman* as you or any gentlemen present; I can trace my family back for six generations, and perhaps you cannot do more'. Spofforth was not the only Australian who was conscious of his English ancestors.[3]

During the tour there was greater scope for Spofforth to resume his rivalry with W G Grace who appeared not only in the Gloucestershire games but played for a number of teams against the Australians: England, the Gentlemen, the

MCC, Orleans and United XI. During this tour W G must have been more satisfied with his form: he scored 340 runs in twelve innings at a very respectable average of 28.3. However, Spofforth was still his nemesis, dismissing him more than any other bowler (five times) and, what was more important, taking his wicket four out of the five times Grace failed (when he scored 12 or less). Grace achieved his highest score against the Australians, 77, when Spofforth was not playing and on the other occasion he passed 50, scoring 61, he was let off when Spofforth missed a return catch. W G dismissed Spofforth three times during the season.

From 15 May until 22 July Spofforth played in every match but was then rested because fatigue was blamed for his indifferent mid-July form. Spofforth returned after an absence of two games, but injured his thigh in the Liverpool game, in which he batted but did not bowl. He then missed another three matches. The enforced break of six matches must have been beneficial when he returned to the bowling fray on 14 August, just two weeks before the historic Test match.

The one Test match at the Oval, beginning on 28 August, came late in the tour. By that time regular play against top competition had begun to take its toll and many of the Australians carried injuries into the Test match. One team member wrote expressing fears that the odds were very much against the tour-jaded injury-ridden Australians:

I am very sorry to say that the incessant toil has interfered sadly with the physique of our men, and if we win Australia will have cause to be proud of her broken-down champions. I wish heartily that this great match had taken place about two months ago instead of now, when the men are all knocked up. Murdoch was unable to take part in the Clifton match (vs Gloucestershire) . . . owing to his having the cold shivers the night before. Alick Bannerman has had his second finger split while in the act of playing the last of the Gloucester match, from W G Grace . . . Palmer has strained himself in the groin . . . Not one in the team is fresh.[4]

While some were fearful of possible failure in the great Test, Spofforth looked forward to the challenge. He later wrote that 'personally I had trained for the match, for the first time in my life'.

The Oval Test generated greater public interest than the match of 27 May 1878 because the Australians had performed well on the tour defeating the Gentlemen and all the leading counties although losing, without Spofforth, to the Players. Despite unsettled weather every vantage point was occupied well before play began at 12.10 p.m. on a rain-affected pitch. One of the largest-ever English cricket crowds, 20,000 paying spectators plus members, attended on the first day.

The English press believed that while the Australians would provide tough opposition England, at full strength, would be too strong on their own turf. On paper this was certainly true. Ten of the English side entered the Test with an 1882 first-class batting average of 24 or better whereas there were only three Australians in this category: Murdoch (36.22), Horan (31.16) and Massie (27.31). The batting average for the English side as a whole was 28.70 whereas the Australian was 20.47. The English bowling averages were also superior. The English averages were: Peate (11.12), Barlow (11.53), Ulyett (14.23). Studd (16.9), Steel (20.4) and Barnes (35). The Australian averages were: Boyle (12.77), Spofforth (13.87) and Garrett (27.20).

Murdoch won the toss and decided to bat but Australia was dismissed for just 63 runs, their lowest total of the tour, in just two and a quarter hours. It was, Spofforth wrote many years later, a 'sorry show ... and [we] were most disappointed. I might speak for myself, and say I was disgusted, and thought we should have made at least 250.' This was certainly the comment of a bowler because the combined total of four innings, on this difficult wicket, was only 363 runs. Two accurate left-handers, medium-paced Lancastrian Dick Barlow (5-19 in 31 overs) and Yorkshire slow bowler Ted Peate (4-31 in 38 overs), were the destroyers.

The Australian bowlers, spearheaded by Spofforth, fought back and dismissed the English side for 101, though they conceded a sizeable lead of 38 runs. Spofforth, who bowled throughout the innings, took 7-46 off 36.3 overs with 18 maidens and was ably supported by Garrett (1-22) and Boyle (2-26). Spofforth 'bowled magnificiently' according to Charles Pardon: 'He, of course, had a wicket that suited him to perfection, and he was able to get a tremendous amount

of "work" on the ball.'[5]

Pardon believed that a heavy downpour on Tuesday morning assisted the Australians because it meant that the saturated wicket was 'bound to be easy for a time' before it dried out when it would become 'difficult'. The greasy ball and the slippery turf also inhibited the bowlers. The Australian opener, Hugh Massie, sensing this opportunity, hit out with a power and brilliance that few others could have matched, scoring 55 runs in even time. With Alick Bannerman holding up the other end the Australians produced a substantial opening partnership of 66. The Australians then suffered a middle-order collapse, sagging to 6-99, and only an innings of 29 by skipper Murdoch held the side together.

Twenty-one-year-old batsman S P Jones, then joined Murdoch with the match poised at a critical stage. They pushed the score up to 114 when a much-discussed incident occurred. After the completion of a run, Jones carelessly 'strayed out of his ground', believing the ball to be dead. Grace then picked up the ball, which had been returned to the wicket area, and 'put down the wicket'. Umpire Thoms gave Jones out on Grace's appeal.

Murdoch expressed his disapproval openly and there was much talk of 'dirty' cricket and debate about 'sharp practice'. There were some suggestions that umpire Thoms had been reluctant to give Jones out, responding to Grace's appeal with the comment that 'If you claim it, sir, out!'. Charles Pardon, who doubted this interpretation, sought out the correct version from Thoms. According to Pardon, Thoms simply uttered the word, 'Out'. The London paper, Bell's Life, also argued this point and claimed that Grace's action was 'legal and fair' in that the ball, technically, was not dead. However, even Bell's Life had to admit that Grace's action 'may not have been a particularly courteous or generous action' and it was 'taking full advantage of the thoughtlessness of a young player'. The journalist disassociated himself from the action: 'I personally cannot say I approve of what Grace did'.[6]

Spofforth himself, according to one source, had had an opportunity to perform the same action on Hornby the day before. When Hornby was out of his ground in similar circumstances to Jones, Spofforth was reported to have observed: 'Don't you know, Hornby, I could stump you now — you're off your ground?' 'Yes,' replied Hornby, 'but surely that's not your game is it?' To which the Demon simply replied, 'Well, no'. The Bulletin, which printed details of this alleged exchange on 28 October 1882, added sarcastically that 'British fair play is getting to be a thing we read of'. The Grace incident is believed to have riled the Demon who is said to have psyched up his team-mates before the fateful second innings declaring that 'it [or, this thing] can be done'.[7]

There has been a measure of English scepticism about this incident. Wisden claimed that 'after the excitement had cooled down a prominent member of the Australian Eleven admitted that he should have done the same thing had he been in Grace's place.' Wisden stood up for Grace when it added that 'there was a good deal of truth in what a gentleman in the pavilion remarked ... that "Jones ought to thank the champion for teaching him something".

Four decades later Spofforth made a reference to the incident. While not stating the extent of his own feeling at the time he did confirm that the Australian team as a whole were affected by the action of Grace:

An unfortunate incident occurred in this match, namely, the running out of S P Jones, but so much has been written of the event that I merely mention it. Anyway, it seemed to put fire into the Australians, and I do not suppose a team ever worked harder to win.[8]

The events of this day created an interesting embellishment of the myth of the Demon. Although he bowled with fierce intensity and the cunning of the Devil himself, his intensity of mind and purpose could be admired greatly because at its core it was intensely moral: not only did he play with great pluck — he refused to be beaten — but he was more moral in his approach to the game than Grace.

While the Australians batted better in the second innings, they were all out for 122 and England had just 85 runs to win in bitterly cold weather under a leaden sky. Whether it was this critical situation, the Jones incident or Spofforth overhearing some derogatory comments in the pavilion, the Demon came out breathing fire in the second innings. Opening from the Gasworks end he bowled flat out, forcing Blackham to stand back for the first time in the match. The dangerous Hornby and the stubborn Barlow both quickly fell to his bowling.

W G Grace and the Yorkshire professional, George Ulyett, who had top-scored in the first innings, then established a substantial and what appeared a match-winning partnership, raising the score to 51. As the score mounted Spofforth first cut his pace, running in off nine paces, and then changed ends in an effort to break the partnership. The removal of Ulyett, by Spofforth, at this score, and of Grace, by Boyle, at 53, gave the Australians a glimmer of hope. Then came what Spofforth later described as 'the most exciting cricket I ever witnessed', with only 32 runs to be scored and 6 wickets still intact:

At this point, the Hon. Alfred Lyttelton and A P Lucas were associated, and played so carefully that at one period no fewer than twelve consecutive maidens were sent down. The bowlers finding it impossible to break through the batsmen's defence, it was decided (at the suggestion of Spofforth) to mis-field a ball in order that the batsmen might change ends, and the stratagem worked, for Lyttelton was bowled at once (by Spofforth).

Lucas was bowled by Spofforth shortly after and from that point on 'we all felt we were on top ... I shall never forget the excitement at this point: it beggars language. By slow degrees, amid infinite breathless eagerness, the wickets were got rid of, and at last England was beaten by seven runs.'[9] A reshuffled batting order had not helped the English cause. Form batsman C T Studd had been held back for an emergency but was left stranded at 0 not out after he came in at number ten. Spofforth, who had bowled throughout the innings, returned figures of 7-44 — almost identical to his first-innings return — off 28 overs with 15 maidens for a match total of 14-90.

England had lost its last six wickets for only eleven runs and the last eight for just twenty-six runs. After that 'I was carried into the Oval pavilion by the crowd', recalled Spofforth, and 'stood on a table to make a speech, but I never remembered what I said'.

The excitement after the historic Test win was captured by 'One of the Team' who wrote the following in *The Argus*:

The vast concourse rushed the ground, and Boyle (other accounts suggest it was Spofforth) was fairly carried into the pavilion by several enthusiastic Australians. I am only speaking the truth when I say that we were as heartily cheered as if we had won the match on an Australian ground before an Australian public. Cries of 'Massie', 'Murdoch', 'Spofforth', 'Boyle' and 'Blackham' were heard again and again from the tremendous throng in front of the pavilion, and each of these players had to go out and bow his acknowledgments amidst multitudinous shouts of 'Bravo Australians', 'Well done, boys', and so on. Never shall I forget the wild excitement of the moment — how, for instance, our manager, Charlie Beal, in rushing out to congratulate us, sent the man at the pavilion gate head over heels; how one man dropped dead in the pavilion from over-excitement; how not only the Australians but Englishmen rushed into our dressing-room and shook hands with us all round; how they mingled champagne, seltzer and lemons, and passed the drink round in a loving cup ... Then, when we were leaving the ground, how the crowd around our conveyance cheered us to the echo; how they almost took Spofforth off his legs in their desire to pat him on the back and shake hands with him for his really superb efforts with the ball; how the ladies from the windows in the Kennington-road waved their handkerchiefs to us, and how all the way back to Tavistock (Hotel) the passers-by looked at us as if we had done something to make us famous for all time.[10]

AUSTRALIA v ENGLAND 1882
The Oval 28, 29 August

AUSTRALIA

First Innings			Second Innings	
A C Bannerman c Grace b Peate	9		c Studd b Barnes	13
H H Massie b Ulyett	1		b Steel	55
W L Murdoch* b Peate	13	(4)	run out	29
G J Bonnor b Barlow	1	(3)	b Ulyett	2
T P Horan b Barlow	3		c Grace b Peate	2
G Giffen b Peate	2		c Grace b Peate	0
J M Blackham† c Grace b Barlow	17		c Lyttelton b Peate	7
T W Garrett c Read b Peate	10	(10)	not out	2
H F Boyle b Barlow	2	(11)	b Steel	0
S P Jones c Barnes b Barlow	0	(8)	run out	6
F R Spofforth not out	4	(9)	b Peate	0
Extras	(B 1)	1	(B 6)	6
Total		**63**		**122**

ENGLAND

First Innings			Second Innings	
R G Barlow c Bannerman b Spofforth	11	(3)	b Spofforth	0
W G Grace b Spofforth	4		c Bannerman b Boyle	32
G Ulyett st Blackham b Spofforth	26	(4)	c Blackham b Spofforth	11
A P Lucas c Blackham b Boyle	9	(5)	b Spofforth	5
Hon A Lyttleton† c Blackham b Spofforth	2	(6)	b Spofforth	12
C T Studd b Spofforth	0	(10)	not out	0
J M Read not out	19	(8)	b Spofforth	0
W Barnes b Boyle	5	(9)	c Murdoch b Boyle	2
A G Steel b Garrett	14	(7)	c and b Spofforth	0
A N Hornby* b Spofforth	2	(1)	b Spofforth	9
E Peate c Boyle b Spofforth	0		b Boyle	2
Extras (B 6, LB 2, NB 1)	9		(B 3, NB 1)	4
Total	**101**			**77**

	O	M	R	W	O	M	R	W
ENGLAND								
Peate	38	24	31	4	21	9	40	4
Ulyett	9	5	11	1	6	2	10	1
Barlow	31	22	19	5	13	5	27	0
Steel	2	1	1	0	7	0	15	2
Barnes					12	5	15	1
Studd					4	1	9	0
AUSTRALIA								
Spofforth	36.3	18	46	7	28	15	44	7
Garrett	16	7	22	1	7	2	10	0
Boyle	19	7	24	2	20	11	19	3

FALL OF WICKETS

FALL OF WICKETS

Wkt	Aust	Eng	Aust	Eng
1st	6	13	66	15
2nd	21	18	70	15
3rd	22	57	70	51
4th	26	59	79	53
5th	30	60	79	66
6th	30	63	99	70
7th	48	70	114	70
8th	53	96	117	75
9th	59	101	122	77
10th	63	101	122	77

* captain
† wicket keeper

London Sporting Times,
30 August.

In Affectionate Remembrance
OF
ENGLISH CRICKET,
WHICH DIED AT THE OVAL
ON
29th AUGUST, 1882,
Deeply lamented by a large circle of sorrowing
friends and acquaintances.

R. I. P.

*N.B. — The body will be cremated and the
ashes taken to Australia.*

The general consensus of the English press was that their batsmen had 'funked it' and had been scared into submission by the Demon. The *Sportsman* typified the mixture of anger and astonishment which greeted the result: it castigated the English batsmen, apart from Grace who had stood up 'like a man', who went down to Spofforth and Boyle like 'so many tailors' dummies' and 'failed lamentably'. With a delightful touch of ethnocentrism, the paper added that 'an Australian eleven has, for the first — and let us hope it will be the last — time, decisively beaten a picked eleven of all England.'[11]

Spofforth did not accept this explanation of why England lost a match that seemed to be securely within its grasp. If there was a 'lack of nerve', it occurred in the Australian first innings when the tourists were bundled out cheaply. However, if there was an English batsman at fault it may have been Alfred Lyttelton 'simply and solely because he did play correctly, fatally correctly'. Lyttelton's failure was not to adopt 'more daring tactics' for had he 'jumped out and hit Boyle, England would have won the match'. For 'the bowler at one end (Spofforth) was ... breaking a foot every ball', while Boyle was 'bowling with machine-like precision' for he 'never could command a break'. The 'extraordinary occasion' demanded 'extraordinary measures' and, while 'Boyle never bowled better in his life', the English batsmen erred in allowing the Australian bowlers to dictate the terms of the match.[12]

This narrow Australian victory, spearheaded by Spofforth, was as important to Australian cricket as the celebrated demolition of MCC on 27 May 1878. The victory established the greatness of the 1882 Australians, for they won the match which really counted. The match also confirmed the reputation of Spofforth both as the world's best bowler and as a big occasion performer. Spofforth's name was forever linked with the Test which began the Ashes tradition because he, unlike Lyttelton, was prepared to gamble. The decision to give away a run, when every run was so precious, was a daring move. The famous advertisement, in 'affectionate remembrance of English cricket which died at the Oval on 29th August 1882' appeared in the London *Sporting Times* on 2 September 1882 and so gave birth to the powerful Ashes legend. It was a topical advertisement as the Cremation Society, founded in 1875, had generated controversy and the first English cremation in modern times took place six weeks after this notice.[13] What was, initially, a humorous invention was elevated into a serious legend several decades later.

Charles Pardon provided his usual balanced assessment of the game. The wicket, as Spofforth himself admitted after the match, could not possibly have suited the Demon more. While there may have been some nervousness on the part of some English batsmen, Pardon believed that in all there was 'not very much to find fault with' the English players:

Spofforth was at his best, and we have no Spofforth; the wicket was a bad one, and we had the worst of it; and though England for the first time (at home) had to lower her colours to Australia, we were beaten by a magnificent eleven, before whose prowess it was no disgrace to fail.[14]

The Australian press, along with the public, wallowed in the glory of the occasion, not only printing long letters from the participants but regurgitating large chunks of the English press description and reaction to the Test. The *Sydney Mail* of 28 October printed large quotations from no less than six English papers: the *Daily Telegraph*, the *Morning Post, World, Bell's Life, Field* and *Spectator*.

The victory was celebrated in two separate poems published by *Punch*, on 9 and 16 September, which both focused on the Demon:

WELL done, 'Cornstalks'! Whipt us,
Fair and square!
Was it luck that tript us?
Was it 'scare'?
Kangaroo Land's 'Demon', or our own
Want of 'devil', coolness, nerve, backbone?

Not even GRACE, of matchless skill
(No worthier in the land),
The 'Demon's' onslaughts could resist,
His awful speed withstand;
By lightning smit, as falls the oak,
The wickets fell beneath his stroke!

Because it was not only one of the most exciting Tests ever but also directly associated with the beginning of the Ashes mythology, the Test has been celebrated ever since. Neville Cardus wrote a chapter on the ninth Test which he described as both the 'greatest' and 'most famous' of all Tests[15] and others, including cricket historian Harry Altham, have echoed this assessment. John Masefield was only four in 1882, but seventy years later he could remember 'a dreadful day' when someone had told him that 'England had been beaten by the Australians'. Being so young Masefield had 'no clear notion' of what the terrible beating meant and wondered whether England could survive as a nation or whether he might become a slave. As a young boy Masefield was captivated by the accounts of the 1882 and 1884 tours, which he discovered in his grandfather's library.[16] The saga of 1882 still moved him late in life and inspired him to write a long poem, '85 to Win',[17] which was published for the first time in *The Times* on 29 August 1956, the day after the completion of the 1956 series which featured another celebrated bowling performance, Laker's 19 wickets in the Fourth Test. '85 to Win' included the following two verses:

> What was this Spofforth, called the Demon yet,
> For men forget but cannot all forget?
> A tall, lean, wiry athlete inly lit
> With mind, and saturnine control of it.
> Is it not said, that he, with either hand,
> Could fling a hen's egg, onto grass or sand,
> Clear seventy yards, yet never crack the shell?
>
> Then when he bowled, he seemed a thing of Hell,
> Writhing; grimacing; batsmen catching breath
> Thought him no mortal man, but very Death;
> For no man ever knew what ball would come
> From that wild whirl, save one from devildom.
> Now the sharp fears came tugging at the heart,
> As Cunning strove with Care and Skill and Art.

Given that the Australians faced much stiffer competition in 1882, they finished with an excellent record of twenty-three wins, four losses and eleven draws. In addition to winning the Test the tourists beat the Gentlemen by an innings and 1 run, though the Australians, minus Spofforth, were beaten by an innings and 34 runs by the Players. Spofforth was unable to stop the tourists losing twice to Cambridge University — by 6 wickets early in the season when he had yet to find form, and later by just 20 runs.

Although Boyle had a slightly better bowling average, Spofforth was easily the leading tour wicket-taker and bowled considerably more than anyone else. He had far more support in 1882 than previously.

Spofforth, who had batted well on occasions on previous tours, finished last on the batting averages scoring just 282 runs at an average of 8.1. It is quite likely that this was a conscious move to save his strength for bowling as Spofforth usually batted last or very close to last. With four batsmen

Australian Bowling Averages in Representative Matches, 1882 Tour

	Overs	Maidens	Runs	Wickets	Average
Boyle	1,208.2	535	1,682	144	12.0
Spofforth	1,594.3	699	2,282	188	12.3
Palmer	1,192.3	515	1,731	138	12.8
Garrett	1,209.2	489	1,759	128	14.0
Giffen	386.3	120	728	32	22.2
Others	165	47	322	8	40.3

scoring over 1,000 runs, and with Murdoch accumulating 1,711, there was less need of a contribution from Spofforth.

Spofforth ended the tour with an enhanced reputation. For since the Lancashire match on 1 June

he has by magnificent bowling fully sustained and even added to his fame.

Whatever else he may have done, he won the England match, and that alone suffices to make him the greatest of living bowlers. For my own part, I am sure that I have never seen his equal on a difficult wicket. His grand break from the off beats the best batsmen, and the wholesome awe he inspired in 1878 and 1880 still remains almost unimpaired by time and use.[18]

The *Pall Mall Gazette* of 29 September commented that 'on bad grounds (as at the Oval against England) he was unplayable, on moderate grounds effective, and on easy grounds rarely expensive'. *Cricket*, 28 September, believed that Spofforth had bowled 'a little slower' than in 1878 and 1880 but 'we class him as superior to any bowler we have'.The 'Red' *Lillywhite'* annual of 1883, was also fulsome in its praise:

In no department of the game did this wonderful team show more proficiency than in that of fast-bowling. The name of Spofforth has become a familiar term, not so much because that distinguished bowler scored one or two marked successes, as that his bowling was always consistently successful, and that more especially, his greatest feats were performed on the most critical and opportune circumstances. No cricketer has shown so conclusively the far-reaching importance of good fast-bowling, and no one, certainly, has proved himself a more plucky, a more energetic, and a more uniformly steady bowler. The possibilities of fast-bowling have never before been so markedly insisted upon — its value to a team, and its immense power as a factor of loss or gain.

This tribute appeared in an article entitled 'The Decline of (English) Fast Bowling', in which the author admitted frankly that the Australian fast brigade, and Spofforth in particular, were far superior to their English counterparts.

Returning to Sydney on the *City of New York* on 18 November, after playing two matches in America, the tourists were met by a crowd of 300 to 400 persons at the wharf. The reception was much smaller than for the 1878 Australians but tours had become a much more routine occurrence. However, there was no shortage of receptions for the conquering heroes who were feted around the country. They were treated to a banquet at Aaron's Hotel, Sydney, where they were praised as 'true men' who had played an honourable part 'in the service of their country', exhibiting a high degree of 'Australian pluck ... endurance, patience, dogged determination, good temper, discipline and united conduct'. One speaker added that 'they could not exorcise our Spofforth ... and they could not expel the demon, to which they attributed his supernatural powers'. Other cities, and even country towns, competed with each other in their tributes. When the team arrived by train at Wodonga at 2 p.m. on 24 November they were given a hearty welcome by an immense crowd at the station, gaily decorated with flags. The team was then conveyed to the Town Hall in three four-horse drays 'amidst continuous cheering from the crowds who lined both sides of Collins-street'. The mayor echoed the refrain which followed the team around the country: they had showed 'plenty of British pluck, energy and perseverance, and that they were true Australians'.[19]

Not to be outdone the Melbourne organisers of a banquet to the Australian cricketers, held on 27 November, included a poem on the program. 'Australia's Victory' not only reflected great pride in the achievement but also mirrored the ideals and ambiguities of Anglo-Australia which referred to an Australian victory secured with 'Grand British pluck':

All England vanquished; can it be?
   A lurking phantom in our Australian sky,
Or an Australian Borealis do we see
   In such great splendour bright and high?
   But another light has dawned upon our shores

In brilliancy supreme; with their honoured stores
Of princely laurels from their English foes.
In friendly battles fought, their duty nobly done,
Has brought Australia to the front rank place!
Though hard the tussle they fought and won,
And made Old England proud of her own race.
Let Britons know that in this the Sunny South,
Her glorious sports are brought to skilful use
By acts, and not by Anthony Trollope's 'blow of mouth'.
We act! We fight! win! and disregard abuse!
The palm of victory 'Our Boys' have won;
The cricket sceptre in triumph now is our own!
Fraught with marvellous pluck — pluck we know must run
Through true Australians from our British sires.
Fairly! Nobly! have their glorious honours come.
Australia longs to-day to praise her every noble son
Of our cricket heroes. All! All! have shown
Grand British pluck beneath a British sun.[20]

By the end of 1882 Spofforth had achieved legendary status. The image of the Demon exerted a powerful influence over cricketers of his generation and beyond. Such was the aura surrounding Spofforth that for years after he retired touring Australian players used to compete with each other to sleep in the room always occupied by Spofforth at the Australian team's London hotel.[21]

The 'Demon' Accused of Cheating

W.W. Read

As was usual, the 1882 Australians did not disband immediately on their return to Australia but played another six games, including four Tests against the seventh English team to tour Australia, which was captained by the Hon. Ivo Bligh. The Australians cleared almost £200 per man for the first three Tests, which meant that the dividend for the entire tour was a very handsome £600-700.

The two overlapping tours provided the usual problems of scheduling. With the Australian team on their way to play a South Australian XV, commencing on 8 December, six of the leading New South Welshmen were unable to represent their colony against Bligh's team, scheduled for 1-4 December. The Englishmen had a hollow victory winning by an innings and 144 runs. *The Bulletin*, which had been full of praise for the Australian tourists throughout the tour, hit out on 2 December against the decision not to play for New South Wales:

The amount of real patriotism about them can be judged by their refusal to play. There are a good many points about this team which the public should know. As soon as all the 'fizz' has gone flat, we shall endeavour to bring these arrogant athletes to their proper level. It is no use casting mud at demigods, so we shall refrain for the present from expressing our opinion of their conduct until they subside into normal insignificance.

The colonial press never wrote in half-tones; one week there was fulsome praise followed by biting criticism in the next. Spofforth must have been all too aware of this fickleness. While his reputation as the world's leading fast bowler was quite secure in England, there were always some doubters in the colonies. Just over a month after the heroes returned from overseas, 'Censor' of the *Sydney Mail*, was promoting Evans and chipping away subtly at the Spofforth legend:

Spofforth is acknowledged in England to be the finest bowler of the day; and those who know how little practice Evans gets must confess that as a manipulator of the leather he is almost as great a wonder as the 'demon'.[1]

Fortunately for cricket lovers a compromise was worked out between the touring Australians and the local cricket authorities. While the tourists did not disband until the end of January, they did make themselves available for the intercolonials, the first of which was begun at Melbourne on 23 December.

Although New South Wales won the match comfortably by seven wickets, Spofforth played a very minor role in the victory, returning match figures of 3-115: the win was secured on the basis of good batting by Murdoch and Alick Bannerman and effective bowling by Garrett and Cleeve. This match marked the beginning of a very difficult season for Spofforth: the season 1882-83 proved disappointing in that he failed consistently to reproduce his English form and, in addition, became the focal point of controversy.

In the First Test, played the following week in Melbourne, Spofforth had to be content to play second fiddle to Joey Palmer whose bowling was described as 'irresistible' in that his 'puzzling deliveries fairly baffled the English batsmen'. His 10-126 set up a comfortable Australian win by nine wickets. One journalist believed Spofforth's relatively poor match return of 4-121 was because the wicket was not 'soft and bumpy'.[2]

Later in the month the Englishmen had their revenge in the Second Test, also played at Melbourne, when they won comfortably by an innings and 27 runs. The Australian attack again focused around Palmer, 5-103, who was supported by Giffen, 4-89. Spofforth went wicketless, 0-57. After the Englishmen scored 294 the Australians collapsed for 114 and 153 when Bates found a spot on the wicket, taking 14-102, including the first English Test hat-trick. The offending spot, the Australians believed, had been caused by the plates on Barlow's boots and provided the Englishmen with an unfair advantage. Prior to this game, Bates had not been a particularly damaging bowler.

There was a great deal of interest in the Third Test in Sydney, which was scheduled as the deciding Test, and attracted a record crowd aggregate of 53,523 over four days. With the Englishmen keen to atone for the Oval Test disaster, the series generated much talk, and even jokes, about the Ashes mythology. The *Sydney Mail* reported on 3 February 1883 that Bligh hoped to 'carry back ... the revered ashes of English cricket' although at this point the Ashes were merely an intriguing concept. There was also no Ashes urn.

The Third Test was full of controversy from the start. Before the match Murdoch complained of the plates worn on Barlow's boots whereupon Bligh had the offending plates removed. Barlow resented this action, arguing that he had always played with the same boots in county games and that 'a suspicion of unfair play has never been entertained against him' during his entire English career. 'Several of the Englishmen' then brought a counter charge against Spofforth, accusing him of 'unlawfully putting spikes in his boots to cut up the turf'. The *Sydney Mail* of 3 February commented further on Spofforth and his boots:

Spofforth brought evidence to show that he only used one nail and a spike — less than any other cricketer uses — in the present match. Spofforth does not use more spikes in his boots than are necessary for him to obtain a fast hold when delivering the ball, but with his extraordinary movements when delivering the ball he would cut up the turf even without spikes.

It was not the first time that this issue had been raised. In addition to the Harris comment of 1880, there were several other references during the 1882 tour. Sydney Pardon wrote that Spofforth 'cuts up the ground' in the match against the Gentleman and implied that it might have been to the advantage of the Australians, but he did not push his argument since the Australians had a very convincing win by an innings and one run. 'Anglicanus', in his tour report, also referred to this match suggesting that the 'Gentlemen were severely handicapped by reason of Mr Spofforth's "third step" (in his follow through) wearing such a hole in the ground that Mr Giffen's deliveries from the opposite wicket were almost unplayable'.[3]

With so much at stake Spofforth rose to the occasion and returned his best figures of the season. Batting first the Englishmen hit up a sizeable total of 247 on a good wicket in fine weather. Spofforth was the mainstay of the bowling attack taking 4-73 off 51 overs and gave, in the opinion of the *Sydney Mail* of 3 February, 'emphatic contradiction to the prevailing belief' that he was 'ineffective on a good wicket'. He 'bowled with wonderful judgment, and infused plenty of mischief into the ball'.

The Australians, by the end of the second day, were very well placed at 1-133, but then rain intervened and gave

England a significant advantage. On a bad wicket the Australians collapsed to be all out for 218. Spofforth, who revelled in the mud, was at times unplayable and took 7-44 off 41.1 overs as the Englishmen totalled just 123 in their second innings. However, the Australians could only reach 83 in their second innings and lost the Test by 69 runs.

Perhaps disappointed with losing such a vital encounter, Spofforth allowed himself to be involved in an incident at the end of the Test. The most direct reference was made to it in *The Age* of 30 January:

After the match was over an allusion was made in conversation to Spofforth having cut up the wicket with his feet. This so annoyed the demon bowler that he struck out at Mr Read, of the English eleven. Fortunately for Spofforth, the genial Surrey secretary is as good tempered as he is muscular and contented himself by smiling upon his ill mannered adversary.

Another version of the incident appeared more than three decades later in the *Sydney Sportsman* of 5 January 1916. According to this article Barlow was aggrieved by criticism of his spikes and, at the end of the day, pointed to the spot where Spofforth had cut up the pitch in the English second innings. An argument then ensued as all the parties involved, including Spofforth, 'went towards the pavilion':

One word led to another, and Barlow made some insulting remark to Spofforth and the Demon replied with a blow which knocked Barlow over the seat. A big fight seemed imminent, but friends dragged Spofforth inside, and Walter Read (a champion amateur boxer) stood in front of Barlow to protect him.

There are some less direct references to this incident in other sources. *The Bulletin* celebrated the event and the controversy with 'A CRICKETING CAROL' in which Spofforth 'shaped (up) quite quick for the affray' to Barlow. The appearance of Read, in this account, spelt the end of the 'fight' because Read refused to respond to Spofforth's overtures. *The Sydney Mail* of 3 February was rather more discreet: while it acknowledged that the debate about boots 'has already led to unpleasantness between some of the players engaged in the match', it argued that it would be better for all concerned 'if no further reference was made to it'

'Song of the Spike', (Bulletin,
3 February 1883)

Song of the Spike.

A CRICKETING CAROL.

'Twas in the dressing room, and lo,
  When all were gathered round
Spoff. cut up rough on Barlow, 'cause
  He cut up rough the ground.

" Those cursed spikes!" the Demon cried,
  " Have spoilt our chance you see!"
" About my spike then" Barlow said
  Just don't you *spike* to me.

" You ploughed it up then," Spofforth yelled,
  Come! how would *you* have liked it?
Our chance has gone all through that spike,—
  It's just what I *ex-spike* ted."

" You lie!" cried Barlow, then Spoff. " shaped"
  Quite quick for the affray;
All thought that spike would cause a great
  Spiketacular display.

Then Read appeared, and said—" Oh, bosh!
  Of this spike we're all full;
To fight about a spike is not
  A bit *respiketable.*"

" I'll go for you!" then howls out Spoff.,
  But Read said—" No, not quite,
I come out here for cricket, I
  Did not come out to fight."

Thus all this row came to an end
  A fracas this of fools
Was this small spike-row you will see

Although it is dangerous to rely too much on newspaper evidence, the appearance of the story in so many places suggests strongly that Spofforth must have shaped up to, if not punched, Barlow or Read or both. The fight at Sydney on 29 January 1883 is the best documented example of Spofforth's occasional volatility. There are some other hints that similar instances occurred at other times. Sam Jones wrote from Auckland in August 1935 that Spofforth had insulted a Frenchman on the ship to England in 1882 and was challenged to a duel.[4] There is also a story that Spofforth was involved in a fight with a team-mate in another shipboard incident. Derek Spofforth, grandson of the Demon, recalls a family story, which may be exaggerated or even untrue. Fred Spofforth, who was then manager of the Star Tea Company, was none too impressed by a gentleman who wanted to take over the Star interests, and hoisted him unceremoniously through a glass door.

Spofforth's occasional outbursts seem quite paradoxical, given that for the most part he was constrained on and off the field, regarded himself as a gentleman and was described as an affable man. Why did this very controlled man, who kept matters very much close to his chest, occasionally resort to physical violence? There are a number of possible explanations. As a forthright individual who was never afraid to mince words, he sometimes got himself into difficult situations: he must have said something outrageous to the Frenchman in 1882. Spofforth's temper was also another facet of his powerful inner drive and his very high standards of perfection. The same forces which caused him to strive well **beyond** the limits of most men on the field to achieve seemingly superhuman ends could get out of hand at times off the field, despite his upbringing. It did not happen very often because Spofforth, more than most persons, harnessed his great physical and mental energy to achieve his goals.

In all probability Spofforth was the first in a long and distinguished line of angry fast bowlers. His anger was much less demonstrable than the modern fast bowler who has developed the art form of aggression which now includes not only glares but also extravagant gestures and heated words with the opposition, umpires and even team-mates.

Spofforth's anger was probably no less intense than that of a Lillee or a Marshall. He was constrained by prevailing social conventions which frowned upon public expression of emotion.

There was probably one other factor involved in the 1883 incident. Although he had a good sense of humour, Spofforth was essentially a very earnest and moral individual who believed in the ethics of fair play and values of the amateur ideology. The suggestion that he was cheating, made by the English professionals, was an unpardonable affront which justified extraordinary measures.

This controversy also raises another central question about Spofforth's character. Was this fast bowler, who chided Grace for sharp practice in 1882 and who later took a very moral attitude on the question of illegal bowling, a man who in the heat of battle stretched the law to his own advantage? Or, more simply, did Spofforth cheat by deliberately cutting up the pitch?

If Lord Harris was reluctant to point an accusing finger at Spofforth, when Bligh reflected on the tour he seemed to imply that Spofforth's action may have been deliberate and unfair:

> though it (the English second innings of the Third Test) began fairly well, it fell away sadly towards the end, the wicket being cut up at both ends by Spofforth's heels to such an extent that Horan became an unplayable bowler; perhaps, if we would, we could say no more than that.[5]

The correspondent of the London *Sportsman* had no such diffidence about spelling out the implications of Spofforth's behaviour. He wrote that 'after working a "spot" at the pavilion end, during which process he bowled with considerable success', Spofforth crossed over, and 'made a hole for himself to pitch into, returned, and, with Horan for partner, quickly got rid of his opponents.' An inspection of the pitch after the innings revealed 'an area about a foot by 18 inches (30-46 cm) scraped into ridges, making the surface uneven to the extent of a couple of inches, and causing the ball dropped on to them to be nearly unplayable'. The practice was 'very annoying' and the scheme was 'so palpable' that there was no doubt in the correspondent's mind that Spofforth was acting unfairly. Spofforth had refined the art of doctoring the pitch to such a degree that he did not even need spikes: 'lately he has adopted a method of screwing his heel into the ground, and can in great measure dispense with spikes'. The journalist concluded that everyone who inspected the damage agreed 'that it was time some steps were taken to stop the unfairness'.[6]

More balanced comments on the controversy were made by another 1882–83 tourist, C F H Leslie who referred first to the 'unpleasant circumstance' before the Test and the English counter objection to Spofforth:

Mr Spofforth replied by showing his spikes, which were of the ordinary pattern and fixed only in the heel; he did not, however, deny that their effect was similar to those worn by Barlow, though he did deny that he caused this effect purposely.

Mr Spofforth, notwithstanding our remonstrance, cut up the wickets very badly, and it was in a great measure owing to this unfortunate propensity that their (the Australian) second innings closed for a small total of 82 (*sic*, 83). This question of cutting up the wicket requires, in our humble opinion, immediate legislation, and it ought not to be left to the umpire to say whether it is fair or unfair play, but rather whether the effect caused is fair or unfair. The Australian umpire, when appealed to, decided that as Mr Spofforth had denied the damage to the pitch to be intentional, it was fair play.

This comment seems to exonerate the Demon of unfair play. For while it reveals Spofforth as a stubborn and doughty competitor who was unwilling to modify his follow-through, Leslie suggested that the damage to the pitch in this instance favoured the Englishmen more than the Australians, who had to bat last on the worn pitch.[7] Being a great competitor and a great bad-wicket bowler, there is no question that Spofforth would have made full use of any spot which he, or others, created. At his worst he exploited a grey area in the law which did not distinguish between 'unfair' intentions and 'unfair' results of a bowling action. Spofforth's case rested on the fact that he did not deliberately set out to damage the pitch; the damage was caused by his natural bowling action and extended follow-through.

With the defeat of the Australians in the deciding Test, the *Sydney Mail* declared on 3 February that Bligh now had in his custody the 'revered Ashes of English cricket'. However, after this 'deciding' Test, another was slated later in the month at Sydney. Prior to this match Victoria, 281, had a commanding win after New South Wales was caught on a sticky wicket and mustered only 49 and 66. Although Spofforth did not do much with the ball, returning 2-75, he had the satisfaction of scoring 26 of the home side's 66 runs in the second innings.

The Fourth Test witnessed another chapter in the intriguing saga of Billy Midwinter, who was picked this time as an Australian. Midwinter had played Tests 1 and 2 as an Australian, and Tests 5 to 8, 1881-82, as an Englishman, and now in Test 13, 1882-83, had rejoined the Australian side. Needless to say the colonial press was not all impressed by this cricket mercenary, even though Midwinter declared that he had now left England for good and considered himself 'an Australian to the heart's core'. He was not happy that he was dubbed 'Anglo Australian' since he regarded it as a term of abuse — which was another shade of meaning of this term — for he felt 'as much an Australian at heart' whether playing in England or Australia.[8] Early in the season 'Censor' of the *Sydney Mail* left no doubts about his opinion about whether Midwinter should play for Victoria: he was castigated in the *Sydney Mail* on 16 December 1882:

Apropos of Midwinter, I would ask seriously, are the cricketers of the colony, and especially those of Victoria, going to submit to another season of vagaries from this very slippery character? One day he is an Australian, the next day an English player. Last season he played with England against Australia, and wanted badly to go to England immediately after as a full-blown Australian cricketer in Murdoch's team. Failing to induce the Australians to take the giant to their arms, he journeyed back to the old country with Shaw's team, and played for his county Gloucestershire during the whole of their last cricketing campaign. In order to ingratiate himself with the colonial cricketers, who will not forget his base desertion of the first Australian Eleven at Lord's, he returned to Australia with Murdoch and his companions, announcing his intention of 'never never' returning to the old country.

Although middle-class Australia admired Australians who returned 'home' and made it there, Midwinter's shifting allegiances and his exploitation of the slackness in international qualification rules made a mockery of Anglo-Australian ideals.

Australia won the final Test of the series by 4 wickets,

more by good batting than bowling: Bonnor scored 87 and Alick Bannerman 63, but the star at the crease was wicket-keeper Blackham who scored 57 and 58 not out. It was a fine performance because prior to this Test Blackham, the only player who had appeared in every Test, had not scored a Test 50. The wickets were shared by the bowlers: Palmer, 4-111, and Spofforth, 3-113, bowled in 'a very in-and-out fashion' and Spofforth came in for some punishment.

Mindful that the Tests had been drawn two all, Bligh quipped that the 'revered ashes' of English cricket must be buried in the Melbourne Cricket Ground because 'his team were going away without them'. He added that Murdoch's team 'must not touch them, as they had no right to do so'.[9] This speech is an intriguing one for several reasons. Bligh admitted, quite candidly, that the Australians had success-fully defended the Ashes despite the flexible programming. It is a more logical construction than the subsequent interpretation of cricket historians that Bligh won back the Ashes by his victory in the Third Test. Given that the last match has Test status, it would be more logical to conclude that 1882–83 represented the first successful defence of the Ashes.

The speech also suggested that Bligh regarded all the talk about the Ashes as a good joke, which had worn well from August 1882 to March 1883, but it was now time to bury it. However, the joke refused to die and some Austral-ian women burnt a stump, or a bail or bails, or even a ball, and presented Bligh with an urn which remained in his house until 1927 and eventually found its way into the Lord's Cricket Museum.

The English public also took a keen interest in who was entitled to claim superior status. Many letters were written to the London *Sportsman* some suggesting that Bligh had 'brought back the ashes', others claiming that the English team were superior and another suggesting that Bligh returned without the sheaf bearing the inscription, 'cham-pionship of the cricket field'.[10] There was clearly a demand from the public for greater refinement of the Test traditions.

The mythology of the Ashes, refined and developed by Clarence P Moody in the 1890s and Pelham Warner in the 1900s, enhanced the tradition of Test cricket. The fanciful

Ashes story was elevated to a serious and spiritual metaphor, a unique concept of sporting success appropriate for one of the most ethereal of games. Developments years after Spofforth's Test playing days assured that his name would be immortalised as the man who was responsible for the Ashes.

The 1882–83 season proved a disappointing one for Spofforth, who had 'but once or twice given us anything approaching his old form'. His bowling, added 'Censor', 'seems to have lost all its "devil" '.[11] Palmer had the best returns in the Tests, taking 21 wickets at an average of 18.9. Spofforth's figures, 18 wickets at a cost of 22.7, would have been much worse but for his Third Test haul of 11-117.

After such an extended period of cricket, Spofforth appears to have headed again to his brother-in-law's Collaroy property at Cassilis, where he could unwind and renew his strength. There was an additional reason for travelling to the north-west of New South Wales as his brother, Edward, was suffering from some form of mental breakdown. Edward died at Collaroy on 15 September 1883 of 'nervous exhaustion', a condition suffered for the past twelve months.

Fred Spofforth must have felt the loss of his only and older brother, who was just thirty-five, very keenly. They both had worked in the same bank and shared a love of sport. The two brothers must have been close to each other: they had spent a month touring Tasmania together in January 1874.

Edward's death may have been a factor in explaining why Fred Spofforth appeared so reluctant to declare that he would join the 1884 tour. The saga of whether Fred would or would not tour fascinated the sporting press from September 1883 right up till March 1884. The *Sydney Mail* declared on 17 November that 'nothing is known as to Spofforth's intentions, but the public all say, "He's sure to go" '. The same paper reported on 1 December that 'Spofforth was in town for a few days last week, looking well after his sojourn in the country', but 'he will not attend practice'. The reporter added that Spofforth would play in the Melbourne intercolonial which began on 26 December but he was absent from both this match and the return Sydney game which started on 8 February. By 22 December the Sydney Mail was taking Spofforth's reluctance to tour sufficiently seriously and suggesting that 'if Spofforth persists in his determination not to go' Turner or McShane should be selected.

The 1884 tour, like the 1878 and 1880 ventures, included an extensive preliminary tour of the colonies to raise funds. At the time of the first match, 1 January 1884, the participation of Spofforth seemed very remote and *The Bulletin* of 5 January announced that the 'Demon Bowler' would not accompany the touring team as 'it is understood that he is at present engaged in the exhilarating pastime of overlanding jumbucks [sheep]'. Even without Spofforth the tourists started on a bright note, notching a mammoth 619 against a Combined XI of New South Wales and Victoria. The 'scientific' Murdoch played a commanding innings of 279 not out, demonstrating that he was 'at the zenith of his powers' and far ahead of all other batsmen.[12]

On 9 February the *Sydney Mail* commented that the touring team had been completed and that Spofforth had 'positively declined' to join it but added that 'if Spofforth can be induced to alter his determination, a place will be found for him at the last moment'. Evans was another non-starter, despite every inducement. His decision not to tour, added the *Sydney Mail* of 23 February, was due to 'family reasons' and owing to 'insurmountable obstacles'.

The same issue of the paper declared that 'Spofforth is the mysterious man' for 'four out of five persons one meets in the street say he is sure to go, yet he himself says otherwise'. The team, added this source, would be 'weak' in bowling without him.

There was at last some hope that Spofforth would tour when he turned out for the Combined XI against the tourists in a match which began on 15 February. The *Sydney Mail* could not hide its joy: 'despite his not having handled the ball for more than 12 months, his straightness was remarkable' and he bowled 'more fast balls than usual'. Spofforth took 4-101 off 212 balls and scored 29 and 14. But even after this return Spofforth did not yet join the touring party's sixth and seventh matches of the tour, which were played in Queensland.

Spofforth joined the tourists at the very last minute. In fact the announcement in the *Sydney Mail* that 'Spofforth, as was generally expected, has joined the team' was published on 15 March, the day that the team sailed out of Adelaide on the P & O steamer *Sutlej*.

Why did Spofforth take so long to make up his mind to tour? Did he ever entertain seriously the idea of not touring? The death of his brother may have been a factor in Spofforth's prevarication but it was probably a minor one as he had been a reluctant tourist before. More probably Spofforth recognised that extended breaks from cricket prior to a tour enhanced his tour performance.

But it is hard to escape the conclusion that Spofforth relished playing out the drama for the benefit of the press and public, who seemed to have sensed that he enjoyed generating media copy and was never really taken in by his act. They knew that Spofforth was never a person who would walk away from a challenge. The weight of evidence suggests that Spofforth was always likely to tour but wanted to do so at his convenience and with maximum publicity. Spofforth enjoyed the limelight. As the star turn he was a law unto himself.

The Finest Tour

G.E. Palmer.

here are only occasional glimpses into the shipboard life of the 1884 tourists. It was reported from Colombo that many of them rose each morning at 6 a.m. and fed the ship's furnaces in temperatures estimated at 146 degrees Fahrenheit (63.3°C). They reappeared a couple of hours later in a lather of sweaty coaldust and after all their superfluous flesh had rolled off in perspiration.[1] During the voyage over, W H Cooper, a leg-break bowler, injured his bowling hand.

Cooper's lack of form seriously unbalanced the attack and stretched the resources of the 1884 side: he was a virtual passenger, playing in only nine of the thirty-two games. With player/manager George Alexander standing in for five games, the remaining eleven tourists had to play virtually every game, playing even when they were unwell or carrying injuries. Spofforth played in every game of the tour. A second problem was that the support bowling was not nearly as strong as in 1882: the useful Garrett was not a tourist, Boyle was not nearly as effective as previously, and Midwinter was a disappointment with the ball though he did contribute with the bat.

Too often the attack came down to Spofforth and Palmer, with some occasional support from Giffen, whose form with bat and ball improved from 1882. The 1884 tour schedule was also much tougher than any previous one: the Test program was expanded from one to three; and there were two games against both the Gentlemen and the Players; the 1882 Australians had only played these sides once each. The tour was probably the most difficult one for Spofforth. The relatively dry summer produced wickets which were hard and true: conditions which favoured the batsmen more than the bowlers and which most scribes believed would not suit the noted mudlark, Fred Spofforth.

The first matches exposed the limitations of the tourists. Whereas the 1882 tourists had begun in a blaze of glory, the form of the 1884 side was very patchy from the start: after six games the Australians had won three and lost three. The losses included morale-damaging defeats by seven wickets to Oxford University, which had a weak and inexperienced attack, and to the MCC by an innings and 115 runs. It was a pattern which was repeated throughout the tour: the bowling attack was thinner and the batting less reliable than in 1882.

W G Grace was very keen to do well against the 1884 side to erase the memory of the 1882 Oval Test and to challenge the view, gaining currency in some quarters, that Murdoch was the champion bat of the world. After scoring just 1 and 30 for Lord Sheffield's XI in the opening match of the tour, W G had his opportunity when he came to bat for the MCC on a very good wicket in fine weather in late May. Murdoch gambled by opening the attack with Palmer and Cooper — the latter bowling for the first time on tour to an unorthodox field, six on the leg and only three to the off. The move was unsuccessful and by the time Spofforth came into the attack, with 30 runs on the board, W G had his eye in and went on to score a very patient 101, which included 51 singles. W G later celebrated his first century against a Spofforth-led attack by scoring two more centuries against the tourists, scoring 577 runs in seventeen innings against the tourists at an excellent average of 38.7.

Just as ominous for the tourists was the fact that other MCC bats were in very good form. The Cambridge and Lancashire amateur, A G Steel, a member of the University side that beat the 1878 team, scored 134 and was in fact the leading English batsman for the season: he scored 635 runs in sixteen innings, averaging 42.5 against the tourists. Nottingham professional William Barnes scored 105 not out in the same innings. Barnes and his fellow county professional, William Scotton, both scored heavily against the Australians. Despite the huge MCC score of 461 Spofforth stuck to his task and was by far the most effective and economical bowler: he returned 4-98 off 57 overs with 20 maidens.

Ill fortune dogged Spofforth and the Australians in a later match against the Gentlemen. After winning the toss the Gentlemen decided to bat on a dry and hard wicket. This time Spofforth had the better of W G, who was caught by Boyle off his bowling for 21. Shortly after Lord Harris, batting with W W Read, hit Spofforth a painful and severe blow on his right arm just below his elbow. Charles Pardon wrote that it was Read who struck the blow but it was almost certainly Harris, who made a point of mentioning the incident because he was to dole out the same punishment in the same match in the 1886 tour with an even more damaging result. Unlike today, when the bowler would immediately retire, Spofforth had to go through the farce of finishing the over, gently rolling the next three balls along the ground. He took no further part in a match which the Australians lost by just four wickets. Spofforth recovered quickly from the injury as he took twelve wickets in the next game against Derbyshire.

It is easy to underestimate, and even overlook, the achievement of Spofforth in 1884 because some of his best performances occurred outside the Test matches. He was in outstanding form in late June and early July and virtually won by his own effort back-to-back games against powerful XIs, the Gentlemen and the Players. The English sides in both matches led on the first innings and it was the Spofforth spirit which twice earnt the tourists memorable wins.

This was a pattern repeated in many matches and Spofforth's strike rate in Test match second innings, a wicket every 26.5 balls, was twice as good as what he achieved in Test first innings, a wicket every 53.8 balls.[2] He saved his best performances for when they were most needed.

After a magnificent 107 by W G in the return match in late June the Gentlemen led by 32 runs on the first innings, 261 to 229. The Australian reply of 219 left the Gentlemen to score 188 to win. An incident at the beginning of the second English innings, when a slips catch was disallowed, riled Spofforth who, according to Charles Pardon, 'bowled his fastest from the Pavilion wicket' and 'Blackham stood back, and there were half a dozen men in slips'. Whether Spofforth bowled to an umbrella field, as this comment seems to imply, cannot be ascertained for fielding terms have changed in meaning: the term 'long slip' was used in this era to refer to third man or short third man (the modern fly slip).[3] Whatever the field, it was effective as Studd was caught 'at slip'. Included in Spofforth's return of 7-68 (match figures of 11-162) were the prize wickets of Grace, Steel, Read, Studd and Ridley. The Australians won the contest by just 46 runs.

The match against the Players followed a similar pattern. The Players, 230, led the Australians 189, on the first innings but collapsed in the second innings for 134 with Spofforth taking 7-43 and match figures of 13-123. The Australians won this game more comfortably by 6 wickets.

Although the match was appreciated by some 60,000 spectators over three days, some of the gloss may have been taken off the victory by the absence of three of the leading Notts professionals, Shrewsbury, Barnes and Flowers, who refused to accept the terms of £10 per man offered by the Yorkshire Committee 'These three,' noted Charles Pardon, 'remarking the enormous "gates" obtained in the Australian matches ... stood out for £15'[4] and when this was refused declined to play. This strike had significant future repercussions for relationships between a professional team, organised by Shrewsbury, Shaw and J. Lillywhite, which came to Australia in 1884–85 and the 1884 Australians.

Considering the Australians played match after match with the same eleven, and given the favourable conditions for batting in 1884, they gave a good account of themselves in the three Tests and were decidedly unlucky to lose the series, one loss and two draws, because Australia was in a favourable position in both drawn matches. *The Sunday Times* even suggested that the English team won the rubber under 'false pretences' because of an archaic rule which allocated only three days for a Test, whereas four days were allocated for Tests in Australia, enabling most to be played out to a finish. English authorities followed a practice which *The Argus* of 16 September 1884 suggested 'was probably framed in old times, when wickets were less perfect, and a three-figure score a rare event'.

Had a fourth day been played in the First Test at Manchester, there certainly would have been a result and the Australians were favourably placed to win. After there was no play at all on the first day, England were dismissed cheaply for 95 on a damp wicket with Boyle and Spofforth taking 6-42 and 4-42 respectively. The Australians then scored 182 and at the end of the second day, when the match was drawn, England was 9-180, an overall lead of just 93 runs. Boyle finished with a total of seven wickets; Spofforth, six and Palmer, four.

Conditions for the Second Test at Lord's were more favourable for batting and England scored what proved a winning total of 379 after the Australians had tallied 229. Australia was well placed for much of the match and at one stage had England 5-135 but a magnificent 148 by Steel altered the balance. Palmer was the best bowler, showing great perseverance in returning 6-111 off 75 overs, while Spofforth 'bowled very finely at times' but was expensive on other occasions returning 2-112 off 55.1 overs. Mostly Spofforth bowled at a slower pace, but at one stage in the Second Test he bowled flat out, placing his field for 'his very fast bowling, and Blackham stood back several yards behind the wicket'.[5] The bowling returns suggest that Murdoch leaned very heavily on Palmer and Spofforth, who bowled 130.1 of the 184.1 overs (over 70 per cent) by six bowlers Clearly the Australian opening duo must have tired in the latter half of the English innings when the last five wickets added 244 runs. The Australian cause was not helped by some dropped chances.

The Australians could still have saved the match but collapsed in the second innings to lose by an innings and five runs. The destroyer, Ulyett, took 7-36 and caused the retirement of another batsman, Blackham, by a 'spiteful kicker'. Ulyett benefited, according to reports, from a patch created by Spofforth's follow-through which seems to provide further evidence that while the Demon's celebrated 'third step' sometimes helped the Australian cause, it actually hindered them on other occasions.

The Australian bats made amends in the Third Test when they ran up a mammoth score of 551 with Percy McDonnell scoring 103, 'Tup' Scott 102, and captain Murdoch recording 211, the first double century in Test cricket. An Australian win looked likely with England at 8-181, but again the Australian bowlers allowed the tail to wag — W W Read scored a century in just 113 minutes — and England reached 346. Palmer, 4-90 off 54 overs, and Spofforth, 2-81 off 58 overs, again carried the attack and when they tired the support bowling was not effective enough to dismiss the English tail. Murdoch, it seems, may have recognised the problem of overbowling his star duo and made the highly unorthodox decision to open with Palmer and a part-time bowler, Bonnor, who took only six wickets on the tour. Spofforth did not enter the fray until 54 runs were on the board. Following on, England was 2-85 at the end of the third day when the Test was drawn. Australia might have won the Test with a fourth day's play.

During the second half of the 1884 tour the Australians came in for considerable criticism, most of it relating to gate money. After it was revealed that the Australians received the entire gate of the Lord's Test, £1,334, many papers recycled the old story that the tourists were greedy gate-money cricketers posing as amateurs. *World* stated that the Australians 'play too obviously for money's sake' in that 'they arrogate to themselves the rank of "gentlemen" and yet are only "professionals" '.[6] The Australians were compared unfavourably with the Gentlemen of Philadelphia, who were touring at the same time. While some papers, such as the *Standard*, added 'Esq.' after the names of the Americans, they pointedly dropped the prefix 'Mr' on the Australian scorecards, suggesting that they were really professionals. One London paper, *Entr'Acte*, lambasted the Australians, publishing a cartoon on 26 July 1884, just after the Lord's Test, with a British Lion addressing a kangaroo with a face which was a caricature of Spofforth's, and whose pouch was full of 'gate money': 'Well you don't mind a good licking, so long as you get the gate-money, do you?' As the best-known tourist, with features which must have delighted cartoonists, Spofforth was singled out as the representative 'gate-money' cricketer.

The Australian press, on this occasion, was much more sympathetic to the tourists. The *Sydney Mail* had written on 8 September 1883, prior to the tour, that the 1878 tourists had excellent terms securing 80 to 90 per cent of receipts at many games. Given the profitability of the Australian tours, terms were much tougher on subsequent tours: in fact, by 1882, the terms rather favoured English clubs, which kept all the stand and half the outer receipts. The same paper argued that the 1882 Australians made approximately half as much from the brief Australian tour as the entire English tour. The Australians did not secure better terms for the 1884 tour as English county clubs refused to part with half of the grandstand gate as requested. The financial arrangements for the Lord's Test were exceptional.

The Argus complained, on 16 September 1884, that 'we have been constantly reminded this season that the Australians take gate-money and the Americans do not, but it has yet to be insinuated that they obtained any of that money under false pretences, by not giving full value for it in a cricketing sense'. 'Censor' in the *Sydney Mail* of 9 August added a refreshing element of realism to the debate, admitting that the Australians were professionals in the strict sense but arguing that he could not understand why such a stigma should be attached to the term 'professional'; the position of professional could be filled with 'dignity and respectability'.

The 1884 Australians were not as successful as their 1882 counterparts: they won 18 matches, drew 7 and lost 7. By the time the dust started to settle on the tour, the English press realised that the side had performed exceptionally well given their lack of luck, their tougher schedule, their injury problems and the dry summer. In addition to the injury of Cooper there were times when Blackham, Murdoch, Spofforth and Midwinter 'had to enter the arena when they were unfit to play'.[7] Assessments ranged from the *Standard*, which described the tour as 'fairly successful', to the *Daily News*, which thought it was 'brilliantly successful'.

What both the Australian and English papers did agree on was that Spofforth had a great tour. *The Argus* of 16 September had no doubt that his 'performance during the tour confirms the long-entertained conviction that he is certainly the most remarkable bowler that ever stepped into a cricket field'. The English journal, *Cricket*, declared on 18 September, that 'in any mention of the bowling ... Spofforth's name must stand out in bold relief, in a position by itself' for he has alone often decided the issue of a match'. 'Censor' of the *Sydney Mail* added that Spofforth had quite eclipsed the other bowlers and that the success of the team was largely due to him.[8] A number of English papers thought that the English batting was as good, if not better than the Australian, but admitted that England had no bowlers who were as consistently good as Spofforth. *Truth* stated that 'we have not — and what is more, never have had — so deadly a fast bowler as Spofforth'.[9]

The Entr'Acte, 26 July 1884, cartoon. Spofforth was a logical representative of the touring team. He was the best known Australian cricketer. He was also a cartoonist's delight.

THE LION TO KANGAROO:—"WELL, YOU DON'T MIND A GOOD LICKING, SO LONG AS YOU GET THE GATE MONEY, DO YOU?"

There are good grounds for arguing that this was Spofforth's most triumphant tour. There was, admittedly, no one match of such heroic dimensions as the 1878 MCC game or the 1882 Oval Test, but his figures overall were superior to any other tour. He took 216 wickets in 1884, 28 more than in 1882, at approximately the same average. What was astonishing about his 1884 performance was that he had far less support at the other end. In 1882 he took 188 out of the 638, or 29.5 per cent of the wickets taken by the Australian bowlers, whereas in 1884, his 216 out of 533 wickets constituted 40.1 per cent of the wickets taken.

Australian Bowling Averages in Representative Matches, 1884 Tour

	Overs	Maidens	Runs	Wickets	Average
Spoffoth	1,586	656	2,642	216	12.5
Palmer	1,247.3	464	2,131	132	16.2
Boyle	738	292	1,172	67	17.3
Giffen	827.3	284	1,623	82	19.7
Midwinter	259.2	115	411	15	27.6
Others	345	81	817	21	38.9

'Censor' was impressed that these figures were achieved in a dry English summer:

It is believed in the colonies that Spofforth is harmless on fast turf. They have never had a drier season in England than the last and on some of the truest wickets Spofforth operated with marked success.[10]

The tour ended on a light note with a match between the Smokers and Non-Smokers at Lord's beginning on 8 September to raise money for the Cricketers' Fund. With Englishmen and Australians mixed in both sides, it pitted Australian against Australian. The game provided one Australian, the 6' 6" (198 cm) big hitter, George Bonnor, with the opportunity to indulge his friendly rivalry with Spofforth. Neither of these players had any doubts about his ability, nor were they reluctant to boast about their success. Appearing for the Non-Smokers, Bonnor must have taken a great amount of pleasure in scoring 124, and punishing Spofforth severely, including one hit out of the ground. Quite possibly Spofforth enjoyed the fun at the end of the tour and served up a few juicy morsels for his friendly rival who was Spofforth's best man when he married two years later.

Spofforth did not return to Australia with his fellow-tourists but left Gravesend on 9 October, a fortnight later, on the P & O steamer, *Ganges*, along with the English amateur, I D Walker. Spofforth almost certainly remained behind to be with Phillis Cadman of Derbyshire, whom he married at the end of the 1886 tour. It was reported in *Cricket*, later in 1884, that Murdoch and Spofforth were 'affianced to two of Derbyshire's fair daughters'. Murdoch in fact married an Australian, Winsome Jemima Watson, whom he met on the voyage back to Australia and married a few weeks after the ship berthed, but Spofforth almost certainly married his Derbyshire fiancee of 1884.

The 1884 tour was the pinnacle of Spofforth's career. He had now completed four outstanding tours in which his bowling had improved on each visit. His reputation was now doubly secure: he was the heroic figure who had performed well in some legendary matches, but he was also the consistent performer who had put Australian cricket on the map and helped to develop some of the traditions of international cricket. But as was so often the case, he did not have a long period to savour his success because the 1884-85 Australian season was a particularly controversial one.

Spofforth the Strike-breaker

T. Horan

T he majority of the 1884 tourists travelled back to Australia at about the same time as the eighth English team, a group of professionals organised by Shaw (manager), Shrewsbury (captain) and J Lillywhite. Included in the English side were the three Notts players, Barnes, Flowers and Shrewsbury, who had boycotted the match against the Australians at Sheffield in 1884. The matter must have still rankled with the Australian players, for the refusal of almost the entire 1884 team to meet the eighth English team in many of the important matches, a counter-strike, was to cast a very long shadow over the 1884–85 domestic season. The Sheffield strike was probably just the trigger for the counter-boycott because there had been differences between the English professionals and the Australian commercials, as they were sometimes called, dating back to 1880 when seven Notts players demanded £20, rather than £10, to play against the Australians.[1] The animosity between Murdoch and John Conway, the Australian agent for the Englishmen, also complicated matters in 1884–85. Whatever the precise reason for the bad feeling between the two sides, *Wisden* claimed it was manifested 'from the moment Murdoch's team landed ... it became evident they (the 1884 Australians) were animated by a feeling of bitter hostility towards Shaw and his party'.

The 1884 Australians, minus Spofforth who had not yet arrived back, refused to play for their colonies in November, when the Englishmen played New South Wales and Victoria. Murdoch's men, who did not disband as a touring unit until after the First Test, had hoped to organise their own matches against the Englishmen, but negotiations had collapsed when Shaw offered them 30 per cent of the gate while the Australian XI demanded 50 per cent. It was a very hefty demand on the part of the Australians, given the convention that the greater expenses of a touring side entitled them to a larger proportion of the gate.

The First Test of the series and the first Test ever played at Adelaide almost did not take place when negotiations over money between the teams could not be resolved. The Australians again wanted half the gate but Shaw offered only 30 per cent. The Australians then offered to play for 40 per cent of the gate but to pay their own expenses and to donate the other 10 per cent to charity, but this offer was also rejected. The game only went ahead after the South Australian Cricket Association (SACA), desperate to stage the match, made terms which 'to the ordinary mind seem very extravagant' by offering each side a flat sum of £450 plus one-third of any profits.[2] The bill for the players was very substantial since it swallowed up the entire gate receipts, which were approximately £900.[3] The SACA gave the Australians and the English close to what they had originally asked for, 50 per cent of the gate. With anticipated match costs of £1,200,[4] the local association raised the gate entry charge to 2s. ground admission and 4s. stand admission. After a smaller first-day crowd and much grumbling in the press, the gate entry charge was halved from the second day on. The association incurred a gate loss of £271 though this was mostly due to bad weather.

The Adelaide arrangements did not endear the 1884 Australians to the colonial press and public, who were 'dead set against' their stance. The *Australasian* of 20 December 1884 noted a view which 'you hear on all sides' which was to let the Australians 'make what they can in the old country' but back in Australia 'let them act a little generously towards our visitors'. Earlier the *Sydney Mail* of 22 November had declared that there was 'great indignation' in Sydney and Melbourne at the 'grasping policy' of Murdoch's team which refused to meet Shaw's unless they got half the gate. The *Bulletin* of 29 November, which had defended the financial arrangements of the 1884 Australians while on tour, referred to their 'impudence' and 'ingratitude' for not playing for their respective colonies against Shaw's team.

Spofforth was still on the high seas when the controversy first surfaced in the press. On the way back to Australia the ship had berthed at Colombo and Spofforth and I D Walker participated in a game organised by the Colombo Cricket Club. Spofforth took 5-15 off 11.2 overs and scored 23. The *Australasian* was amused by a reference to Spofforth as the 'demm bowler' in the Colombo press and quipped that either this paper could not get Spofforth's nickname right or maybe they thought he was a 'demm good bowler'.[5]

It is not clear whether Spofforth intended to play against the 1884–85 Englishmen because it was later suggested in

Cricket, on 29 January 1885, that it was 'his intention to resume his station life directly on his return'. As was the case after previous tours, Spofforth must have looked forward to an extended break from the game. However, by the time he reached Australia, if not before, he was notified of the death of his brother-in-law, Charles Farquhar Clive, who had died at the Collaroy property on 31 October, at the age of thirty-seven. Spofforth proceeded to join his bereaved sister, Anna, at Cassilis after the *Ganges* arrived at Sydney on 28 November.

The Australians, without Spofforth and Midwinter, who had congestion of the lungs, were easily defeated in the Adelaide Test by eight wickets. The Australian bowling, with the exception of Palmer (5-81 and 1-23) was ineffective.

The controversy over gate money came to a head at the time of the Second Test, which began on 1 January 1885 at Melbourne. The 1884 Australians had disbanded by this time, the Adelaide Test being the last match of the tour, but because of the ongoing debate over gate money, they continued to operate as an informal group with George Alexander acting as their spokesman. Unlike the SACA, the organisers of this Test, the Victorian Cricketers' Association (VCA), took an uncompromising stand and the English professionals, encouraged that local opinion was flowing strongly against the 1884 Australians, also took a tougher stand, offering the Australians only £20 per man, which was less than half the amount they received in Adelaide. Just before the Test Alexander was desperately backpedalling: he reduced the demand to 40 per cent of the gate and then wrote that the team was 'willing to accept 40 per cent of the net profits, our intention being to hand the same over to the Melbourne charities, after paying our bare expenses'.[6] Having overplayed his hand in the Adelaide and Melbourne negotiations, it seems Alexander was now trying to save face.

None of the thirteen Australian tourists played in the Test, which was an event without precedent in Test cricket. A few of the English professionals had boycotted matches against the Australians on previous tours, but no strike had involved an entire team, nor had it occurred in a Test match. Outraged by the action of the local players, the VCA suspended the Victorian players involved in the strike —

Blackham, Bonnor, Boyle, McDonnell, Palmer and Scott — from future matches organised under its jurisdiction. The ban, imposed on 13 January, was not removed until 11 November 1885. The press echoed almost unanimous support for this action: the *Sydney Mail* criticised the 'selfish policies' of the Australians while the semi-official English journal, *Cricket*, went further to describe the boycott as 'unpatriotic'.[7]

Bulletin, 7 March 1885.

Their True Colours.

The strike did not involve the whole side, however. Only eight of the thirteen actually withdrew from the Test: Murdoch, Bannerman, Blackham, Bonnor, Boyle, McDonnell, Palmer, Scott. Another two, Alexander and Cooper, did not have to withdraw because their form was not considered good enough for selection: they were not even chosen for the Victorian practice squad. Alexander, however, supported the 1884 strike. Another two appear to have been unavailable for the Test: Giffen could not get leave from work and Midwinter was ill. Then there was the thirteenth man, Spofforth, who right from the start declared publicly that he was totally against the strike. Spofforth, who was probably still at Collaroy at the time of this Test, sent a letter to an English gentleman, during the Test, in which he expressed 'his thorough disgust at the action of his recent comrades of the Australian Eleven'. He added that 'if he can possibly manage it', he planned to play in the match between the tourists and New South Wales to begin on 24 January 1885.[8] Other sources confirm that Spofforth publicly repudiated the action of his fellow tourists in boycotting the Second Test.

Spofforth made no bones about his disagreement with his former colleagues over gate money as soon as he arrived back in Australia. When the *Ganges* berthed at Melbourne on 23 November Spofforth had been met by his former colleague, Tommy Horan, who noted that Spofforth was uncommonly well after the long sea voyage. Horan believed that Spofforth could enter the field in 'rare buckle after a few days on the shore'. 'Felix' then went on to report Spofforth's views on the actions of the 1884 Australians, which were published in the *Australasian* of 29 November:

He (Spofforth) does not intend to play with the Australian Eleven against the Englishmen in Adelaide, and he regrets very much the position taken up by his comrades in connection with the now very fully ventilated question of gate-money. The want of tact and good management on the part of the executive of the Australian Eleven has surprised the 'demon' not a little ... If Spofforth can manage to do so, he will play in the intercolonial; he would also like very much to play for United Australia against the Englishmen, and he thinks such team should be composed of seven or eight of the present Australian Eleven, and the remainder from New South Wales and Victoria.

It is unfortunate that Spofforth did not set down, either

In the Toils.

The criticism of commercialism in cricket is a longstanding one.
(Bulletin, 7 March 1885)

at the time or later, more precise reasons why he felt so strongly about this issue and why he turned his back on his close colleagues, and most notably Murdoch. Spofforth's stance does, however, establish that he set great store on principle and was prepared to speak up for what he saw as right even if it meant jeopardising close friendships built up over four tours. He implied that the Australians were asking for too much and not recognising the principle that a visiting team had claims for a larger share of the gate-money revenue. Spofforth's stance must have been deeply hurtful to Murdoch. The team's action was not supported by its most famous member, whose stance undermined what was otherwise the united position of the 1884 Australians. But

Spofforth was a law unto himself. He was a fierce individualist who was willing to stick his neck out to defend a principle come what may.

Former team-mate, Horan, was one to support Spofforth's stand. His condemnation of the strikers in the *Australasian* of 27 December 1884 conveyed some of the heat generated by the issue:

our association (VCA) should show some backbone in this matter and take notice of these refusals. If every member of the recent Australian team disappeared from the country tomorrow, cricket would still flourish in the land. Indeed, according to their action since they came back, it would be a good thing for Australian cricket if they never played here again.

Although a second-string Australian XI batted well in the first innings, they did not provide very much resistance to the Englishmen, who won the Melbourne Test by ten wickets. Only some 23,000 spectators attended the four days of the Test, whereas for the equivalent contest in 1882-83 a crowd of around 50,000 turned up for just three days of cricket.

The strike continued throughout January, despite savage criticism from the colonial press. *The Bulletin* published a cartoon on 24 January, captioned 'Their True Colours': it featured the Victorian contingent of the 1884 team outside a tent of the Victorian Cricketers' Association and standing on a mat labelled 'Gentlemen Amateurs' but with a flag unfurled declaring, 'Professional players who keep a sharp eye on the gate money'.

Immediately before the match between New South Wales and England, commencing on 24 January, the New South Wales Cricket Association (NSWCA) met to consider an appeal from the VCA to support its stance and some unusual correspondence from Bonnor, Alick Bannerman and Spofforth. The suspended Victorian, Bonnor, who had played for Victoria against New South Wales only a month before (in a match beginning on Boxing Day 1884), but who had subsequently moved to New South Wales, wrote that 'he would not take part in matches against the English Team, but would if desired play for NSW in the next (February) Intercolonial'. Alick Bannerman wrote 'declining to take part in matches v Englishmen unless Messrs Bonnor and Murdoch played'. Spofforth's letter was more routine: he stated that owing to an injury to his ankle and pressure of business he was unable to play for the colony against the Englishmen but 'would endeavour to take part' in the Intercolonial and Combined (Test) match.[9]

The NSWCA was unwilling to endorse the tough action of the VCA against the striking players. While it did not condone the action of the strikers, it was rather more concerned with making a success of the upcoming Sydney Test and viewed the suspensions as a Victorian domestic problem. The NSWCA adopted the following moderate resolution towards the strike:

That although the association cannot endorse the action of the NSW contingent of the late Australian Eleven, in refusing to represent the colony in the matches against the Englishmen, this committee does not consider that it comes within its province to demand any further explanation, or to take any further action with regard to such refusal.

One NSWCA member, C W Beal, manager of the 1882 Australians, moved an even more parochial amendment that the association 'does not endorse the action' of the VCA, but it was lost.[10]

The differing responses of colonial associations underline how unfederal each was and how colonial officials jealously guarded their own bailiwicks. Rather than assisting the strike, the lack of coordination between the officials from one colony to another may have been a factor in the collapse of strike action. The softer line of the NSWCA made it easier for some of the strikers to cut their losses and to return to the Test fold. There was the great irony that the suspended Victorians who could not even play for their colony in Melbourne, were able to represent their country in Sydney.[10]

When the match between New South Wales and the Englishmen began on 24 January, Murdoch, Alick Bannerman, Bonnor and Spofforth were absent from the colonial side. Murdoch had not even bothered to answer the local association's invitation to play.

Spofforth was fit to play against Victoria on 13 February but he must have been a little rusty. His presence enabled New South Wales to win by just three wickets. Spofforth had a long spell in both innings taking 1-72 off 188 balls and 5-

100 off 251 balls. He scored 36 runs when he opened the batting in the first innings.

Spofforth's opening batting partner was Bonnor. It was an unusual situation to say the least. The local association had turned down Bonnor's January request to represent New South Wales in the intercolonial but, when Evans had withdrawn at the last moment, Bonnor was selected. 'Judex' of the *Sydney Mail* argued beforehand that the selection of Bonnor would undermine the 'representative character' of these contests and that a residential qualification of six months should be introduced.[11] During the 1880s many of the conventions of cricket were still being established.

The Englishmen met a much stronger XI when the Third Test began at Sydney on 20 February. Perhaps encouraged by the stance of Spofforth, three of the strikers — Alick Bannerman, Bonnor and Scott — joined him in the Australian side. This exciting match, played on a rain-affected pitch, did not begin all that well for the Australians who slumped to 9-101 before a last wicket stand of 80 between Garrett (51 not out) and Evans (33) rescued the side. It was a measure of Evans' decline that the leading all-rounder of the 1870s now batted at number eleven and bowled only eight overs in the two innings.

After the Englishmen put on 31 for the opening stand Spofforth almost took his second hat-trick in Test cricket. After he caught and bowled Shrewsbury, Ulyett 'fluked' his first ball for two runs but was clean bowled by the following ball, a Spofforth yorker. Barnes was then stumped off the next ball fortuitously: the ball bounced off the keeper's pads on to the stumps. With Spofforth taking 4-54 and Horan 6-40 the Englishmen trailed by 48 runs, totalling 133.

After the Australians scored 165 in their second innings, the Englishmen were set 214 runs to win. Their start was not very promising: Spofforth, bowling fast, uprooted Scotton's leg stump and, after he removed three more batsmen, the Englishmen had slumped to 6-92. A century partnership between Flowers and Read then lifted the score to 194 and with only twenty runs to get and four wickets in hand an English victory seemed probable. It was at this point that Captain Massie must have instinctively leaned on the man for the crisis situation, who beat Read with a slow straight ball and bowled him for a fine innings of 56. Spofforth's Victorian and Test colleague, J W Trumble, commented later that this 'was the cleverest ball I ever saw bowled'. The slow ball had come along in 'action, delivery and flight apparently a reproduction of its predecessor' and 'Read played forward to it and completed his stroke before the ball had arrived' and 'he then tried to pull his bat to cover his wicket, but it was too late preventing the ball getting through to the stumps'.[12] After a run out and a wicket to Trumble the Englishmen moved to 9-207 with Flowers, 56, still at the crease. With just seven runs required for an English victory 'the spectators were now in the wildest state of excitement, and watched every ball closely'.[13] It was left to the Demon to execute the *coup de grâce* when Flowers was caught by Evans at point off his bowling, Australia winning the Test by just six runs, one run closer than the 1882 Oval Test result. Spofforth returned match figures of 10-144. He bowled almost half the total overs bowled by the Australian team: 96.1 out of 201.2.

The Australians were close to full strength for the Fourth Test at Sydney, with four more rebels returning: Blackham, Giffen, McDonnell and Palmer. Murdoch, who was practising law in the New South Wales country town of Cootamundra, remained the only notable absentee. After England won the toss they batted and hit up the good score of 269. Although Spofforth had a relatively moderate return of 2-61 off 29 overs, he was not far from the limelight. The Englishmen believed that Horan's excellent return of 7-117 was caused by the Spofforth follow-through: for after 2-52 'Giffen now began to get difficult, owing to the "demon" having torn up the pitch, and several balls played very queer'. Later Flowers was bowled by Giffen, 'another undeniable one on the sore spot'.[14] Spofforth did not have everything his own way as Read, when 37, was caught off a no-ball — a relatively rare occurrence in this era.

The Australians secured an advantage of 40 runs on the first innings, chiefly because of a hard-hitting 128 by Bonnor, who reached his century in even time. Then heavy rain fell overnight. Spofforth and Palmer revelled in a sticky wicket, and were 'unplayable' with the ball 'breaking and kicking dreadfully'. After the Englishmen totalled only 77

(Spofforth 5-30 and Palmer 4-32), the Australians easily won the Test by eight wickets.

The final and deciding Test was played at Melbourne in the following week. Spofforth came to bat with Australia awkwardly placed at 9-99 in fine conditions and proceeded to play an entertaining and rapid-fire innings of 50 — his first and only Test half-century — and helped Australia to a more respectable total of 163. Several times Spofforth 'ran fa: up the wicket' to hit the ball and his innings included a long low hit off Barnes for five (now six) which cleared the pavilion gate. It was, as *Wisden* put it, a 'rattling innings' hit in 'most vigorous fashion'. The Englishmen then hit up the very large, and winning, total of 386 which was made possible by a number of dropped chances. Particularly damaging was an easy chance missed by McShane off Spofforth when Shrewsbury was just six; he went on to score 105 not out. Spofforth returned 2-71 off 49 overs. Australia lost three early wickets in the second innings and could only reach 125, leaving the English easy victors by an innings and 98 runs.

Although the Englishmen won the series by three Tests to two and retained the Ashes, Spofforth could be satisfied with his performance. When he played Australia had won two out of three Tests and he was easily the best bowler with 19 wickets for 306 at an average of 16.1 per wicket. Giffen took 11-348 (av. 31.6) in three Tests and Palmer took 11-171 (av. 17.1) in two. Reviewing the 1884-85 season 'Censor' of the *Sydney Mail* declared that 'Spofforth is still the demon of old, and he keeps up his batting amazingly'.[15] James Lillywhite noted that 'on almost every occasion when England has been defeated (in 1884-85), it has been by the aid of the "demon" bowler, Spofforth'.[16]

Although the strike had been settled by the Fourth Test, there was much criticism of those involved for the rest of the tour and throughout 1885. *The Bulletin* published another cartoon on 7 March 1885 which showed Australian cricket caught in the tentacles of an octopus entitled 'L.s.d.'. Then there was a reported cable from the MCC in March that the 1884 tourists, with the exception of Spofforth, would not be welcome on the next tour and that they would be debarred from playing at Lord's, the Oval and Trent Bridge. *The*

Bulletin of 14 March declared that it would 'serve 'em right' because 'Murdoch and his company have at last wrung the neck of the goose that laid their golden eggs'. This opinion was echoed in the same day's *Sydney Mail,* which argued that 'Murdoch's Eleven, in their thirst for gold, have brought the stigma on themselves'.

A report, which appeared in the *Sydney Mail* a few months later, suggested that English cricketers and the general public were 'very much disgusted' with the behaviour of the 1884 Australians towards Shaw's team and the reception of the next Australian team was likely to be 'frosty'. There was, by contrast, nothing but admiration for Spofforth:

The English public always make an idol of him, both in the field and out. If he visits England again he will find himself 10 times more popular than he ever was, all in consequence of his conduct in the late cricketing dispute.[17]

It is ironic that, in many respects, Spofforth seems to have been more popular in England than in Australia. Perhaps this was because he often saved his best performances for England. Perhaps, too, this was because the Australian press and public demanded much more of their heroes.

Although the 1884–85 tour was not a financial disaster, the Test crowds were down by almost 50 per cent on the previous one and the profits were greatly diminished.[18] Much of the blame for the strike focused on the captain and the instigator, William Murdoch, whom *The Bulletin* referred to sarcastically as the 'giant' and the 'Australian Great Man'. It was not the first time that the paper had criticised Murdoch. Two years before it had not been impressed by a paragraph in the *Cootamundra Herald,* which it believed would 'enthral the upper crust', that Murdoch was about to return to Cootamundra to settle down to business. 'It's about time that William resumed his profession as a gentleman' and 'gave the gate-money racket' a rest, suggested *The Bulletin* of 10 March 1883, for 'we consider him a bore'. On 17 February the same paper had declared that Murdoch has 'had his day' for 'Billy is getting too fat'.

There are good grounds for believing that Murdoch quit senior cricket for five years because he was vilified by all sections of the colonial press and criticised by officials and the public for his stand in 1884–85. There are hints that he took the criticism badly. He did not bother to turn up to the function after the Victorian intercolonial and it was left to Garrett to reply on behalf of the New South Wales team. He did not bother to reply to the invitation of the NSWCA to play in the Third Test. He alone of the strikers, did not play against the Englishmen in the latter Tests. There was the excuse of attending to his Cootamundra law practice and on 8 December 1884 Murdoch married the heiress, daughter of a Bendigo gold-mining magnate, Winsome Jemima Watson. By late 1885 Murdoch had moved to Melbourne where he was admitted to the Victorian Supreme Court. Despite pressure to play for Victoria, he did not play once for his new colony between 1885 and 1890.

Murdoch must have become so fed up with cricket politics that he turned his back on the game to concentrate on his profession and family life. Although he had a weight problem from 1883 on, Murdoch's talent and enthusiam for cricket had not been extinguished, or at least could be rekindled, because he returned to captain the 1890 Australians and was a very successful captain and player for Sussex from 1893 to 1899. Had he remained in international cricket during these years his reputation might have been even greater because he was undoubtedly one of the best batsmen in the world from 1880 to 1885 and certainly the premier Australian batsman.

There were a number of reasons why the strike of 1884–85 failed. It was not well organised either in terms of the shaping of player demands or in terms of publicity. By the time of the Melbourne Test the strikers were in disarray and the withdrawal of labour held out no promise of any improvement in revenue paid to players. The VCA reacted savagely, punishing the Victorians who had undermined their Test match, while the NSWCA had no inclination to take up what it saw as a Victorian cause because it conflicted with its own self-interest. Perhaps, too, the NSWCA was shrewd and independent enough to note that the strike was virtually over in January and there was no reason why their star players should be penalised further. The unwillingness of the star of the 1884 Australians to support strike action was another important reason for its failure. Spofforth may have strained a number of friendships but he alone was shrewd enough to question the basis of the strike action.

The short-lived withdrawal of services in 1884–85 was a preliminary skirmish for a far more serious strike when six of the best Australian players withdrew from the 1912 tour to England. This strike was a culmination of three decades of debate about issues such as private interest and public control, the rights of players, and acceptable levels of commercialism and professionalism. It was not until 1912 that the Australian Board of Control for International Cricket, formed in 1905, fully established its authority as the organiser of Australian cricket.

Spofforth was a key figure in one of the most important decades in the emergence of the modern game. Not only did he play a pivotal role in the rise of Test cricket and its symbols, but he was also involved in some of the critical debates about the structure and organisation of the game.

The End of an International Career

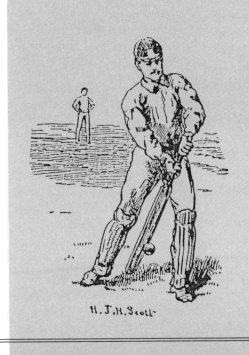

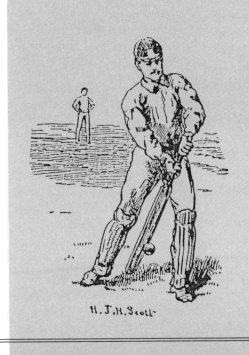

CHAPTER 12

H.J.H.Scott

New South Wales lost another champion cricketer when Spofforth followed Murdoch to Melbourne. Spofforth joined the National Bank of Australasia and became the first officer-in-charge of a new branch opened at Moonee Ponds on 1 June 1885. Cricket was a likely factor in his appointment because the Chief Manager of the National Bank of Australasia, Grey Smith, who was vice president (and later president) of the Melbourne Cricket Club, encouraged his employees to involve themselves in the game and believed that 'a graceful batsman or talented bowler was as desirable an officer in his eyes as a neat penman'.[1] In joining the Melbourne Cricket Club, Spofforth formed a distinguished international quartet with Palmer, Blackham and Bruce.

Later in 1885 the press turned its attention to the proposed tour of England and when Spofforth made his usual declaration that he would not tour the statement was taken with a grain of salt. By this time sections of the English press had become aware of his game of reluctant tourist. *Cricket* commented on 24 September that the Demon has 'expressed his intention not to come this time' and 'the English newspapers have reproduced this report as conclusive'. While 'it is quite possible that he may not come', the reporter noted that Spofforth had previously refused 'in equally emphatic terms'. The Australian critics, who had all been 'quite sure he would join the (1884) team' were proved right.

During November J. Lillywhite wrote a letter to 'Censor' of the *Sydney Mail*, giving his advice 'to bring Spofforth, even if they have to give him a thousand down', but added that 'they must not bring any of Murdoch's late team, even if each of them offered to give £100 to be selected. They would only spoil the trip.'[2] Spofforth had still not declared his hand by 9 January 1886 but the *Sydney Mail* was not worried for 'Spofforth, as usual, avers that he will not join the team; but when the "Demon" says "no" he generally means "yes," or rather he does the reverse of what he says!' Spofforth was in fact listed as a tourist in the next issue of the *Sydney Mail* on 16 January.

The colonial press may have been a little more hopeful because Spofforth turned out for Victoria against his former colony in a match which began on Boxing Day 1885. Having resided six months in Melbourne, and turning out for the Melbourne Cricket Club, he was eligible to play for Victoria.[3] Murdoch, who had only been in Melbourne for approximately a month, and was eligible to play for New South Wales but not for Victoria, did not play in the game. Much to the dismay of the *Sydney Mail*, Bonnor turned up again in Melbourne since 'no one knows whether Bonnor belongs to Melbourne or Sydney'. Although the paper urged the NSWCA to 'discountenance this bird-of-passage sort of business', Bonnor appeared for New South Wales.[4]

Spofforth seems to have relished bowling against his former team-mates and his bag of 10-138 helped secure a big Victorian win by an innings and 69 runs. Spofforth's attitude to his former colony was rather different to that of Murdoch, who was pressured to represent Victoria in following seasons, but stated that:

I have learnt and played all my cricket ... in and on behalf of New South Wales and I don't mind telling you that whenever she has an eleven in the field I wish them to win, no matter by whom they are opposed, and that being so I could not play against them.[5]

Although this comment may disguise Murdoch's real reason for not playing first-class cricket, it is ironic that the Victorian-born Murdoch should feel more passionately about this issue than the New South Wales-born Spofforth. Being a great competitor and an individualist, Spofforth seems to have had no such qualms.

By this time Spofforth had an established reputation both as a legendary bowler and as a character. An incident from the same intercolonial underlined that he very much enjoyed the latter role. The youthful J W Worrall took a spectacular catch off Spofforth's bowling, jumping sideways to clutch a powerful Bonnor drive in his left hand, a shot which 'spun me around in mid-air, with my left arm forced round to the back of my neck'. Worrall was quickly surrounded and praised by some of his celebrated team-mates, who included Blackham, Horan and others, but to Worrall's dismay and puzzlement Spofforth never came near 'to give me a word of encouragement or pat me on the back'. However, after a few more Spofforth overs, the Demon 'condescendingly' turned to Worrall and quipped: 'Worrall, keep your eyes open, for I am still bowling for you.' Worrall enjoyed the joke enormously.[6]

Worrall later recounted another celebrated incident when two strong personalities, Spofforth and umpire Jim Phillips, clashed at the Sydney Cricket Ground. Spofforth, like another heady bowler of a previous era, T W Wills, was keen to establish psychological dominance of everyone on the field and this included the umpires. In the days before the crease was widened, Spofforth, who was then representing Victoria, went outside the crease and bowled several no-balls when striving for extra variation. He was called by the umpire, whereupon Spofforth 'became nettled':

Going outside deliberately he was in the act of delivering the ball when Phillips 'called'. But the cunning old fox held tight to the ball, and Phillips had of necessity to reverse his decision. Things went on quietly for a while until Spofforth failed in another attempt at trapping the umpire, covering up his intention by remarking, 'Oh, Phillips, my foot slipped this time'. Big, burly, red-headed Jim of Dimboola, with brown eyes, made no remark and as he had the face of a sphinx the game proceeded. But he was only biding his time, and at last, when the bowler had delivered the ball with his foot fairly planted behind and within the crease, Phillips yelled out in stentorian tones, 'No ball': 'Oh, Phillips,' said Spofforth, 'I have never bowled a fairer ball in my life.' 'I know that,' said the umpire, 'but my tongue slipped that time.' That incident ended the feud, and all the rest was peace.[7]

Spofforth must have enjoyed this exchange because he embarrassed another umpire many years later when he was playing club cricket for Hampstead.

The 1886 tour differed from the previous four in two significant respects. Due to the controversy emanating from the 1884 tour and spilling over into the 1884-85 Australian season, there were a number of moves to take the organisation of tours out of the hands of the cricketers and vest them in the hands of the associations. The VCA attempted to liaise with the associations of New South Wales and South Australia, anticipating the need for a national organising authority to have greater control over international matches. When this move fell through the Melbourne Cricket Club took over the organisation of the 1886 tour and its Secretary, B J Wardill, became tour manager. What this meant was that the players were engaged on a fixed contract, rather than on the basis of a joint stock company, with the Melbourne Cricket Club attracting the profit or losses of the tour. No longer were the Australians criticised as gate-money cricketers.

Another difference was that there was no obvious replacement for Murdoch as captain. The merits of three pretenders were canvassed in the press in February 1886: Jack Blackham, Tom Garrett and Dr Henry J H 'Tup' Scott. Blackham, who had been Victorian captain since 1882–83, was the only one with Test captaincy experience: he captained Australia in the Third Test of the 1884–85 series. As a shrewd and highly experienced skipper of New South Wales, Garrett had much to commend himself. The man with the least captaincy experience, Melbourne University-educated Scott, who had performed well with the bat on the 1884 tour, was chosen ahead of the others. 'Censor' hoped that Scott had not been chosen for his 'speaking abilities' for 'if a speech-making captain is required, it would be easy to elect one in addition to the cricketer'.[8] Such qualms were well grounded because, whereas captaincy had been the Australian strength on four previous tours — Gregory and Murdoch were shrewd, imaginative captains who maintained team morale and discipline — the easy-going Scott was unable to contain team quarrels which bedevilled the 1886 tour.

In the same article that 'Censor' talked about a 'speech-making captain' he added that if, a 'mashing' captain could be chosen 'the choice would lie between Bonnor and Spofforth'. It seems likely that 'Censor' was suggesting that both men were 'showy' individuals with an inclination to boast, and there is some evidence that they had similar personalities: mostly they were men of few words who preferred action to talk; mostly they kept matters very much to their chests;[9] but when roused they were more than willing to boast or engage in very straight and blunt speech. They were both all-round athletes: Bonnor was also a good boxer, rower and swimmer.

Until he captained Derbyshire in 1890, Spofforth does not seem to have ever been considered seriously as a possible Australian or even colonial captain. With his keen cricket brain and ability to inspire a side, he might well have been a good choice for the 1886 tour and it seems surprising that his name was not even canvassed. Possibly there was a prejudice in this era in favour of a batsman-captain. More probably there were other reasons: Spofforth was too independent, too much of an individualist to be a good leader.

When the team left Australia in March 1886 it did not look a bad one on paper. Although some English authorities were reported to be unsympathetic to the return of any 1884 tourist other than Spofforth, another five had been members of that side: Blackham, Bonnor, Giffen, Palmer and Scott. Garrett and S P Jones, members of earlier tours, added to the experience of the side. Then there were five players on their first tour: Bruce, Evans, Jarvis, McIlwraith and J W Trumble. There was the usual uncertainty about Evans, who had been 'seriously ill from a severe sunstroke' which the *Sydney Mail* of 14 November 1885 stated had 'affected poor Evans's mind'. Three weeks later he was 'fit and well' though 'somewhat thin' and by 23 January 1886 he was batting and bowling with his 'customary energy'. Evans was, this paper argued, a man to be emulated by the other colonial players, because 'there is an amount of earnestness about that cricketer which entirely belongs to himself'. The *Sydney Mail* of 6 February hoped that this 'popular cricketer' who was a 'really good bowler' on a 'sticky' would have a good tour and predicted that, if the season was wet, he might well be as destructive as Boyle in 1878.

Spofforth was, however, far less impressed by this reticent champion who seemed forever reluctant to put his reputation on the line outside Sydney. When Spofforth learnt that Evans, approaching the age of thirty-seven, had finally decided to tour, he backed himself to take over 100 wickets more than Evans. The boast, which surfaced in the *Australasian*, may well have been a light-hearted throwaway comment which no one other than the reporter took seriously. However, it might also have been a barbed humorous comment, because that rings true with the Spofforth personality. Spofforth had good grounds to be fed up with the promotion of Evans by the colonial press, for Evans had time and time again absented himself from testing situations. Nor was Evans the only colonial bowler denigrated by Spofforth. In his later reflections Spofforth showed no reticence in criticising the performance of Frank Allan at Lord's in 1878 and Harry Boyle at the Oval in 1882. However, given that Spofforth and Evans were team-mates in 1886, the boast was hardly inclined to add to team morale and cohesion.

The story was aired by Felix (Tom Horan) in the *Australasian*, which was usually a reliable source. Although Horan had referred to Spofforth as the 'greatest living bowler' on 25 November 1885, he was not too impressed by Spofforth's boast. 'If Evans shows anything like his old inter-colonial form when he used to beat the demon time after time in bowling average, Spofforth's chance of winning the wager will, I fancy, not be particularly bright.'[10] The comment was not particularly realistic because Evans had rarely reproduced his good form of the mid-1870s. Perhaps Horan was angered by the Demon's denigration of his rival.

Spofforth was in fine form during a wet May which marked the beginning of the tour. On a wet and difficult wicket, he proved irresistible in the fourth match of the tour against Oxford University, returning 9-18 and 6-18 and clean bowling eleven batsmen. He also had good returns in the second match against Notts (6-58 in the first innings) and the fifth game against the North of England (7-19 in the first innings). After the fifth game of the tour Spofforth had taken 31 wickets at a cost of 6.1 per wicket.

Spofforth had missed the third game of the tour against Surrey through indisposition and Evans had a rare oppor-tunity to open the bowling and to bowl a long spell: in the match he bowled 81.3 overs, of which 41 were maidens, and returned match figures of 6-84. One of the puzzling facts of the 1886 tour is why Evans was so much out of favour with the captain, for he only bowled 506.3 overs on the entire tour. Evans was by far the most economical bowler on the tour, bowling a very high proportion of maidens (251) and only conceding just over a run an over (615 runs). But he was not as penetrative as hoped, taking only 30 wickets for the tour at a cost of 20.2 each wicket. In the representative matches he took only 4-172 (132 overs and 65 maidens) at a cost of 43 runs per wicket. Felix of the *Australasian* commented after the tour that while Evans had done 'very badly' he had 'not been given a proper chance' especially in bowling when he was rarely tried until the batsmen were well set.[11]

Then occurred an event in the sixth game of the tour, against the Gentlemen, which had a far-reaching effect on Spofforth's future as a world-class bowler and which also greatly affected the fate of the touring team. After Spofforth had dismissed W G Grace cheaply for the second time in the young season he suffered a severe injury to his right hand, breaking (dislocating in some accounts) his third finger. The villain of the piece, Lord Harris, who had inflicted a similar injury on the same hand in the equivalent match in 1884, later wrote that:

He (Spofforth) followed up his ball very far, and as I probably jumped in, he was very close, too close to put his hand in exactly the right place; else he was ordinarily a very good field to his own bowling, but so full of nerves, that a hard blow made more difference to him than to many.[12]

But this time the injury was far worse. Spofforth did not play again for almost four weeks and, in the opinion of Harris and other critics, 'he was never the same bowler after the second (1886) injury'. The tour figures bear out this contention: after his injury he only took another 56 wickets for 1,309 runs at a cost of 23.4 per wicket.[13] After his injury Spofforth had only one 10-wicket haul, against Gloucestershire, when he had the satisfaction of removing W G Grace twice.

Punch was among the well-wishers for a speedy recovery of England's favourite Australian cricketer:

Disabled by accident, Spofforth?
That's hard! To the world let it go forth
Punch wishes you cure
As prompt as it's sure;
Good luck, lots of wickets, and so forth![14]

Propped up in bed in his pyjamas, his bandaged finger in a splint, Spofforth was visited by a journalist from the *Pall Mall Budget* who found the Demon more than willing to expound on a variety of matters which were duly published in early June.[15] The reactions of an English journalist to Spofforth throw light on the English perception of the man.

The meeting was 'very like an anti-climax' because while Spofforth had a 'satanic glamour' the journalist was clearly charmed by a very affable star. The journalist added that 'demon though he be, (he) is excessively modest, like all who have achieved world-wide fame'. The 'concentrated look from his piercing eyes' and a 'demoniacal smile' were all 'very good natured'. When asked whether he ever lost his temper or got violent 'when he was hit about', the Demon retorted 'not a bit' for 'I may feel disappointment if a man misses a catch, but angry if runs are got off me — never'.

The interview, entitled 'The Demon Bowler on Bowling', also reveals much about the Spofforth personality. It is quite clear that he relished the idea of talking (and writing) to the press, expounding earnestly on the art of bowling and embellishing his role in the development of the craft. He also had a keen eye for the noteworthy comment, even if it was at best a half-truth, and he told that journalist that 'I never practise' and 'I seldom play in Australia — half a dozen times a year'. Such a statement cannot be accepted on its face value by the youth who disciplined himself bowling alone for hours on end and by the veteran cricketer who kept himself in such fine fettle that he was a useful cricketer well into his fifties. It also seems at odds with the senior cricketer who practised every day on board ship on the off chance that he might get a game with the 1888 Australians and the veteran cricketer who always preferred to purchase a house with a billiard room so he could practise his bowling run every day. The word 'lazy' suggests a lack of discipline and involvement in the game which does not fit the Spofforth make-up. What Spofforth described as 'laziness' might better be referred to as a conservation of energy, in less important phases of a game, for the big occasions when it really counted.

An even more questionable statement was that 'in the early days of Australian cricket, and before the visits of the English cricketers, no bowler had discovered how to break (presumably cut) a ball. This was an art I found out for myself.' However, there were some franker revelations about how it had not been easy to rise to the top:

I did throw once, but when I found that out, after the difference had been explained to me ... I went to work and corrected it. Ah! it is not easy to make a name. I tried and tried again for years. If I bowled well they said it was luck; and if I took wickets it was luck; my break was luck again or the wicket.

The article also provided examples of Spofforth's thoroughness and thoughtfulness. In his younger days he used to 'propound mentally the most difficult combinations to overcome a batsman' and then try out these ideas at practice where he welcomed the criticism of an English professional.

Spofforth did not stay very long in bed, but made the most of his convalescence. *Cricket* reported on 17 June that he 'has been during the last few days wasting his sweetness in the country air of Derbyshire', courting Phillis Marsh Cadman. He must have spent most of this time at The Cedars, the substantial grey mansion of the Cadman family which still stands on the hill above the picturesque village of Breadsall, just two and a half miles (4 km) north of the town of Derby.

Spofforth's grandchildren believe that Phillis was the twenty-first or the twenty-second child (and the youngest or second youngest) in the Cadman family, but census data suggest that Phillis was the sixth daughter, and eighth child, out of ten.[16] Her father, Joseph Cadman (c. 1817–97) was born in Quardon, Derbyshire, and was a grocer in Salford, Lancashire, from 1838. He married Phillis Marsh, who was born in Salford and was possibly a decade younger than him, in the mid-1840s. Joseph prospered in business, acquiring more and more shops. By the mid-1850s the Cadmans had moved to 75 Downing Street, Ardwick, now a Manchester suburb, and it was there that Phillis was born. They must have lived in a substantial house because nineteen people were listed there when the 1871 census was taken.[17]

By the time the Cadmans purchased The Cedars, in the early 1880s, Joseph was a wealthy man. His business, which became known as the Star Tea Company from the mid-1870s, had shops (tea, druggist, grocery, wine and spirits), warehouses, cafes and hotels in London and many provincial towns, including Derby, in England and Wales. The business was very much a family operation and when it was converted into a limited liability company on 13 April 1892 virtually all the shareholders were from the Cadman family. When Joseph died in 1897 his probate was a very substantial sum: £94,703 11s. 11d.

Spofforth rejoined the tourists on 28 June, just two matches before the First Test. Although he performed satisfactorily in his comeback match against Lord March's XI at Chichester, returning 8-103, he struggled from this point on. In fact Spofforth 'continually complained of the weakness of the finger that had been injured' and the 'difficulty he found in imparting anything like the old spin to the ball'.[18]

Despite this disadvantage Spofforth was by far the best Australian bowler in the three Tests. The bowlers, headed by Spofforth, made a close game of the First Test. After Australia scored 205 and England 223 the Australian batsmen could only muster 123, with Spofforth scoring 20 not out. England scored the 106 required to win, but not before the Australian bowlers had taken six wickets. Spofforth returned match figures of 6-122 and Palmer 4-52.

Thereafter the Australian batsmen failed dismally in the next two Tests, recording successive totals of only 121, 126, 68 and 149. Batting proved the Achilles' heel for the 1886 tourists, with only Jones, Scott and Giffen playing an occasional innings of substance. Compounding the tourists' problems was the fact that much of the bowling was ineffective in the next two Tests and England scored 353 and 434 to win them by an innings and 106 and by an innings and 217 runs, respectively. Spofforth battled on through both these long innings and was the only bowler to have respectable returns: 56 overs, 26 maidens, 73 runs, 4 wickets (Second Test) and 30.1 overs, 12 maidens, 65 runs, 4 wickets (Third Test). In the three Tests he was head and shoulders above the other bowlers taking 14-260 (av. 18.6) compared with Garrett 8-222 (av. 27.8); Trumble 5-110 (av. 22); Palmer 5-177 (av. 35.4) and Giffen 4-234 (av. 58.5).

Compared with his tours of triumph, the 1886 tour was a disappointing one for Spofforth as it was for most of the other Australians. He took only 89 wickets (compared with 216 in 1884) at an average of 17.1 (12.5 in 1884). Reviewing the disasters of 1886, 'Censor' of the *Sydney Mail* suggested on 2 October that 'our old players are not to be relied upon' for 'they are getting stale, and their retirement is necessary for the restoration of our cricketing prestige'. Garrett, Evans and Spofforth, this journalist added, 'have seen their best days, and there can be found more trustworthy batsmen than Bonnor in our junior ranks'.

Some English opinion, as usual, was a little kinder to the Demon. The 'Red' *Lillywhite Annual* of 1886–87 suggested that Spofforth's 'injury, it may be fairly argued, was one of the main reasons for the non-success of the team'. However, even a fit Spofforth would have found it hard to prop up the Australian batting in 1886. A London paper listed the following reasons for the failure of the tourists: the weaknesses of the batting; the failure of McIlwraith, Evans, Bonnor and Spofforth 'to maintain their respective reputations'; a wet May; disunity and lack of confidence in the captain.[19]

Spofforth's 1886 tour performance was more meritorious than the bald figures would suggest. In 1886 he played in only half the tour games (nineteen out of thirty-eight), being absent for two extended spells; the first owing to injury and the second, at the end of the tour, when he got married. In previous tours he had rarely missed a game. While his wicket haul in 1886 was much less than that of Giffen (162 wickets), Garrett (129) and Palmer (110), Spofforth had the best average in the nine representative games.

Australian Bowling Averages in Representative Matches, 1886 Tour

	Matches	Overs	Maidens	Runs	Wickets	Average
Spofforth	7	320	126	554	29	19.3
Garrett	9	697	332	839	40	20.4
Palmer	9	436.2	169	720	29	24.2
Giffen	9	482	213	742	25	29.2

Phillis Marsh Cadman and Frederick Robert Spofforth were married on Thursday, 23 September 1886, at the Breadsall parish church. The bride was twenty-two and the groom thirty-three. Phillis had expressed the wish that the

*Spofforth did not escape the
cartoonist's pen even on his
wedding day.* (Bulletin)

wedding should be as 'quiet as possible' but by 1 p.m., the appointed hour, the church was crowded and the village had been decorated with triumphal arches with appropriate mottoes and the church gates were also festooned with mottoes declaring 'May God bless you' and 'May love sanctify the union'. Phillis was attended by four bridesmaids who each carried handsome bouquets of red, white and blue, the colours of the 1886 Australians. The male section of the bridal party must have towered over the female, because Phillis was comparatively short, 5' 3" (160 cm), and Fred's groomsman was George Bonnor. The only other cricket representative appears to have been Mr Richardson from the Derby County Cricket Club. Had this official known that Spofforth would later expose his financial dealings he might have been less keen on this link between an Australian cricketer and a daughter of Derbyshire. Among the wedding presents was a timepiece from Lord Harris.

The reception at The Cedars must not have been a lengthy one for the Spofforths departed on the 3.40 p.m. train for London. One possible reason for the haste was that the newlyweds needed to complete preparations for the voyage to Australia. They left London on the *Orizaba*, on 30 September, just a week after the wedding.

Fred and Phillis Spofforth sailed for Australia along with two other cricketers, Tom Garrett and John McIlwraith, and their wives. The other tourists had left on 9 October on the *Arawa*, bound for a short tour of New Zealand, 22 November–8 December. Spofforth, Garrett and McIlwraith were to settle their wives in Melbourne, then travel to Hobart to join the team in New Zealand.

It seems likely that the Spofforths planned to settle in Australia. Apart from his continuing cricket career, Fred Spofforth also returned to the National Bank, joining the East Collingwood branch. His immediate family — his mother, his three sisters and their families — were still living in Australia.

When the *Orizaba* arrived in Melbourne on 14 November the cricketers were the subject of 'some good-humoured chaff' by the crowd at the wharf for the 'small success' of the 1886 Australians. However, Spofforth and Garrett were more preoccupied with attempting to find their luggage so they could join the team in Hobart en route to New Zealand. McIlwraith, whose luggage was discovered, left for Hobart the next day, while Spofforth and Garrett left Melbourne on 17 November and travelled directly to New Zealand. Spofforth did not take his new wife on the short tour and she was left, presumably with friends, in a totally new country for several weeks.

Spofforth, who had carried all before him on his two previous tours of New Zealand, was completely out of form and took only 17 wickets at 10.5 each. He trailed well behind three other bowlers: Palmer took 53 wickets at a cost of 7.5, Evans snared 34 wickets at only 3.2 each, and Garrett returned 19 wickets at a cost of 7.5 each.[20]

Even before Spofforth had departed for New Zealand the ninth English team, organised by the old firm of Shaw, Shrewsbury and Lillywhite, had arrived in Australia for another tour. Playing against New South Wales in late November, when the 1886 Australians were still in New Zealand, the English professionals were bundled out twice for very low scores, 74 and 98, and New South Wales won the game easily by six wickets. The secret of the colonial success was its fast bowlers: Charles Thomas Biass Turner, who became known as 'The Terror', took 6-20 and 7-34, and his partner in crime, John James Ferris, appropriately nicknamed 'The Fiend' (and also 'The Tricky'), returned 4-50 and 3-49. Both had an outstanding season, by the end of which they were established as the country's opening duo. Turner, an inch or two under six feet (c. 175 cm), had a low front-on action, moved the ball both ways off the pitch and generated considerable pace off the pitch. He was a deadly bowler on a sticky wicket. Ferris, shorter in stature than Turner at 5' 6" (167 cm), was an accurate left-hand bowler who could also move the ball both ways and was an ideal foil for Turner.

Spofforth had a very poor season in comparison. Possibly he was suffering from too much cricket. Barely a week after the last match in New Zealand the 1886 Australians played three matches against the English XI which occupied most of them from 17 December until 11 January and were played at Melbourne and Sydney. Then he may have been preoccupied in setting up his household in

Melbourne, for Phillis fell pregnant almost immediately after their marriage. The serious injury sustained on the 1886 tour was probably another factor.

Historians have not recognised the three matches between the 1886 Australians and the English professionals as Tests, even though matches set up on a similar basis after previous tours have been recognised.[21] Australia lost two and drew the other match. In none of the six innings did Spofforth take more than two wickets and took only 6-253 (av. 41.2). The Demon was able to get a lot of help from the Sydney wicket. It 'behaved frightfully' and balls from Spofforth 'bumped sometimes as high as the batsman's head'. On several occasions the Englishmen dropped their bats and wrung their hands after being hit. But even on this wicket 'Spofforth's bowling was knocked all to pieces' and he returned his worst figures of 0-67 (132 balls) and 0-14 (9 balls).[22]

Spofforth did not play in the Melbourne intercolonial, when Turner and Ferris starred in the second innings, but he travelled to Sydney in late January for the return intercolonial and was selected in the First Test against the tourists. Although overshadowed by Turner and Ferris who took eight and nine wickets respectively and were responsible for an easy New South Wales win by eight wickets, Spofforth had a good match — his only worthwhile outing of the season — on a bowler's wicket. He wisely reduced his pace to medium, trusting to break instead of pace, and took 6-47 in the first innings and 1-14 in the second. The *Sydney Mail* of 29 January 1887 commented that 'his trundling was a great improvement on what was recently seen against the Englishmen, and it is possible that he is coming back to something like his old form'.

In the Test match played on a very wet wicket a week later, Spofforth must have felt more of an observer than a participant. Debutant Test bowlers Turner and Ferris bowled unchanged to dismiss England for just 45 runs. Then they did most of the bowling in the second innings, with Spofforth only being called on towards the end of innings: he took 1-17 off 48 balls. Ferris, by contrast, returned match figures of 9-103 off 315 balls and Turner took 8-68 off 250 balls. It must have been a frustrating Test for Spofforth —

it turned out to be his last — because England won by thirteen runs despite their first-innings debacle. Spofforth had the minor satisfaction of taking three catches.

Spofforth virtually played no more senior cricket in 1886-87. He was selected for the intercolonial against South Australia, which began in Melbourne on 11 February; he was not selected in the Second Test, which began in Sydney on 25 February; nor did he play for Victoria against the Englishmen, a match which started on 4 March.

Reviewing the season, Tom Horan commented that Turner and Ferris had emerged just at the right time to 'worthily fill the places of the veterans', Spofforth and Evans, who 'are going down the hill, as well, indeed, they might after their long years of splendid service'. The figures for Turner, Ferris and Spofforth were most unflattering for the Demon. Whereas Turner had taken 70 wickets for 538 runs at an outstanding average of just 7.68 and Ferris had returned 47 for 689 (av. 14.66), Spofforth had taken just 14 for 331 (av. 23.69). It marked, so the colonial press believed, the end of Spofforth's international career.[23] But although he now played less and less senior cricket, he had not yet given up the idea of playing more international cricket.

Towards the end of the season Spofforth, along with the other leading Australian players, was asked his views on the possible change from four to six-ball overs. Spofforth's meticulous answer was published in the Melbourne *Sportsman*:

As to increasing the over to six balls, he really could not see any obstacle in the way. It would not place any undue strain on the bowler. If anything, it would give him a slight advantage in varying the balls sent down to the batsmen ... The change, would doubtless, save some thirty minutes to fifty minutes per day from the time occupied in changing positions in the field. He estimated that a change in field occupied on the average about forty seconds.[24]

The Spofforths' first son, Reginald Markham, was born at Moonee Ponds on 15 June 1887, his second name suggesting that his father was an admirer of another achiever, his cousin Markham Spofforth.

Early in the 1887-88 season there was some newspaper talk that Spofforth would be one of the sixteen tourists to visit England in 1888. But more informed sources doubted whether he was bowling well enough or was interested enough to tour again. While the New South Wales team, spearheaded by Turner and Ferris, easily beat both the English touring teams, Shaw's professional team and Vernon's amateur team, the Victorians had a 'bad time' against Vernon's team because 'Spofforth and Boyle have long ago dropped from the front rank of bowlers'.[25] Spofforth in fact played in very few of the major matches and none outside Melbourne: he was absent from the Victorian game against Shaw's XI, only played in one of the intercolonials and did not play in the only Test match. In his one intercolonial match — and his last — he was bowled sparingly, taking 1-30 off 66 balls and 0-22 off 60 balls. The Victorian captain leaned rather more on Harry Trott, who took 6-60 off 201 balls, and Hugh Trumble, 7-93 off 186 balls. The best bowlers, however, were Turner (9-114) and Ferris (8-108) and New South Wales won the game by two wickets.

During the season Spofforth opened the Melbourne Cricket Club bowling with a twenty-year-old recruit, Hugh Trumble. Spofforth was, in fact, upstaged by the youngster who won the bowling average for the club: Trumble took 36 wickets, average 6.77; Spofforth returned 27 wickets, average 8.07.[26] The young pretender, at the beginning of an outstanding international career (141 wickets and two hat-tricks), must have relished the opportunity of bowling alongside such an established star.

Despite Spofforth's lack of match play and form in 1887–88, there were still some who advocated that he be sent on tour. 'Point', a correspondent of the *Sydney Mail*, suggested on 3 March 1888 that the inclusion of Boyle was a 'weak spot' and strongly argued for Spofforth's inclusion:

I would like to know whether our old friend Spofforth has been asked to go. He was the backbone of former teams, and if he be judged on recent performances in Victoria, his arm does not seem to have lost any of its former cunning ... Turner may fill Palmer's place, but Spofforth's never.

'Cricket Gossip', also of the *Sydney Mail*, did not share this view. Referring on 17 March to rumours that Spofforth would tour, he stated that 'Anyone who has followed Spofforth's career must see that his day for cricket has gone by'.

Spofforth had other things on his mind during the 1887–88 season. Only months after the birth of their first child Phillis fell pregnant again, and Spofforth was also confronted by the problem that his wife did not like living in Australia, possibly because she missed her family.[27] The unhappiness of his wife must have led him to entertain seriously the possibility of returning to England. Joseph Cadman may have played a role in the return of Fred and Phillis Spofforth to England. It is highly likely that he made an offer to his son-in-law to join the Star Tea Company possibly as far back as September 1886 and, if not, by letter some time between then and 1888.

It may not have been an easy decision for Spofforth to leave Australia and leave his own immediate family, including his mother, Anna, who was to die three years later. There is a family story that he drove a hard bargain, agreeing to join the Star Tea Company on the condition that he would become its manager within a year. But the bargain, if indeed it was made, may not have been as hard as it seems. Joseph, in his mid-seventies in 1888, was probably looking for a member of the family to take over the company.[28] It was an obvious choice to groom his celebrated son-in-law, who had a good background in business as a bank manager, as the future managing director.

Whether or not it was an easy or difficult decision, the Spofforths made up their mind to return and settle permanently in England and booked a passage on the *Orizaba*, which left Melbourne on 8 June 1888. The evening before, Fred Spofforth and a very pregnant Phillis were guests at a farewell dinner at the Oriental Hotel. The chairman of the meeting, Frank Grey Smith, who was by then chairman of the Melbourne Cricket Club, regretted that 'they were about to lose the benefit of his services' as a cricketer and banker. He was followed to the podium by William Murdoch, who traced their close association from the days when they had met as youths when Balmain challenged the Glebe. It was not the end of their association, however, as Murdoch, also acting out Anglo-Australian ideals, was to follow Spofforth to England a few years later: he too was to die an Englishman.

In his speech Murdoch suggested that Spofforth would arrive in England (in late July) to be of some possible assistance to the 1888 tourists who had left Australia some two months earlier. Murdoch added that he hoped that Spofforth, 'whatever his success in England, would never be found opposing an Australian eleven'.

Spofforth replied that up until the injury of 1886 he 'had never been in better form' and 'he was convinced that he had not lost his powers as a bowler'. He then added, 'Australian associations would ever remain very dear to him'. However, while Spofforth 'cordially agreed with Mr Murdoch in the hope that he would get to England to be of some service to the Australians', he could not accept Murdoch's hope that he would not play against Australia 'if England paid him the compliment of picking him'. Spofforth added that 'if as a member of an English team he was instrumental in beating an Australian eleven, he would feel all the more proud of it for the sake of Australia'. His audience, made up of many who believed fervently in Anglo-Australian ideals, cheered this comment.[29]

The nationalist *Bulletin* was not all that impressed by this effusion of Anglo-Australian ideals. It made two sarcastic comments about Spofforth's departure in the issue of 9 June:

Spofforth, the erstwhile demon bowler, having come in for money, leaves next month to take up residence in England.

If Turner keeps up his present form with bat and ball the Britishers will forget all about Spofforth who at his best was only a one-part demon.

A week later *The Bulletin* ridiculed the remarks made by Spofforth in his valedictory oration. Spofforth, it argued, would not be of much use to the Australians who were short of batsmen rather than bowlers; nor would the Britishers need any extra bowling resources with Briggs already taking 5-15 against the Australians. The paper then proceeded to denigrate the performance of Spofforth:

The long'un, in his day funked the Britishers, who (Grace always excepted) had lapsed into a mechanical style of batting unfitted to master a new method of attack. But they have come to modify their former opinion of Spof's powers very considerably.

On 28 July *The Bulletin* compared Spofforth unfavourably

with Turner, who in the last seven matches had taken 80 wickets for 428 runs at an average just over 5.3: 'Spofforth, even in his Demoniacal days, never equalled this!'

The Bulletin's barbs did not in any way disturb the Demon. Five days out of Melbourne, when off the coast of Western Australia, Phillis gave birth to their second son, Edward Ralph. Meanwhile Spofforth took 'as much exercise as possible on the voyage' in case 'he was wanted against England' for the Lord's Test match.[30] The possibility of Spofforth's recruitment was not as remote as *The Bulletin* believed because it was clear that after Turner and Ferris the Australian support bowling was not adequate.

The Return to England

A damaged hand.

J M'C Blackham   W.G Grace

T he Spofforths arrived in England on 15 July 1888, the day before the First Test at Lord's, and there was considerable conjecture in the English press as to whether his services would be recruited to the Australian cause. The 1888 tourists had an outstanding bowling pair in Turner and Ferris, who had carried all before them, but the support bowling of Worrall, Lyons, Edwards and Boyle had proved inadequate. The team also suffered from the loss of batsman and change fast bowler, S P Jones, who was seriously ill. The tour management recruited the Australian-born Cambridge Blue, S M J Woods, who bolstered the Australian bowling in the Tests but did not play with the tourists in any other games.

Turner and Ferris bowled Australia to victory in the Lord's Test, but Australia lost the next two Tests and the series mainly because of poor batting: the Australians failed to reach three figures in four out of six innings. However, the lack of support bowling was a contributing factor: *Cricket* noted on 1 November that Woods 'did not bowl at all up to his University form'. After the tour more than one English commentator discussed whether it would have been better to recruit Spofforth and *Cricket* noted cautiously in the same issue that 'it is open to question whether it would not have been good policy to have utilised on his arrival in England the valuable services of Spofforth for the later matches'. 'Anglicanus', the English correspondent of the *Sydney Mail*, put the case for Spofforth rather more forcefully:

the general opinion outside the Australian circle was that, his great reputation being no mean consideration, he would have formed a decidedly greater acquisition to the eleven than Woods. Spofforth has played but little cricket this summer, but for the Gentlemen of England against I Zingari, at Scarborough, he bowled very finely, and showed plainly that the demoniacal right arm has by no means lost its cunning.[1]

It is not known precisely why Woods was preferred to Spofforth. He was not an Australian cricketer in the strict sense of the term, having played no first-class cricket in Australia whatsoever. Born at Glenfield, New South Wales, he had completed part of his secondary education at Sydney Grammar and Royston College but migrated to England permanently at the age of sixteen. He completed his education at Brighton College and Cambridge University. Perhaps someone on the team resented Spofforth's past behaviour as a prima donna who could pick and choose when, and under what circumstances, he would tour. Such behaviour was tolerated when Spofforth was at his peak, but now his form had begun to decline there may have been less sympathy for his eccentricity and individualism.

Spofforth was probably not all that disappointed not to resume his international career, because he had plenty to occupy his mind. His first task was to settle his young family in a house in Derby City: the Spofforths rented a property at 24 Kedlestone Road for two years. The next priority was to involve himself in learning the business of a tea merchant in the Star Tea Company: he started off as the Midlands representative of the company. From this point on he concentrated his efforts far more on a career in business. Although he retained a great love for the game and played county and club cricket for another sixteen years, it was now time, as Spofforth had written way back in 1879, to get on with 'more serious pursuits'. Unlike so many other ambitious cricketers, Fred Spofforth was not one to dwell on some past pinnacles of greatness. He was ready to direct his ambition in another direction.

However, Spofforth still wanted to play some cricket and let it be known that he was willing to play for Derbyshire in 1889. The county was keen to obtain the services of the Australian star because the years following Derbyshire's demotion to second-class status in 1888 'were among the darkest in the history of the club. Morale was low, the accounts were in the red, defections to other counties were rife and the playing record abysmal.'[2] There was, however, one snag: a residential rule which required a two-year qualification period.

The Derbyshire Committee, meeting in November 1888, formulated an amendment to the rule since it was thought that there would be little objection to the idea of Spofforth assisting a second-class county in 1889. The amendment was rejected by the County Cricket Council on 10 December 1888 by twelve votes to two, but the February Annual General Meeting of the Council left open the possibility of

Spofforth playing for Derbyshire providing each of their opponents consented to his appearance. Yorkshire was the only county, Spofforth later wrote, 'which treated me in a fair and courteous manner', accepting the proposal readily. Spofforth appeared in the two games against this county in 1889. He chose not to play against Surrey and Notts because their acceptance was more grudging and belated.

Spofforth attended the annual meeting of the Derbyshire Club on 27 February 1889 and became a member of the new committee. The statement of accounts revealed a very unhealthy financial situation: it was reported that the amount owing to the bank had increased from £227 6s. 5d. to £808 7s. 5d.

'The question of Mr F R Spofforth playing for Derbyshire,' commented the semi-official *Cricket* on 16 May 1889, 'has caused a good deal of vexation of spirit, and not a small quantity of ink slinging.' Spofforth nudged the controversy along when he gave a frank interview on the subject which was published in the *Birmingham Daily Mail* of 10 June. While accepting the right of the Marylebone Cricket Club and the Cricket Council 'to disqualify me', he contended that 'I have more right to play for Derbyshire' than Midwinter to play for Gloucestershire and Burns, the Lancashire professional, to play for Essex. Spofforth argued that he believed he had 'a moral right' to play for Derbyshire because he had not come there as a professional cricketer, he had come to Derbyshire for business and private reasons. Had he come to England solely for the purposes of advancing himself in the cricket world, 'Derbyshire would have been the last county I should have chosen to call my own'. He then added the revealing comment reflecting his Anglo-Australian ideals: 'personally, I regard myself as an Englishman, but other people seem to take a contrary view'.

On 13 June *Cricket* scolded Spofforth for his outspokenness ('Mr Spofforth has never been averse to confiding his opinions to the interviewer') and disapproval of his disqualification, arguing vigorously that Spofforth had got his facts wrong and that Midwinter, born near Cirencester, Gloucestershire, and Burns were both entitled to play for their respective counties. *Cricket*, in a legal sense, stood on the firmer ground, but there were strong moral grounds for speaking out against the narrow-mindedness of some of the stronger county clubs which opposed some much-needed assistance for a battling county.

When Spofforth turned out in the match against Yorkshire on 10 and 11 June, which was reported in the same issue of *Cricket*, the match report had a facetious heading: 'Derbyshire (with Mr Spofforth) v. Yorkshire'. The first game played at Derby in 1889, it created great local interest and Spofforth, relishing the occasion of finally playing for Derbyshire, turned in an outstanding performance:

33 overs, 11 maidens, 45 runs, 7 wickets;
20 overs, 8 maidens, 36 runs, 8 wickets.

It was not enough to secure a Derbyshire victory. Yorkshire won by 54 runs, but the spirited bowling was obviously a tonic for the local followers and reporters of cricket. The correspondent of the *Derby Mercury* declared that Spofforth 'retains his old cunning with the ball' and 'it was simply marvellous how he mowed the Yorkshire wickets down' on the second morning. The reporter added:

His pace is not fast, though it was varied, as it always is. The secret of his success is that he can vary both pace and pitch without in any way altering his action . . . On Tuesday morning the batsmen did not seem to understand him a bit — the ball when it pitched hung a bit and then twisted off into the wicket. Probably there was a bit of vertical spin on it.[3]

Spofforth did not have a chance to repeat this performance in his only other county match of the season as the return game against Yorkshire at Sheffield was spoilt by rain and he did not bat or bowl.

Apart from the two county games, Spofforth kept turning his arm over, appearing for clubs with suitably colourful names such as Littleover Free Lances and Belper Meadows, and regularly mowing down inferior opposition such as the Gentlemen of Cheshire and Staffordshire. In the two county games and some fifteen club games he took 112 wickets at a cost of only 478 runs with the average per wicket of 4.3. His returns appeared in the 'Pavilion Gossip' column of *Cricket* of 27 December 1889 because Spofforth sent the match details to Harry Boyle, who came on the 1890 tour as manager. It was not too difficult to guess what Spofforth had in mind: 'Mid-on', cricket correspondent of the Melbourne *Leader*, noted that 'I presume from the same source that "Spofforth will be willing to assist the Australians in their principal matches next year" '. The fact that William Murdoch came out of retirement to lead the 1890 Australians may have added to Spofforth's interest in playing for Australia again, because Spofforth greatly admired Murdoch as a captain. It was not to be the last time that Spofforth felt the urge to return to the international cricket stage.

The annual meeting of the Derbyshire Cricket Club, held on 25 February 1890, was a particularly stormy one. The committee report referred to the 'great evils' of player indiscipline with players staying up late and drinking to excess during the period of a match. One player 'could neither bowl nor field' on the last day of the Essex match because he 'had been drinking and smoking until four o'clock that morning'.

An even more startling revelation was the announcement that the popular assistant secretary and former captain, Samuel Richardson, had been embezzling funds of both the cricket and football clubs and had robbed the club systematically over the past decade, leaving it with a debt of nearly £1,000. Richardson, who had pocketed money for a large number of match tickets and who had appropriated considerable portions of gate receipts, absconded to Spain, changed his name and became court tailor to King Alfonso. He lived to a ripe old age.[4]

'The whole unhappy affair,' according to club historian John Shawcroft, was 'brought to light by Spofforth'. It is highly likely that Spofforth discovered the frauds when he audited the books. At the 1890 meeting Spofforth and J H Richardson were appointed auditors for the club and it seems probable that he had performed that role in the preceding year. Later that year Spofforth wrote an article on 'Cricket in Derbyshire' for the 1890 *Derbyshire Cricket Annual*, in which he confirmed his role in exposing the fraud. The Demon, as usual, was quite unapologetic for his strong moral stand:

Unfortunately the past season will ever be remembered on account of the defalcations of the late assistant secretary. It seems almost incredible that the things brought to light should have taken place, as no one in the sporting world of Derbyshire was so popular. By some people I have been greatly blamed for the part I took. To those I can only answer, if I am ever placed in the same position again I shall do the same as I have done; but let us hope that the stumbling block to success has been removed, and that Derbyshire will resume her old position.

Not surprisingly, Spofforth was elected captain of the Derbyshire XI for 1890. In the same *Derbyshire Cricket Annual* Spofforth set down some of his thoughts about what he hoped would produce 'brighter results' for Derby. One reason, he suggested, why Derbyshire had not been success-ful was that the 'Derbyshire crowd have been educated to defeat, and so have the players'. The team, he wrote, 'must go in to win'. One reason, Spofforth added, for the club's loss to Yorkshire in 1889 was that 'many of the side would not strain their utmost'. There was a great reluctance of bowlers to bowl into the wind: their general answer was that 'It's no use my trying from that end'. There was also the perennial problem that Derbyshire consists of 'ten bowlers and a wicketkeeper' but 'this want of batting' was due 'to the players not getting sufficient practice'.

Although Spofforth played in six of Derby's fourteen games in 1890 — he was available only for the home games because of business commitments — he obviously did much to restore the club morale and self-respect. The club won seven, drew two, and lost five matches; a great improvement on previous seasons. Spofforth, as usual, led from the front. In his first match of the season, against the Australian tourists, he returned 3-34 and 6-42 in a drawn game. In his next game some of the Spofforth resolve rubbed off on his Derby team-mates and they beat Yorkshire by an innings and 25 runs with Spofforth taking 2-84 and 4-20. His most outstanding returns were against Leicestershire: 9-56 and 5-58 and 19 not out and 2. Although he played in less than half the season's games, he topped the bowling: 240.1 overs, 66 maidens, 496 runs, 42 wickets, 11.8 average. Perhaps the victory which gave Spofforth the most pleasure was when his side travelled to Sheffield, without their captain, and beat Yorkshire by 52 runs.

Just before the season began Phillis gave birth to the

Spofforths' third child and first daughter, Dorothy Velce, who was born on 19 May 1890 at 24 Kedlestone Road. Dorothy became an artist whose paintings were accepted by the Academy but were not hung. Most of her paintings were in the genre of social realism but she did paint some cricketers including a watercolour of Jessop which is in the Lord's Cricket Library.

Spofforth only played one more match for Derbyshire — against Leicestershire, 18-20 May 1891, when he took only 2-106 and scored 10 not out and 32 — because in 1891 he moved to London and settled at 59 Broadhurst Gardens, Hampstead, where they lived until 1900 when they moved up the road to Trefancha, 111 Broadhurst Gardens. There seems little doubt that Spofforth was sent to London to expand the Star Tea Company and to establish its headquarters in London, or that he was being groomed by his father-in-law to run the company. Begun as a family business in the early 1870s, the Star Tea Company was converted into a limited liability company on 13 April 1892 and was listed on the London stock exchange with an authorised capital of £80,000.

Caricatured by daughter Dorothy.

Although Joseph Cadman did not die until 14 April 1897, it seems highly likely Spofforth had already taken over most of the daily operations of the company. Joseph died at his residence at 28 Adelaide Crescent, Hove, which suggests he may have been in retirement. The London operation of the Star Tea Company was located at 292/314 Old Street, EC2: the premises comprised a handsome block of buildings of large warehouse space, completely equipped with the necessary plant and apparatus and with all facilities for carrying on a large business, including cold storage, and bacon smoking stoves.

When Joseph Cadman died he left a successful and expanding company. While Spofforth married into money, and inherited a business with great potential for growth, he was never one to rest on his laurels. He threw himself into the business of being a successful tea merchant with as much relish as he applied himself at cricket. He was shrewd enough to establish a close association[5] by 1899 between the Star Tea Company and a much larger and much older tea company, Ridgways, which began in 1836 and was a household word. Spofforth was listed as a director of Ridgways by 1899.[6]

With Spofforth at the helm, the Star Tea Company also expanded its capital from £80,000 to £200,000 in 1908, following very large annual profits in the preceding five years. The shareholders received a very handsome dividend of 19 per cent for 1907–08 and the dividend figure was even higher in the war years, rising to 20 per cent in 1915 and 25 per cent from 1916 to 1921. A share bonus of 50 per cent was issued in 1919–20. The company had done so well that arrangements between it and Ridgways were changed in 1922, with the Star Tea Company assuming the dominant role. As Spofforth put it in a letter to the stock exchange authorities, 'the position will be reversed and this Company (Star) will hold the control of Ridgways, Limited'.[7] With the expanded role of the Star Tea Company, Spofforth became head of an empire with a capital of £925,000 and the combined businesses operated 433 shops, more than twice as many as it owned in 1908.

Not surprisingly, Spofforth died a wealthier man than his father-in-law with probate listed at £169,268 gross

(£164,034 net). There seems little doubt that he was a shrewd, astute and respected businessman and that the mental energy, physical toughness and driving ambition which took him to the top of the sporting tree also made him a good businessman. He was and is one of the fortunate few of the stars who had a life beyond sport and who could successfully switch their ambition from the world of sport to that of business. One reason for the successful transition was that he virtually retired from first-class cricket in 1888, at the age of thirty-five, to concentrate on business, though he did play the occasional game for the Gentlemen and the MCC until 1897. Spofforth could easily have played regular county cricket for a decade after 1888, and after his move to London in 1891 there was some newspaper discussion that Spofforth might turn out for Middlesex.

But with business taking priority, Spofforth was content with club cricket, mostly played on Saturdays, and he joined the Hampstead Cricket Club (HCC) for the remainder of the 1891 season. The decision to join his local club proved a most agreeable one because the HCC was one of the most distinguished club sides in London. Founded in 1867, it had its own attractive undulating ground at Lymington Road and already boasted one future Test player and future England captain in A E Stoddart, who joined the club in 1885 at the age of twenty-two. Stoddart rattled up an astonishing score of 485 in just over six hours when Hampstead scored 813 in a day against the Stoics in 1886. In 1893 the club ranks were augmented by Gregor McGregor, who had been the English Test wicket-keeper since 1890. The club could also boast of a number of players who also represented Middlesex, such as G Thornton and Ahsan-ul-Hak. Spofforth did not play in a great many games in 1891, but he headed the bowling averages, a feat which he repeated in nine of his next fourteen seasons.

A second daughter, Vera Ethel, the last of their four children, was born at 59 Broadhurst Gardens, Hampstead, on 6 November 1891. Vera became her father's favourite because she more than Reginald, Ralph or Dorothy seemed to have inherited the Spofforth sporting talent. Twice Spofforth watched Vera play in the semi-finals of Wimbledon, the mixed doubles in 1922 and the women's doubles in

1923. On the first occasion she was thwarted by a combination which included the champion female player of the day, Mademoiselle Suzanne Lenglen. Vera, who had married James Stewart Youle, played as Mrs Youle. She was also a very fine billiards player and had the distinction of becoming the English open champion on her very first attempt, in the ladies' division, when she was in her seventies.

By 1891 two other prominent Australian cricketers, Murdoch and Ferris, had followed Spofforth's path to England, and in Murdoch's case, the move was a permanent one. Captain of the 1890 Australians, Murdoch had only shown glimpses of his former batting prowess on tour, but had not given up hopes of playing for Australia again. The immediate reason for migration was to join the Sussex Club because there were many in Australia who believed that he was past his prime and too old to play again for his country, although Murdoch would have liked to be a member of the 1893 touring side.[8] Murdoch, it seems, had again become disillusioned with Australian cricket and set out for the fresh pastures of county cricket where he answered his critics with his excellent form for Sussex from 1893 to 1899, scoring 5,799 runs at an average of 24.7. However, his main reason for settling in England was that he, like Spofforth, believed in Anglo-Australian ideals: that Australians were Englishmen in the Antipodes and that the ultimate achievement was to return to the font of English culture. In an interview published in the *Cricket Field* on 16 July 1892, Murdoch stated that 'English country life suits me very well'. He added that 'some day or other I hope to go back to Australia' but 'not to live there, for I have settled in England now — but to see the old country again'.

While many Australian critics believed that Australia could dispense with Billy Murdoch, there was consternation when twenty-three-year-old Ferris left the country in March 1891 to qualify for Gloucestershire, for over the past two tours he and Turner had been the heart of the Australian attack, which was decidely thin in support bowling. W G Grace, who lured Midwinter away from the 1878 Australians, again seems to have played a role in recruiting another Australian to the county which was, in 1891, strong in batting but weak in bowling. In order to reduce the qualification period, on 24 June 1890 and while on tour with the Australians, Ferris signed an agreement 'for the tenancy of a small house near the County Ground at Bristol', presumably at the suggestion of Grace and with the help of the county club. It was an unorthodox and presumably secret agreement made before the two Test matches of 1890. Ferris then returned to Australia to settle some business matters and play some domestic cricket, representing New South Wales in several matches before returning to England in March 1891. Because of this fiddle with the residential rules, Ferris was able to play for Gloucester in 1892 rather than 1893. It was not certain whether Ferris intended, like Murdoch, to settle permanently in England. A bank clerk in Australia, he joined a Gloucestershire stock-broking firm.

There were many in the cricket world who looked upon the move to Gloucestershire as a mistake, because the Gloucestershire attack was weak and Ferris had to 'do an immense amount of work under very great difficulties'. The critics were proved right because Ferris 'was soon worn out' after three seasons with the county and was never the same bowler subsequently. Ferris could have stayed with Gloucestershire after 1894 but 'his disposition was such that he could not brook failure' and he returned to Australia in 1895, where he played twice for New South Wales and once for South Australia, but 'could not recover anything like his old form'. He was one of the first colonials to enlist in the Boer War, with the Imperial Light Horse, but died on 21 November 1900 of enteric fever, and was buried at Durban, aged only thirty-three.

Eight years before, in March 1892, Ferris had visited South Africa and had played his last Test, representing England as a member of W W Read's largely amateur side. Another member of the side was the wicket-keeper batsman, William Murdoch, who also played his final Test. Strangely, while Murdoch had more than a year to qualify for Sussex and while Ferris was still months off qualifying for Gloucestershire, both were deemed eligible to play for England, admittedly for a second-string Test side against an opposition yet to establish itself as formidable. While Murdoch had an ordinary Test, scoring 12 runs and achieving one stumping, Ferris was the architect of an easy English win by an innings and 189 runs: he had match figures of 13-91. Ferris in fact had to carry the English attack on tour and there were 'a good many people' who blamed his limited success with Gloucestershire on 'the wear and tear' of the South African tour which 'seemed to have upset him considerably'.[9]

While Ferris struggled with Gloucestershire in 1892, taking only forty-six wickets at a cost of 28.3 each, and Murdoch waited to become eligible for Sussex, Spofforth was enjoying an excellent season for Hampstead, taking 77 wickets at a cost of just 8.4 each. The following seasons proved even better: he took 110 wickets at a cost of 7.2 each in 1893 and 200 wickets at a cost of 5.9 in 1894. Spofforth hit the headlines in both 1893 and 1894 when he twice took all ten wickets in an innings against Marlow: returning figures of 10-20 and 7-20 in 1893; and 4-27 and 10-14 in 1894. There was a suspicion, suggested David Frith, biographer of Stoddart, that 'some of these wickets were surrendered to his reputation' and there was an admission that one of his bowling colleagues had helped Spofforth obtain all ten wickets in 1894. Pawling, the only other bowler used against Marlow in 1894, 'afterwards stated that when Spofforth got the first 7 wickets in the second innings, so as to help him to get all the 10, he bowled fast and well outside the off stump and succeeded in keeping down the runs and not taking a wicket.'[10] During 1893 Spofforth produced an outstanding batting performance in the match against Uxbridge. Arriving late for the match, he was not called on to bowl as Stoddart and Thornton had dismissed the Uxbridge side cheaply. 'The rest seems to have done Spofforth good' because the Demon then 'amazed everyone with an innings of 155' which put a Stoddart innings of 68 'in the shade'.[11]

By all accounts Spofforth was a popular club member at Hampstead and he was elected to the club committee in 1894. While there was some of the never-say-die Spofforth spirit still in evidence, he seems to have been more ready to entertain his team-mates with his humour on the field and to acquire a reputation as a raconteur off it. But even a more relaxed Demon was still an inspiring cricketer to some of the younger cricketers of Hampstead, including club historian F R D'O Monro, who joined the club in 1896. Monro later recounted various anecdotes concerning Spofforth's time at Hampstead.[12]

After Spofforth had bowled an over to a new batsman, on one occasion, Monro warned Spofforth about the form of the batsman: 'Spoff that man is a dangerous batsman, he made 100 last week'. Spofforth retorted that 'he's a rotten bad cricketer' and 'sure enough', noted Monro, Spofforth 'had him next over'.

There was another occasion when Spofforth, like most fast bowlers, was decidedly unhappy about some dropped chances in slips off his bowling during a pre-lunch session. Since he was often inclined to boast that Australian cricketers were superior to the English, Monro commented to Spofforth during the luncheon interval: 'I expect even in Australia your slips sometimes missed catches off you'. Spofforth replied instantly: 'Never, I trained them'. Monro received the following fanciful explanation:

In the part of Australia I came from there are hedgerows and on a Sunday I used to get some stones, put them in my pocket and take out my slip fieldsmen for a walk. I walked on one side of the hedge, they on the other, I threw the stones into the hedge, and they caught the sparrows as they came out.

Monro does not record his reaction to the popular Spofforth pastime of leg-pulling.

In another match Spofforth was 'rather naughty' when he repeated a prank which he had played on the Australian umpire, Jim Phillips:

The foot of Spofforth's hind leg went over the crease and Gregory (umpire of the Stoics) promptly no-balled him. The next ball the foot of Spofforth's hind leg went 6 in. over the crease and Gregory (good umpire that he was) promptly shouted 'No ball', but Spofforth held the ball and didn't bowl and there was a bit of an altercation. Apparently it was a bit of Spofforth's playfulness because he had done this before.

Spofforth reflected at length on his club experiences in an interview, 'Chats on the Cricket Field', which was published in the *Cricket Field* of 13 August 1892. Senior statesman Spofforth was more than willing to hand out advice:

I like it (club cricket) very much indeed. One meets so many men whose batting is very little inferior to first-class, and the matches are very enjoyable. But I have often noticed that there never seem to be any bowlers who have a chance of being better than they are at present, and I believe that the English system of practice is altogether to blame for that. When men go down to the nets, merely for a quarter of an hour's batting to the professionals, what can you expect? You can't afford to make experiments in a match when your opponents are strong, and so only a few men ever get a chance of knowing whether they can bowl or not. We had something like London club cricket about Sydney, but the play was not as good as it is here.

Spofforth admitted that he seldom had time for practice but he still believed that he could perform well in the first-class game:

I am generally only able to play on Saturdays, and so I don't bowl as I should if I had more opportunities. You see, it is twenty years since I began to play first-class cricket, and as one gets older it becomes more and more difficult to bowl without constant practice. Besides, one loses much of one's 'go', even though one may gain in other ways, but I think I could get most of it back again if I tried. At present I seldom bowl really fast, because I get stiff on the next day. If the match lasted three days, the stiffness would wear off.

Murdoch helped make arrangements for the 1893 tour and still entertained the hope, even after he had played for England against South Africa in 1892, that he might be called upon to join the 1893 Australians. Spofforth, who turned 40 in 1893, no longer harboured hopes of joining a touring side as his business commitments gave him time for only the occasional first-class game. Even so there were some English commentators who stated publicly that he would have helped the tourists, who lacked a form fast bowler: Turner and Giffen were not as penetrative as on previous tours and Hugh Trumble was only beginning to emerge as a front-line bowler. After his 1893 return against Marlow, *Cricket* once again pushed the case of its favourite Australian, suggesting on 20 July that:

There are good judges, and not a few of them, who are of the opinion that the Australian team would not have done a bad stroke if they had been able to secure the services of a fast bowler, even as Spoff now is. At all events, he would have furnished the variety which has been at times so sadly lacking in the Australian bowling.

Being the competitor that he was, Spofforth relished the next best thing, which was appearing in the occasional match against Australian touring sides. On the following tour he had the opportunity to represent Wembley Park against the Australians, captained by G H S Trott, on 8 and 9 June 1896. The badly rain-affected wicket was tailor-made for the Demon and he bowled splendidly, taking 11-106, but the Australians were not embarrassed as they won the match easily: the weak Wembley Park batting crumbled before the bowling of Trott, Trumble and Giffen. In his other first-class game of the season, Spofforth took 9-82, assuring a win for the South of England against Yorkshire at Scarborough.

Although Spofforth was now almost forty-three and was a part-time club cricketer, he believed that he was bowling better than ever and that he was good enough to perform well in Test cricket. He was present at the Oval for the final and deciding Test of the series beginning on 10 August 1896. Inspecting the wicket which was seriously rain-affected — there was no play until 4.55 p.m. on the first day — he had pleaded with Trott to allow him to play for Australia, guaranteeing to remove the English team for less than fifty runs and had fumed on the sidelines when Trott, not surprisingly, did not accede to this highly unorthodox suggestion. England, 145 and 84, defeated Australia, 119 and 44.

Much later Colonel Philip Trevor noted, in the *Daily Telegraph* of 5 June 1926, that all public performers are the worst possible judges of 'their own intrinsic merits' and that this dictum was certainly true of Spofforth, who operated under the illusion that he was a better bowler in his maturity:

He was definitely and seriously of the opinion that in his strenuous manhood he was never as good a bowler as he became in his middle age, when, because his natural force had abated, he had taken to bowling slow-medium pace, and you could not convince him to the contrary.

This astute comment suggests that even the great cricketers operate under some illusions in regard to their own ability. But it also illustrates Spofforth's confidence in his own talent that, even at age forty-two, he believed he could draw on his own powerful inner spirit to once again subdue opposition batsmen. It was this daring — courage to the point of foolhardiness — which had made Spofforth such a great performer.

A Time for
Reflection

P. S. McDonnell

From the mid-1890s Spofforth played less frequently for Hampstead, although he usually occupied a place high in the club averages.[1] He had more time to reflect and write on the game and over the next decade produced three major essays which covered autobiography, comments on Australian and English cricket and his views on the art of fast bowling. Undoubtedly all these articles were commissioned by editors who were eager to capture the thoughts of one of the more formative cricket personalities around. However, they also provided the hero with an opportunity to consolidate his position in history, a possibility which would not have escaped the Demon. In the introductory paragraphs of his first essays he commented that 'I may perhaps be allowed to say, without seeming egotistical ... to realise that within the bounds of my own experience lies the growth of Australian cricket, almost from its rough, untutored beginnings to what was perhaps its keenest hour of triumph, the remarkable defeat of England in August, 1882'.

Spofforth's first essay, published in two parts in the *New Review* in 1894, traced the development of Australian cricket from the 1860s to the triumphs of 1878 and 1882. By any standards, the short essay in two parts was a fine and evocative piece of cricket journalism and one of the best, and now much-quoted, pieces on Australian cricket in this era. He had a keen eye for telling detail and wrote about an earlier era when 'artisans and gentlemen played together in all the clubs, and if the ordinary boots got slippery, off they came; even socks were discarded by the artisan, if they were thought to add to the comfort'. Then there was the story of how Mr E M Grace, the only amateur on the 1863-64 English side, was much 'studied and copied' and how many Sydney cricketers always wore a white handkerchief hanging down from their belts 'a la Grace'. The narrative was also spiced with many colourful anecdotes such as scrambling round the New Zealand countryside with the huge kitbag in 1878.

Cleverly blended with entertaining illustrations were a number of astute observations about cricketers and techniques of bowling, batting and fielding seen through the keen eyes of a young man who had studied closely and analysed thoroughly the strengths and weaknesses of his contemporaries and the visiting Englishmen. Candour also enhanced the narrative, Spofforth admitting that at one point in his career he used to throw, though not deliberately.

The essay focused more on the 1878 tour and the triumph at Lord's than on any other tour or match, suggesting that this tour had the greatest impact on Spofforth even though he achieved better figures on later ones. Reading Spofforth's account of the departure of the team from Australia, the reaction to the victory at Lord's and their triumphal homecoming at the end of the tour suggests that it was the most memorable of his tours.

Although Spofforth was a more mellow and relaxed cricketer in the 1890s, he was still a man of strong principle and threw his weight behind the anti-throwing campaign that had been championed by Lord Harris for more than a decade. Spofforth wrote to *Sporting Life* on 25 January 1897, urging the authorities to take strong action against 'this practice of throwing', which 'is growing rapidly'. He argued that there was scarcely a first-class county 'which does not include a "thrower" amongst its cricketers'. He also singled out one of the 1896 Australian tourists:

with the last eleven there was one who hardly ever delivered a 'fair' ball, and although I am quite aware I may raise a 'hornet's nest' about my head by mentioning names, I allude to McKibbin who, I shall always maintain, should never be allowed to play under the existing rule.

It was only 'fair', Spofforth added, that he should also name an English 'thrower', Bobby Peel. The criticism of Peel was not so severe because Spofforth believed that he only threw the occasional ball. Spofforth recommended strong action against throwing by a committee of the captains of the first-class counties under the chairmanship of Lord Harris.

McKibbin, who bowled medium-paced off breaks, did not get a second trip to England. Some have claimed that 'when McKibbin was named as a chucker' by Spofforth 'it virtually ended McKibbin's international career'.[2] While Spofforth's name must have added great moral weight to the anti-throwing cause, there were others who must have played an equally significant role. *Wisden* also condemned the 'unfair bowling' of McKibbin.

The fast bowler, Ernest 'Jonah' Jones, was another of the 1896 Australians criticised by *Wisden*, though he was not named by Spofforth in 1897. (Jones was later exonerated by

Spofforth, who stated in a 1902 interview that he never saw Jones throw.) During the 1896-97 Test series Jones was no-balled for throwing by Australian umpire Jim Phillips, though he recovered from this setback and bowled within the law later in the series. During the 1896 tour Jones had also attracted comment because he appears to have pioneered the modern bumper. On 21 May *Cricket* described a 'famous' ball of Jones, which created 'terror' but which did not secure a wicket: it was a ball which pitched half-way along the pitch, came off quickly and gave the batsmen just time to get their nose out of the way. It remained to be seen, noted *Cricket*, whether the English fast bowler, Richardson, could develop a similar ball.

Bumpers had not been part of the fast-bowler's reper-toire in the time when Spofforth played international cricket. There are references to 'bumpers' in press reports in the 1870s and 1880s, but they were balls which bounced awkwardly off an uneven pitch. 'Bumpers', in this era, often 'bumped' off a good length and provided bowlers such as Spofforth and Evans with catches at point.

Spofforth played his last first-class game in 1897, returning 2-58 and 1-51 at Scarborough on 20-22 August. More relaxed in his middle age, the Demon enjoyed these occasions both on and off the field. 'My most treasured recollection of Spofforth,' wrote Dr Roy Clayton who was a schoolboy in the 1890s and attended many festival games, 'is of the great bowler sitting on the steps of a bathing machine, munching maids of honour out of a paper bag. He was extremely partial to these cakes, which in those days were made to perfection in a small shop in Westborough.'[3]

There were still some occasional tussles against strong opposition, such as in 1900 when Hampstead played a two-day game against the MCC at Lord's which included an all-Australian confrontation between Spofforth and Albert Trott which was 'full of fire and incident'. While Spofforth was out first ball to Trott in the first innings and took only 1-84, he did score 11 off one stroke (including several overthrows), under the net boundary experiment in the second innings. 'The exertion and humour of it all,' noted David Frith, 'must have left old Spofforth little enough breath.'[4]

A few years earlier, on 15 April 1897, *Cricket* had referred to stories in several Australian newspapers that Spofforth 'has decided to return to Australia'. Given that Spofforth was so active in consolidating the Star Tea Company at the time, it is highly unlikely that he was seriously contemplating returning to Australia on a permanent basis. However, there could have been an element of truth behind the rumour in that Spofforth may have been keen to visit his sisters and their families and to renew other acquaintances. Spofforth did visit Australia four years later, his visit coinciding with the English 1901–02 tour. A number of photographs survive, including one taken of Spofforth when he was in Sydney at the time of the Fourth Test, depicting an erect Edwardian gentleman impeccably attired in boater, winged collar, three-piece suit and cane. Spofforth was photographed alongside some of his former team-mates Dave Gregory, Alick Bannerman, Massie and Garrett. Spofforth also visited Melbourne for the Fifth Test where Tom Horan, alias Felix, reported in the *Australasian* that 'he is looking in grand condition with all the old well-known springiness of action in his movements'. Horan also reported that the Spofforths were returning to England on the *Omrah* along with A C Maclaren's team and the 1902 Australians.

During his visit to Australia Spofforth had plenty of opportunity to provide good copy for the Australian press. A summary of one such interview, which was republished in *Cricket* on 27 March 1902, indicated that Spofforth was his usual forthright self and that he, like so many former heroes, was inclined to remember the past more favourably than the present:

He considered that the only first-class bowler in England was Rhodes. The old bowlers had fallen off and no one had come forward to take their places. There was a great deal of throwing. He knew fifteen or twenty good bowlers who threw at times. He never saw Jones, the South Australian throw, but he was convinced that Mold threw at times. He did not see how they could well stop throwing. He did not think that at present there was a wicket-keeper in the same street as Blackham. 'Ranji' was certainly the best batsman in England, Fry was next and Maclaren third.

Spofforth continued to play club cricket into his fifties and the longer he played the more accolades he attracted from the English cricketing fraternity, becoming the revered elder statesman, along with Grace, of English cricket. *Cricket* published a feature article on Spofforth on 29 January 1903, based on an interview by W A Bettesworth, which stated that 'just as the name of Dr Grace is known all over the world — to Archbishops of Canterbury and to street arabs — as the representative batsman, so Mr Spofforth is known as the representative bowler'. *Cricket* added that even though Spofforth was now forty-nine, 'he bowls so finely at times that it is not difficult for anyone who meets him to imagine how good he must have been in his prime'. Spofforth, as usual, provided some good and even startling copy for the interviewer. Commenting on why the Englishmen 'did not do so well against the Australian bowling', he floated the idea, topical in an era when Social Darwinism was much in vogue, that 'at the present time Englishmen, as a race, are too highly strung', with their nerves letting them down in the big matches. When asked what were the chief defects of English cricket he opted for a more orthodox reply that 'its failure to allow originality to develop, and its tendency to make a cricketer a machine'.

Later in the same year Spofforth published 'In the Days of My Youth: Chapters of an Autobiography' in *M.A.P.* ('Mainly About People', a popular penny weekly) on 28 November 1903. The title suggests that he harboured the idea of writing more chapters, but none eventuated. Although Spofforth enjoyed expressing himself in print, he was probably too much a man of action to produce an extended piece of writing.

The *M.A.P.* article provides a number of clues as to how Spofforth saw himself in terms of identity. His was a 'very old Yorkshire family' going back to before the Conquest of 1066. Looked at in this light, the colourful and often hair-raising adventures of his family in Australia and New Zealand were intriguing but brief imperial interludes in the history of an English family.

However, Spofforth did not undervalue the experiences of his ancestors on the frontiers of colonial civilisation. Rather, he saw them in a romantic light, lusting for adventure and acquiring great toughness and pride in surviving hardship and even adversity. In a sense his career was an

LONDON COUNTY CRICKET CLUB.

CRYSTAL PALACE.

"ST. ANDREW'S."
LAWRIE PARK ROAD,
SYDENHAM, S.E.

Telegraphic Address:
"GRACE SYDENHAM."

July 24ᵗʰ 1901

My dear Spoff

I am sorry to say
I am not playing at Hampstead
so cannot accept your kind
invitation to dine afterwards
you will be sorry to hear
Old E. his second wife died
this morning, telegram just
arrived, she has been ill
some time, but we did not
know it was so serious until
last week, they kept it to
themselves. and told no one, so
it has given us rather a shock.
I expect we shall have a fair
team, Murdoch may play but
his leg is bad again and
he wants to rest. Believe
me

Yours very truly

W. G. Grace

extension of a romantic imperial adventure, except that it took place on a new frontier, the international cricket field.

It is intriguing from a modern point of view to note that 'the days of my youth' did not end, according to Spofforth, until he moved from Derby to London when he was aged thirty-seven. Possibly this rather broad definition of youth occurred because the concept of adolescence was still a relatively new one. However, it also suggests that 1891 was a turning-point in Spofforth's life. Before that he pursued youthful adventure on the cricket field, but after then he concentrated on the adult pursuit of business.

The article again included some colourful anecdotes revealing various aspects of a keenly honed sense of humour. Spofforth, who could be serious and solemn on occasions but who did not suffer from undue modesty at other times, had the saving grace of humour, some of which was directed at himself:

Playing at a gold-mining town in Australia, called Sandhurst ... and while walking to the cricket ground two little 'nippers' picked me out. The elder said: 'That's the Demon — that's him'. The younger glared with his mouth wide open, and then came in front and looked up in my face. The elder again said, 'That's him, Jimmy; what do you think of him?' Jimmy answered, 'I'd like to have his nose full of gold dust'.

During his last few seasons with Hampstead Spofforth's bowling was sometimes collared, as was the case in the match against Birchington House on 7 and 8 August 1903 when opposition batsman A E Clark scored 239 not out in just two and a half hours and with the support of A F Bryan, 137, the opposition declared the innings closed at 6-570. On a very hot day Spofforth bowled in short spells and did not give up: Clark enjoyed a certain amount of luck in his innings, hitting Spofforth off 'the edge, back and shoulder of his bat' much 'to Spofforth's indignation'.

Spofforth was honoured at the 1903 club annual dinner. The cover of the menu card featured yet another caricature, designed by G Hillyard-Swinstead, of the club vice president. Spofforth, horned and with bat wings, was depicted in the act of bowling while the pavilion tent, labelled victims, was full to overflowing. It was yet another incarnation for the man who had been caricatured variously as demon, cricket and kangaroo.

During the 1903 season Spofforth aired his views to the editor of *Wisden* as to why the Gentlemen rarely produced a 'really first-class bowler' and was encouraged to put down his views which appeared in the 1904 edition under the heading 'Schoolboys' Bowling 1903'. Spofforth contended that the 'sons of gentlemen don't succeed as bowlers'

The Demon canonised.

HAMPSTEAD CRICKET CLUB

ANNUAL DINNER

because 'they don't do the necessary work when young'. Spofforth argued that success in bowling was achieved by those who worked hard, who often started at an early age and who had greater 'elasticity to the muscles'. The young 'professional' had an advantage in that 'he had no one to instruct him' and 'bowls just as he likes on some village green where the pitches are bad'. Furthermore 'he has no one to prevent him practising every day as much as his school hours will allow'.

In the same article Spofforth also made an interesting comment as to why Australia was producing a significant number of country cricketers:

I might add that most of the Australians who have gained fame have come from country districts where the grounds are comparatively bad, and on coming to the metropolitan grounds had to suffer severe checks in wicket taking and it is owing to this fact that most of them use their 'headpiece'.

Spofforth bowled with mixed fortune in his last two years of cricket with Hampstead. He bowled 16 overs without success (0-21) against the boys of Tonbridge School on 4 June 1904 before retiring with a split finger. Club historian Monro suggested that it was a fine feat for the students and 'the two boys who went in first must have had a stern struggle',[5] but one suspects that a mellow Demon may have bowled well within himself to encourage his youthful opponents. After an extended break due to illness (probably this injury), he returned in August to take 7-19 against Charlton Park, finishing off the innings with yet another hat-trick.

Right up to his final season, 1905, Spofforth was a dominating presence at HCC. After the Hampstead skipper won the toss against a very strong Oxford Authentics side, which was brought together by A J Webbe — one of Spofforth's opponents in 1878 — Spofforth had a look at the pitch and 'called out to him in his high pitched voice: "Put 'em in"'. The Hampstead captain followed his advice. 'Spofforth, having been instrumental in having the other side put in, threw his whole soul into the attack and bowled as well as he had ever done in his life' to secure a victory for Hampstead by twelve runs.[6]

Prior to his final season Spofforth was again honoured

at the annual dinner at which he was the chairman and also the focal point of another menu card. During the evening one speaker pointed out that Spofforth had taken 886 wickets for the club at a cost of a little under eight runs apiece:

The cover of the menu card at the dinner of the Hampstead C.C. was from a very clever design by Mr G. Hillyard-Swinstead. It represents the Chairman, Mr Spofforth, with a background of 'Hampstead Warriors' of present and past days. Conspicuous in the centre and just behind the Chairman is Mr Stoddart carrying the flag of England (a reference to the tours of Australia).[7]

The toast of Hampstead.

Spofforth's greatest honour, however, was to take pride of place both in terms of photos and text in the Beldam and Fry classic, *Great Bowlers and Fielders*,[8] which was published in 1907 and 'dedicated by kind permission to the Demon Bowler'. He was fortunate that George Beldam, a county cricketer and the pioneer of cricket action photography as it was then called, had visited the Hampstead Cricket Ground in October 1904 and taken a remarkable set

223

of photos of the Demon in action. Beldam was himself fortunate that a fifty-one-year-old bowler was willing to participate in the experiment, because many of the photos depict a decidedly elderly fast bowler. One photo, however, became a classic because it captured Spofforth's high leap at the moment before delivery and shows him perfectly balanced with his right arm extended high. It is such a good photo that it creates the illusion of a much younger bowler.

In Beldam and Fry's book, Spofforth was provided with more space than any other great bowler. He wrote the initial chapter, 'On Bowling', which was illustrated by a large number of Beldam's photos. Spofforth's chapter included a certain amount of advice for would-be bowlers, urging them 'to work really hard at it' when they were young because 'in all games the early work and teaching have much to do with success in after life'. 'Laziness' was the reason, he believed, why there is hardly one first-class amateur bowler. Spofforth then contradicted a remark — probably a startling throwaway that sounded good at the time — made more than a decade ago about how he seldom practised:

For my own part, I am still a believer in practice; and scarcely a day passes in the winter that I do not go through the *delivery* of at least twelve balls. By this I mean that without any ball in my hand I bowl at least seventy-two balls a week, with all the power I have, at some imaginary crack batsman. This can easily be done, even in a room or passage; and to this alone I attribute the fact that I am still able to bowl long after the allotted span of a bowler's career.

Spofforth's grandchildren believe the houses that he owned always included a billiard room containing a suitable long passage for winter practice.

In addition to practice, Spofforth was meticulous in every aspect of the game, including the tools of trade. 'Bowlers,' he regretted, take 'little interest in the ball' for unlike the batsman, who owns his bat, bowlers do not own their ball. He took a keen interest in the composition of a ball because a poorly made one was likely to soon get soft on the hard grounds of Australia:

Although it is not generally known, Wisden's Special Crown Balls were made to my instructions, at my special request, in 1890, and have been kept the same ever since. I shall always remember Wisden's old ball-maker being called up to take my instructions; he simply looked at me and said, 'I have made cricket balls for forty years!' I told him that did not matter, and was proceeding with my instructions, when he stopped and looked at me, and said: 'It's nearer fifty', and turning to the manager said, 'They will cost 2s. 6d. a dozen more to make.' But he made the balls (six), and I have always given the old man credit for making them as he did.

The chapter in *Great Bowlers* also provides some Spofforth comments on his own bowling. He distinguished between two kinds of break from the off: finger-spin and cut, 'the latter is the the method the writer most frequently adopted'. He defined 'cutting' as deviation created 'without any twisting action of the fingers'. The advantage of bowling off-cutters was that 'break produced by cut can be combined with deceptive variation of pace'. He added that 'not even members of my own side, could tell when I was bowling fast, slow, or medium, and that prince of wicket-keepers, Blackham, always received a sign of what to expect'.

'On Bowling' also demonstrates that a once innovative thinker, who anticipated and even introduced future trends in technique, was becoming more orthodox and even conservative in his middle age. Spofforth was dubious about the potential of what he called 'side swerve' — swing in modern terminology — which had come into vogue around the turn of the century: the principal practitioners were the Englishmen Arnold, Hirst and G W Beldam; the Australian M A Noble and North American J B King. Spofforth distinguished between 'vertical' and 'side' swerve. Bowlers of his era found, probably because of the larger and less polished ball, that 'vertical' swerve (or curl as it used to be called) achieved more than 'side' or horizontal swerve to the right or left. By imparting 'check spin' bowlers such as F E Allan and Alfred Shaw were able to cause the ball to have an 'upward flight' or to drop suddenly. In 1906 Spofforth was unable to grasp the future potential of side swerve which soon became the orthodoxy of swing. He argued that he did not believe that anyone could 'get the swerve unless he overpitches the ball, and this over-pitching is going to be expensive'. He also added that:

it will take a great deal to convince me that anyone can get a short-pitched ball (to) swerve in the air, or that anyone can swerve with the wind straight behind him, or that anyone can swerve to any great extent on a perfectly calm day.

Spofforth was such a sceptic about swing bowling that he asked whether the new tribe of swing bowlers 'would not be just as successful if they did not swerve at all'.

By the time he retired from cricket Spofforth was the respected great fast bowler and revered elder statesman of English cricket. Although there were times when he seemed to have an equal standing with Grace, he was not placed on quite such a high pedestal. Spofforth was an Anglo-Australian whereas Grace was the archetypal Victorian Englishman. Probably more important was the fact that Spofforth's years of triumph, 1878-86, were but a brief interlude when compared with the extended career of 'The Champion' or 'The Old Man' who dominated the world of cricket for almost four decades.

Life After Cricket

Lord Harris

Retirement from cricket gave Spofforth more opportunity to spend time with his family. By all accounts he was a strict Victorian father and was somewhat remote from his children. When the Spofforths went to Australia in 1901–02 (Reginald) 'Rex' and (Edward) Ralph were bundled off to boarding school. The girls were also sent off to boarding school because Spofforth believed that it was a means of making them more independent.

Several of the grandchildren believe that Spofforth's sons, being run-of-the-mill cricketers at best, were rather overshadowed by their illustrious father, who did not really think a great deal of them until they proved themselves in the war.

While Spofforth may have kept matters very close to his chest and have been seemingly indifferent to his sons, his occasional boasting to others about them suggests that he was interested in their development and approved of their independence of character. During an interview in 1922 he stated that:

One of my sons, R M Spofforth, gave promise of becoming a first-rate bowler. When he was a youngster I sent him to a preparatory school in Yorkshire, of which the principal was Mr Ernest Smith, an Oxford MA, who captained the Yorkshire eleven for some time. He told me that the boy had the makings of a really fine fast bowler. The youngster went on from the preparatory to a big Public school, and came under the tuition of the old pro there. The pro. said to him: 'Look here, you know, I can't have you bowling like that. You must bowl slow, and learn to break and swerve.' The boy said, 'My father told me to practise fast bowling, and that is what I am going to do.' In consequence of that the pro. managed to keep him out of his house eleven, and my boy gave up cricket altogether for a time.[1]

Spofforth's son-in-law, Stuart Youle, who married Vera, was a reasonable cricketer who was in the second eleven at Oxford University and who played for the Oxford Authentics. A good all-round sportsman who represented his country at hockey shortly before the First World War, Youle plucked up courage to ask his famous father-in-law to pass on some tips about bowling. Spofforth refused. He believed that it was better for Youle to find out the hard way, as Spofforth himself had done, rather than being spoon-fed. After Youle went to the war and was injured, so that he was unable ever again to play cricket, Spofforth did relent to pass on his tips about bowling, demonstrating his grips and general technique. Youle wanted to be a schoolmaster but Spofforth declared that teaching was not good enough. So Youle became a businessman, a Lloyd's underwriter, instead.

With his business prospering, the Spofforths moved south of the Thames to a much grander house, Ashley House, Oatlands Drive, Walton-on-Thames, where they lived, c. 1911-20, before they moved to Ditton Hill Lodge, in the village of Long Ditton not far from the outer London suburb of Surbiton, Spofforth's final property. Both houses were set in substantial gardens which enabled Spofforth to indulge his love for gardening. The once fire-breathing Demon became an ardent floriculturalist and his non-competitive groups at the Surbiton Chrysanthemum Show were always much admired.[2] He also kept bees at Ashley House.

Spofforth became a much more mellow individual in retirement, though he enjoyed practical jokes as much as ever: he was, in the words of his grandchildren, a 'tremendous tease'. He enjoyed witnessing the stunned looks on the faces of visitors who were asked to admire Spofforth's multicoloured rose bushes, achieved by splicing roses from several bushes on the one plant. Spofforth also loved to tell visitors that a polished Seychelles coconut kernel, which served as a doorstop, was actually an elephant's kidney.

Jas Scott believes that even the editor of *Wisden*, Sydney Pardon, had his leg pulled. In October 1912 Spofforth wrote to the *Sportsman* advocating that two runs should be given to the fielding side for every maiden over that was bowled. *Wisden* labelled this an 'astounding suggestion' and added that:

Never, I should think, has such an absurd proposition been put forward by a first-rate expert. The proposal would not bear a moment's examination, and but for the weight that attaches to Spofforth's name the letter would probably have been consigned to the waste-paper basket. I think Spofforth must have rushed into print without realising what his proposal involved. Leaving aside the encouragement to bowlers to adopt the off-theory, or any other expedient to keep down the runs, the whole notion is contrary to the true spirit of cricket. Imagine the position of two batsmen coming together, perhaps on a nasty wicket, with the result of a big match entirely dependent on their success. What could be more grossly unjust than to penalise their side, even if they found it necessary to play for half an hour without getting a run?[3]

Writing many years later Scott commented drily: 'we are inclined to the belief that this was just another instance of Spofforth's favourite pastime'.[4]

On 18 February 1911, Murdoch died while watching a Test against South Africa at the Melbourne Cricket Ground. Given that Murdoch was born, bred, and married in Australia to an Australian wife and that his greatest achievements were as an Australian Test captain, it is surprising that Murdoch was not buried an Australian. But his body was embalmed and shipped back to England where he was buried at Kensal Green, a north London suburb, on 18 May. Like Spofforth, he had reasserted his English identity.

If the death of Murdoch came as a shock to Spofforth, he must have had some intimations of his own mortality when two heroes were struck down in 1915: first there was the death of Victor Trumper on 28 June, followed on 23 October by the death of the Victorian legend and Spofforth's arch rival, W G Grace.

The news of the death of Victor Trumper must have taken Spofforth by surprise, for Trumper was not only a much younger man, aged thirty-seven, but he was also a hero who had come to the fore a generation or two after Spofforth. Coming from a working-class background, Trumper was more identifiably Australian and never thought of England as home. Journalists, searching for a new kind of hero to express a sense of nationalism which grew much stronger in the 1890s, played a role in elevating and, to some extent, romanticising working-class heroes such as Trumper in cricket, Dally Messenger in football, Les Darcy in boxing and many others.[5]

The death of the Grand Old Man represented the end of a significant era of cricket. Grace was more than a cricket hero, he was one of the best-known and most-admired Englishmen of his generation. Spofforth must have been one of the more prominent mourners at Grace's London funeral on 26 October and later added his reminiscences to the *Memorial Biography of Dr W G Grace* which was published in 1919.[6]

Spofforth's tribute to his former arch rival is a most revealing statement because he could not resist continuing their rivalry beyond the grave. In the process of eulogising W G, Spofforth was also stating a case for his own greatness, measuring his performance against that of the master batsman.

Spofforth stated that it was his theory that 'most people did not bowl so well to Grace as they did to other batsmen' as 'they were a bit afraid of what he would do to their balls ... I am sure this was the case not only with professionals, but with a good many amateurs' but it was 'never in my case'. Spofforth was one individual who was never cowed by Grace. Spofforth added that 'the figures Sir Home Gordon has shown me of what Grace did in matches against me, 37 innings, 1,042 runs, 28.16 average, considerably less than his general average (a career average of 39.55 and a Test average of 32.29) bears out my theory that I never had any particular difficulty in getting him out.' Spofforth then added that he had cleaned bowled W G seven times.

Spofforth also could not resist telling one anecdote of how he had outfoxed Grace:

A C M Croome says that W G told him that on any wicket he never knew when I should bowl him. This may have been due in part to my artfulness. I always had a silly mid-on for him and that invariably worried him. I used to put my fingers round the ball in odd ways when bowling to W G just because I knew he watched my hand so closely. Once he hit a single off what was merely a long hop, and when he came to my end he asked 'What were you trying to do with that ball?' I had not been trying to do anything except to lull him into inattention, but I replied: 'You are the luckiest bat in the world; it's just my bad luck that I did not get on a big break from the off and send you back'. The very next ball he had from me, he was ready for me to try that big break. I knew he would be, I was sure his great leg would come in front to allow him to reach the ball. So I sent a perfectly straight one dead at the leg-stump, which hit him hard on the pad. 'How's that?' 'Out,' said Luke Greenwood, and as W G walked back grumbling and growling, he added: 'I can't help it; no, not if you was the Prince of Wales hisself'.[7]

Spofforth, like Grace, had been an enthusiastic supporter of the war effort. During the war a journalist had been introduced to a 'tall, athletic man, with a keen face and hair turning grey, who had a fine feeling about the war and a sounder knowledge of the food question at home than any man I have met lately'. The man, whom he discovered was Spofforth, recounted that 'his two sons have been in the thick of the fighting since the start, and his two daughters are nursing' and added that 'I'd rather see the war won than make a penny profit'.[8] While there is no reason to doubt Spofforth's commitment to the cause, war proved a great boon to the Star Tea Company, which produced record profits. The Spofforths also entertained troops, mainly Anzacs, who were convalescing in a nearby hospital. *The Bulletin* reported on 13 November 1917 that F R Spofforth 'took the Kaiser's off-stump last week when he invested £20,000 of his co.'s funds in one of the war-bond tanks that are selling around Blighty'.

The same journalist recounted another tale that suggests how quickly heroes of the cricket field fade in the public memory:

Mr Spofforth, having retired from the cricket field and become lost to the public eye, while building up a great business, was thought by many people to have died. One day he was present when the Australian cricketer was being discussed by strangers to him.
'Poor Spofforth! He's dead!' said one of them.
'What did he die of?' asked F R S
'Drink, I think,' was the reply.

On 19 July 1917 Spofforth received a letter from Lieutenant-Colonel Henry W Hill that his son, Second Lieutenant Reginald 'Rex' Spofforth of the 5th Middlesex Regiment, attached to the 4th Battalion, had been wounded, though not seriously: 'a piece of shell passed through the muscles of the left arm between the elbow and the shoulder'. Rex was injured

in action with an A.A. gun and doing splendid work keeping back the German aeroplanes. Whilst he was shooting at one, another German plane directed a battery of heavy guns on to the A.A. position. Your son and four other men were wounded. Your son with his customary gallantry, arranged for the disposal of the wounded and the withdrawal of the gun to another position ... On July 10th, Lieut. Spofforth performed a very gallant action in assisting Capt. Hall who was seriously wounded to a dressing station under a very heavy barrage fire.

Several years after the war Australia and England played the hundredth Test match at Trent Bridge, Nottingham, 28-30 May 1921, a Test which Australia won by ten wickets. To mark the occasion the editor of *Cricketer*, Pelham Warner, invited Spofforth to write on the 1882 Oval Test but the article when published on 28 May was entitled, 'Two Historic Matches'. While Spofforth regarded the 1882 Test match as 'the most exciting game', he viewed the demolition of the MCC in 1878 as 'the most interesting (game) I ever played in' after which 'I found myself famous almost at once'. The Oval Test of 1882 may have occurred long ago 'yet I can recall almost every incident in that famous game as well as if it had been played last week'.

The dismissal of W G in the second innings of the 1878 match was still savoured by Spofforth: 'I began bowling to "W G", and Mr Murdoch behind the wickets missed him off my first ball, much to my sorrow; but the next ball knocked his leg bail thirty yards, and I screamed out "Bowled".'

Spofforth, who had not chosen to play in the very first Test, slipped quietly into the Australian dressing-room on the occasion of the hundredth Test and presented each of the Australian team members with an inscribed gold medal to mark the occasion. One player, H S T L 'Stork' Hendry, was playing in his first Test: it was a unique occasion when a player whose life span covered the era of the first hundred tests presented a medal to a player who was still alive at the time of the thousandth Test. Hendry recalled this occasion in 1986: 'the appearance of Spofforth was a great surprise, he hardly spoke a word and simply wished us well for the match'. The medal was inscribed simply though the initials were incorrect:

E L Hendry Esq.
England v. Australia
100th Test Match
Won by Australia
Presented by F R Spofforth Esq.
May 1921

Hendry lost this valuable medal for a time, but noticing a strange taste to a cup of tea, he discovered that the missing medal had been carefully hidden in a tea pot to fool any would-be burglars.

If the cricket public were not totally aware that the Demon was still soldiering on, the successful tea merchant was certainly well known in the business community. Spofforth was featured in a volume, *Notable Londoners: An Illustrated Who's Who of Professional and Business Men*, which was published in 1921-22. His listed business activities included Managing Director of Star Tea Company and Ridgways Limited and Chairman, Albion Tin Works. No doubt he paid for the privilege of appearing in this volume and supplied a suitably flattering photo — one which appeared in *Cricket* as long ago as 1902 — revealing a much younger man in his late forties.

On 29 November 1922 Spofforth wrote an official letter to The Imperial and Foreign Corporation, outlining the new arrangement between the Star Tea Company and Ridgways: 'The Star Tea Company Limited, which has carried on a successful and increasing business for many years as tea, grocery and provision merchants, has recently reconstituted and increased its capital for the purpose of enabling it to acquire the Ordinary Share Capital of Ridgways, Limited'.

Spofforth's grandchildren, Derek, Pamela, Jean and John, have shadowy memories of visiting their famous grandfather at Long Ditton. Not all the images are flattering. Jean and John recall that Spofforth was very quiet and undemonstrative to his grandchildren. Pamela remembers Christmas at Long Ditton when she was given a doll's pram 'by a tall lean man, with bushy eyebrows and a hooked nose', who 'sort of stared'. Spofforth, who was full of confidence on the cricket field and at his business, had a 'sort of shyness' and a 'stiff upper lip' which resulted in this social and emotional aloofness. Pamela noted that Spofforth was not a particularly gracious recipient of presents: once, when her mother Winifred had given Spofforth a box of his favourite cigars, he hardly said thanks at all and he had pushed them under the chair.

There are also family stories that attest to Spofforth's inner drive and his intensely high standards. When he suffered a bad leg injury, probably during the Hampstead phase, he refused to have it encased in plaster, which had recently become part of medical practice. Instead, he made his own strapping and helped his recovery by hobbling round the billiard table once every hour during the night. He made an astonishing and rapid recovery.

The Spofforths and their daughter, Dorothy, travelled to Australia in 1924, arriving at Fremantle on 19 January 1925. Fred and Phillis Spofforth shared a British passport and he was listed as a 'British subject by birth'. Spofforth's second return visit to Australia also coincided with an English cricket tour and the Spofforths arrived in time to watch the last few Tests of a series which Australia won 4-1. J W Worrall, who played with Spofforth for Victoria in the late 1880s, later wrote that he 'looked in such perfect health, and was upright as ever'.

During the English summer of 1925 Spofforth suffered an attack of ptomaine poisoning after which he never recovered his normal health. Not long before his death Lord Harris visited Spofforth on his sick bed. 'We had a chat about old times,' recalled Harris, and Spofforth was 'keenly interested in past as well as present times.' As Harris left the room Spofforth made an interesting comment which suggests not only a fine sense of history but also that he was facing up fearlessly to the reality of his own death: 'The doctors say I shall see the first Test Match (12-15 June 1926); but I made my reputation in May (1878); you knocked me out in May (1886); and I shall go out in May.'[9] Spofforth died on 4 June 1926. The listed symptoms of death, chronic colitis and failure of his intestines to absorb fat, were of eighteen months duration.

He was buried at Brookwood Cemetery on 8 June. Among the mourners were Clem Hill and Dr Rowley Pope, representing the Australian cricket team, and Lord Hawke. Spofforth was buried according to the rites of the Church of England. The granite slab that marked his grave bore the simplest of inscriptions, with no hint of his past greatness nor of any hope of future life:

IN LOVING MEMORY OF
FREDERICK ROBERT SPOFFORTH
DIED JUNE 4, 1926 AGED 72 YEARS

The tributes were fulsome. *The Times* declared on 5 June that 'he was beyond question the greatest bowler of his generation' and was 'regarded by many as the greatest bowler who ever lived', while the London *Daily Telegraph* argued that 'no one ever bowled with his head so earnestly and so malignantly'. J W Worrall wrote in the *Australasian* of 12 June that 'there is no doubt that he was the greatest bowler of all time'. Such a view was endorsed by one of Spofforth's fellow-tourists, J W Trumble, who wrote a lengthy article in *The Times* a few years later, on 26 July 1928, headed 'The World's Best Bowler'.

Two of Spofforth's contemporaries, while endorsing the above sentiments, expressed their admiration a little more cautiously. Lord Harris, in a *Wisden* tribute, concluded that 'what we must judge performances by are the circumstances and conditions of the time when they were done, and taking those as the criteria, I do not see how any bowler can be held to be better than was F R Spofforth'. The Earl of Darnley, in the same issue, concluded that Spofforth was 'one of the very best bowlers that the last 50 years have seen, unquestionably; possibly the best of all'.

But there were some who proffered admiration with some reservations. Writing in the London *Daily Telegraph* on 5 June 1926, Colonel Philip Trevor suggested that 'he was a very great bowler, and had he retired in, say 1884, he would probably rank to-day as the greatest of all bowlers'. Trevor argued that a performer, like Spofforth, was the worst judge of his own performance and that he suffered under the illusion that he was a better bowler in his middle age, bowling 'slow-medium pace', than in his prime. There was also some debate about whether Spofforth was a genuine fast bowler: in a letter to the editor of the same paper which was published on 7 June, Robin H Legge stated that 'I for one, cannot understand the present depreciation of the pace of Spofforth's bowling. It was terrific at times.' There were also those who asked questions about the Spofforth legend out of ignorance. Lord Harris had a revealing conversation with M A Noble, who played for Australia not much more than a decade after Spofforth, making his debut in 1898.

I was talking to Mr Noble early in the season at the Oval, and he told me that Spofforth was seriously ill, and then put to me the astonishing question, 'Was he a great bowler?' It was about the equivalent of asking if W G was a great bat. 'About the best I ever played,' was my reply; 'but did you never see him?' It was another shock to find that Noble, with whom I had never played, had never seen him bowl.[10]

Old cricketers and the cricket public love to compare the bowlers and teams of one era and another. Was Spofforth a better bowler than C T B Turner? How does he compare with a Lindwall or a Lillee? Comparisons between the players of different eras are anachronistic. The judgements are mostly subjective.

Various more objective comparisons have been suggested. On one score, Spofforth's contemporary Turner, who was timed at 55 miles (88.5 km) per hour, does not compare well with the moderns. But on another score, Spofforth does. Philip Derriman, who set out to pick an Australian all-time eleven, looked at the proportion of wickets taken by a bowler as a percentage of the total wickets taken in his era.[11] Using this measurement, Spofforth makes Derriman's eleven, which suggests that in terms of wicket-taking he was head and shoulders above his contemporaries. Spofforth was the only pre-1900 cricketer to make this team. The major problem in making comparisons is that conditions changed so much from one era of cricket to another. The ball, the wickets, the science of batting and bowling were all very different in Spofforth's day.

A surer method of evaluation is to dwell on the Demon's impact on the cricket world of his time. Almost all the pundits of this era agree that he was the great thinking bowler. He was, as Tom Garrett put it, 'the most brainy bowler that I ever knew'; Englishman A C Maclaren noted that he combined an 'exceptional knowledge of the game' with 'a wonderful brain'; while J W Worrall commented he was a man of 'rare mental energy' who was a master in strategy and resourcefulness and who 'quickly sized up a batsman and soon realized his strong and weak points'. Maclaren and Worrall provided two examples to support their case. 'His pet scheme was to leave the batsman's favourite shot open, purposely taking the fieldsmen away, and then bowl a ball to tempt the batsman to bring off his favourite shot, which he felt would prove his undoing, the ball defeating the batsman on many occasions.' Then there was the Spofforth bluff. When two batsmen were well set and scoring freely, he then 'proceeded ostentatiously to alter the positions of his field, packing several of them behind the wicket and down the gully as is done for very fast bowling' and 'started his run to the wicket at top speed' before delivering a well-disguised slower ball which produced a soft return catch.[12]

Spofforth's keen brain led him to make a study of the art of bowling: J W Trumble claimed that 'as a student in the art of bowling Spofforth stood out from all other bowlers'.[13] Not content to stay within the tradition of fast bowling which he inherited he made a detailed study not only of fast bowling but he 'then studied medium-pace and slow bowling, his objective being a completely disguised combination of the three paces ... Nobody ever fooled good batsmen with the slow ball so completely as did Spofforth.' W G paid Spofforth the ultimate compliment by stating that 'however well he might be set, he was never sure that "Spoff" would not bowl him out the next ball'.

A prominent Golden Age cricketer and astute writer, C B Fry, had no doubt whatsoever about Spofforth's unique contribution as the first great fast bowler:

Spofforth ... appears to have been the first naturally fast bowler to discover that the subtle variations of pace and deceptive tricks practised by a slow-medium bowler like Alfred Shaw might with advantage be imitated and developed in conjunction with sheer speed. On this score it is justly said of him that he founded a new school of bowling ... In fact, to all appearances he was a very fast bowler. But appearances were deceptive. By subtle differences in the way he held the ball in his hand he varied the pace of the ball without in the least varying his style of delivery. Consequently, the batsman opposed to him never knew at what pace the ball was coming.[14]

Biblio-
graphical
Note

W.L. Murdoch
caught by Lord Harris.

N o biography, or extended study, of Fred Spofforth has ever been written. The man who attracted extensive media attention and was the subject of many feature articles has been ignored since his death. Since 1926 there has been only an occasional article or chapter on Spofforth such as R L Arrowsmith, 'Brief Lives: F R Spofforth', *Journal of the Cricket Society*, 1983 and the occasional chapter such as Ralph Barker, *Ten Great Bowlers* (Chatto & Windus, London, 1907).

Writing a biography of a sportsman who died more than six decades ago is not an easy task since there are no persons alive whom I could locate who actually saw the Demon bowl. I am fortunate that Spofforth himself wrote a number of short articles and letters which have enabled me to develop some measure of understanding of a complex and at times baffling personality. Since this is the first major study of Fred Spofforth, it is worth providing a list of his output: articles and reported interviews.

They include:

Letter to the Editor, *Sydney Mail*, 15 November 1879.

'Cricket in Derbyshire', *Derbyshire County Annual*, 1890.

'Australian Cricket and Cricketers: A Retrospect' and 'English Cricket and Cricketers: A Retrospect', *New Review*, Vol. 10 (1894), pp. 507-16, 626-36.

Letter to the Editor, *Sporting Life*, 25 January 1897.

'In the Days of My Youth: Chapters of Autobiography', *M.A.P.*, 28 November 1903, pp. 672-74.

'Schoolboys' Bowling 1903', *Wisden*, 1904, pp. 333-4.

George W Beldam and Charles B Fry, *Great Bowlers and Fielders: Their Methods at a Glance*, Macmillan, London, 1907.

Letter to the Editor, *Sportsman*, October 1912.

Lord Hawke et al., *The Memorial Biography of Dr W G Grace*, London, 1919, pp. 104-05, 130-2.

'Two Historic Matches', the *Cricketer*, 28 May 1921, pp. 7-8.

Reported interviews and speeches

'Mr F R Spofforth', The *Cricket Field*, 13 August 1892, reprinted in W A Bettesworth, *Chats on the Cricket Field*, Merritt & Hatcher, London, 1910, pp. 443-49.

'The Demon Bowler on Bowling', *Pall Mall Budget*, June 1886, reprinted in *Cricket*, 23 September 1886.

The *Australasian*, 9 June 1888.

The *Birmingham Daily Mail*, 10 June 1889.

Cricket, 27 March 1902.

The *Sydney Morning Herald*, 14 February 1933.

Notes

1 A Day of Cricket Legend

1 Spofforth, it seems, preferred Fred to Frederick. His most common signature of both formal (including as chairman and managing director of the Star Tea Company) and informal letters was Fred R Spofforth.

2 F R Spofforth, 'Australian Cricket and Cricketers: A Retrospect' and 'English Cricket and Cricketers: A Retrospect', *New Review*, Vol. 10 (1894), pp. 507-16, 626-36.

3 F R Spofforth, 'Two Historic Matches', *The Cricketer*, 28 May 1921, p. 7.

4 *Globe* quoted in P E Reynolds, *The Australian Cricketers' Tour Through Australia, New Zealand and Great Britain in 1878*, J W McKenzie reprint, Cambridge, 1980, p. 22.

5 Charles W Alcock, ed., *James Lillywhite's Cricketers' Annual*, 1879 (Red Lillywhite), James Lillywhite, Frowd & Co., London, p. 1.

6 It was the first of two first-class hat-tricks in a calendar year as just seven months later Spofforth took the first hat-trick in Test cricket, at Melbourne on 2 January 1879. His third hat-trick was achieved against South of England, during a match played on 11-12 September 1884 at the Oval.

7 Reynolds, *Australian Cricketers' Tour*, p. 20.

8 There has been continuing debate about whether Spofforth took 4-16 or 5-16 in the second innings, as to whether Wild was bowled by Spofforth or Boyle. The weight of evidence, newspaper and contemporary, favours the 4-16 figure.

9 Spofforth, 'Two Historic Matches', p. 7.

10 Reynolds, *Australian Cricketers'* Tour, pp. 21-22.

11 The *Pall Mall Gazette*, 28 May 1878.

12 Spofforth, 'Australian Cricket and Cricketers', p. 628.

13 Lord Hawke, *Recollections and Reminiscences*, Williams and Norgate, London, 1924, p. 207.

14 *Australasian*, 12 June 1926.

15 'Country Vicar' (Rev. R L Hodgson), *Second Innings*, Hutchinson, London, 1933, p. 35.

16 Dr Roy Clayton, who saw Spofforth bowl at Scarborough, an unidentified newspaper clipping, dated 25 March 1951, in the collection of the Spofforth family.

17 Spofforth, as suggested later, was prone to 'impulsive exaggeration' and the moustache in question may have not been of quite such impressive dimensions.

18 Spofforth, 'Australian Cricket', p. 628. The English *Cricket and Football Times*, for instance, of 2 May 1878 commented that Spofforth 'rushes up to the wickets like a demon'.

19 Presumably this name came from the French and referred to Spofforth's wolf-like face or his wolf-like (devastating) bowling.

20 See, for instance, Clifford Bax, *Rosemary for Remembrance*, Frederick Muller, London, 1948, p. 110. Although this was not a cricket book — it was a book of Hampstead reminiscences — and published more than two decades after Spofforth's death, Bax simply mentioned that he saw 'the Demon' play in 1898 assuming that his audience was well aware of who 'the Demon' was.

21 *Cricketer*, 22 August 1953.

22 *Vanity Fair*, 13 July 1878.

23 Quoted in Reynolds, *The Australian Cricketers' Tour*, p. 23.

24 *Sydney Morning Herald*, 26 November 1878.

25 F R Spofforth, 'Australian Cricket', p. 631.

2 The Spofforths: Colonial Adventurers and Buccaneers

1 F R Spofforth, 'In the Days of My Youth: Chapters of Autobiography', *M.A.P.*, 28 November 1903, pp. 672–74. Unless otherwise identified Spofforth quotations in this chapter will be from this article.

2 Captain Ralph Spofforth, author of an unpublished manuscript, 'A New History of the Spofforth Family', has argued that the Spofforth family tree prior to the Reformation contains 'grave inaccuracies and is 'merely conjectural'.

3 *Howden Explored*, Georgian Society for East Yorkshire, Howden, 1979.

4 Edward Walford, *County Families*, Robert Hardwick, London, 1874.

5 Robert Senior was a clerk of the Halmote and Temporal Courts, which were held under the stewardship of the Bishop of Durham in the 1780s. Robert Junior was

appointed by the Bishop to the post of Coroner of Howden and Howdenshire from 1787 to 1823. Robert Junior was also appointed Clerk and Treasurer of the Court of Sewers for Howdenshire in 1802.

6 When Robert Senior died in 1827 his probate listed property — land, farms, cottages, tithes, tenements, marshgates, closes — not only in Howden but in North Duffield, Eastringhton, Blacktoft, Hemingbrough, Skipwith, Drax and elsewhere — valued at approximately £7,000.

7 Information supplied by the Principal Librarian, Battye Library.

8 Rica Erickson, General Editor, *Dictionary of Western Australia 1829-1914*, Vol. 1, *Early Settlers 1829-1850*, University of Western Australia Press, Nedlands, 1979, p. 317.

9 Grey suggested that the party left the next morning (7 May) but Roe suggested that it was the day after (8 May).

10 George Grey, *Journals of Two Expeditions of Discovery*, T and W Boone, London, 1841, Vol. II, pp. 98-115.

11 Ibid., Vol. I, pp. 147-49.

12 Jas Scott, 'A Cricketing Miscellany: Being a Collection of Odds and Ends', unpublished manuscript, Sydney, 1942, p. 61, NSWCA Library.

13 If Edward's birth date of 28 November 1805 is correct, he was actually forty years old.

14 This material is based on the research of Peter Reynolds published in *Leichhardt Historical Journal*, No. 10 (1981), p. 14; No 14 (1985), p. 42.

15 Edward's death certificate, 1875, lists that in addition to two sons and three daughters there was another 'female deceased', a child who almost certainly died in infancy.

16 S N Hogg, 'Biographical Sketches', Mitchell Library, MSS712/4. The Spofforth family also owned a 'little cottage', part of the site of 136 Darling Street, Balmain, which remained in the family until 1878.

17 T W Reese, *New Zealand Cricket 1841-1914*, Simpson & Williams, Christchurch, 1927, p. 78; T W Reese, *New Zealand Cricket 1914-1933*, Vol. II, Whitcombe & Tombs, Auckland, 1936, pp. 112-13.

18 R F Holder, *Bank of New South Wales: A History*, Angus

& Robertson, Sydney, 1970, Vol. 1, *1817–1893*, p. 214.

19 Eric Harrison, *KohuKohu*, a booklet published by the Kohukohu Historic and Arts Society, 1983, p. 17.

20 His biography has appeared in A H McLintock, ed., *An Encyclopaedia of New Zealand*, Government Printer, Wellington, 966, Vol 2, R E Owen, Wellington, 1966 and E H Scholefield, ed., *A Dictionary of New Zealand Biography*, Department of Internal Affairs, 1940; Harrison, *Kohukohu*, p. 17.

21 *Dictionary of New Zealand Biography.*

22 *Leader*, 9 June 1888.

23 Philip Derriman, *True to the Blue: A History of the New South Wales Cricket Association*, Richard Smart, Sydney, 1985, pp. 39–40.

3 The Education of a Fast Bowler

1 F R Spofforth, 'Australian Cricket and Cricketers' and 'English Cricket and Cricketers', *New Review*, Vol. 10 (1894), pp. 507–16, 626–36. Unless otherwise identified, quotations from Fred Spofforth in this chapter will be from these articles or from 'Days of My Youth' *M.A.P.*, 28 November 1903, pp. 672–74.

2 This was probably on 17 March 1864, when Hayward and Caffyn (rather than Hayward and Carpenter, who also batted on that day), played substantial innings against the New South Wales XXII.

3 H S Altham and E W Swanton, *A History of Cricket*, Allen & Unwin, London, 4th ed., 1948, p. 111.

4 Richard Daft, *Kings of Cricket*, Arrowsmith, 1893, p. 75.

5 *Cricket Field*, 13 August 1892.

6 Richard Cashman, 'The Rise and Fall of the Australian Cricket Club 1826–68', *Sporting Traditions*, No. 5, Pt 1 (November 1988), pp. 112–30.

7 *James Lillywhite's Cricketers' Annual*, 1879 (Red Lillywhite), James Lillywhite, Frowd & Co., London, p. 5.

8 W F Mandle, 'Games People Played: Cricket and Football in England and Victoria', *Historical Studies Australia and New Zealand*, Vol. 15, No. 60 (1973), p. 519.

9 R L Arrowsmith, 'The Height of the Bowling Arm Between 1864 and 1884', *Cricket Quarterly*, IV, 1966, pp. 35–37.

10 Jack Pollard, *The Formative Years of Australian Cricket 1803–93*, Angus & Robertson, Sydney, 1986, p. 140.

11 'O.B', a schoolfellow of Spofforth at Eglinton College, 'in the early sixties', *The Bulletin*, 17 June 1926.

12 *Sydney Morning Herald*, 16 February 1933. R L Scrutton, who described himself as a friend of Spofforth, was a member of the Glebe Club some '70 years ago'.

13 Pendrill, who was the son of Dr Pendrill of Clifton, Gloucester, was educated at Eton and St John's College, Oxford. Pendrill died on 21 January 1872 and the college was closed in 1878.

14 Grammar has produced ten Test players, seven of whom played in the pre-1914 era: R C Allen, J W Burke, P C Charlton, A Cotter, H Donnan, H S T L Hendry, F Iredale, S P Jones, F R Spofforth, S M J Woods. In addition Grammar, was the school of Eric Barbour, Jack Chegwyn and commentator Alan McGilvray.

15 *Sydneian*, XII, September 1878. It is unclear why 'Our Special Cricketomaniac' referred to the figures of 7-11 since Spofforth did not achieve such figures in any of the main matches of the 1878 tour. Either he secured these returns in a minor match or the poet got his figures wrong.

16 This event appears to have occurred in 1871 after Spofforth had ended his college life. Possibly the drawing master who taught him in 1869 introduced him to the Newtown Club in 1871.

17 Jas Scott, 'A Cricketing Miscellany', p. 53.

18 David Frith, *The Fast Men*, Horwitz Grahame, Cammeray, 1981, p. 69.

19 R F Holder, *Bank of New South Wales: A History*, Angus & Robertson, Sydney, 1970, Vol. I, p. 407.

20 They were published by R. Bone, Sydney, 1865. Max Solling discovered a copy of this publication in the Fisher Library, University of Sydney.

21 *Australasian*, 9 June 1888.

22 Philip Derriman, *The Grand Old Ground: A History of the Sydney Cricket Ground*, Cassell, North Ryde, 1981, pp. 6-7.

23 Spofforth wrote, in 1903, that 'the following season' (after his first season with the Albert Club, that is 1873-74) 'I was elected to play for New South Wales v. Victoria, but declined'. Since there was no intercolonial game in

this season, with the visit of the third English team, this comment must have referred to the match of February 1873. This statement seems at variance with the comment in the *Sydney Mail*. He gave no reason why he declined to play.

24 *Sydney Mail*, 4 March 1876.
25 Richard Fotheringham, 'Early Sporting Diplomacy: The Case of R A W Green', *Sporting Traditions*, No. 5, Pt 2 (May 1989), pp. 173-86.
26 *Sydney Morning Herald*, 11 February 1939 quoted in Scott Bennett, 'Professional Sculling in New South Wales', *JRAHS*, Vol. 71, Pt 2, p. 130.
27 Ibid., p. 132; and Bennett, *The Clarence Comet: The Career of Henry Searle 1866-89*, Sydney University Press, 1973, p. 13.
28 *Sydney Morning Herald*, 18 August 1884, commenting sometime later on this happening.
29 W F Mandle, 'Cricket and Australian Nationalism in the Nineteenth Century', *JRAHS*, Vol. 59, Pt 4 (December 1973), pp. 225-37.

4 Intercolonial and International Cricketer

1 *Sydney Mail*, 21 February 1874.
2 W G Grace, 'W.G.': *Cricketing Reminiscences & Personal Recollections: W.G. Grace*, Hambleton reprint, London, 1980, p. 376.
3 *Cricket Field*, 13 August 1892.
4 George W. Beldam and Charles B. Fry, *Great Bowlers and Fielders: Their Methods at a Glance*, Macmillan, London, 1907, p.13.
5 Lord Hawke, Lord Harris and Sir Home Gordon, eds, *The Memorial Biography of Dr W G Grace*, Constable, London, 1919, p. 104.
6 Grace, *Cricketing Reminiscences*, p. 84; Lord Hawke et al., *Memorial Biography*, p. 104; W G Grace, *Cricket*, J W Arrowsmith, Bristol, 1891, p. 380.
7 *Sydney Mail*, 27 March 1875.
8 London *Sportsman*, 31 March 1883.
9 Philip Derriman, *True to the Blue: A History of the New South Wales Cricket Association*, Richard Smart, Sydney, 1985, p. 23.

10 Living in the country may have made it more difficult for Evans to attend the major games played in Sydney. He was based at Penrith in the 1870s but moved to Yass and later Albury, in the early 1880s, where he was an Inspector of Forests.
11 *Sydney Mail,* 4 and 11 March 1882.
12 *Cricket,* 6 May 1886, quoting a report in the *Australasian.*
13 Derriman, *True to the Blue,* pp. 21, 26.
14 *Australasian,* 27 March 1875.
15 Ibid., 18 December 1875.
16 Ibid., 4 March 1876.
17 *Conway's Australian Cricketers' Annual,* 1876-77, F F Bailliere, Melbourne, 1877, p. 21.
18 This cup was also donated to the Australian Gallery of Sport in 1988.
19 Derriman, *True to the Blue,* p. 41.
20 Quoted in the *Sydney Mail,* 24 March 1877.
21 Ibid.
22 *Sydney Mail,* 17 March 1877.
23 The total crowd for the four days was approximately 21,500.
24 *Australasian,* 24 March 1877.
25 *The Argus,* 2 April 1877.
26 *Sydney Mail,* 1 December 1877.

5 The Technique of a Fast Bowler

1 C B Fry, 'The Australian Bowlers in England'. Publication is unknown. The clipping is in the Spofforth Family files.
2 Lord Hawke, *Recollections and Reminiscences,* Williams & Norgate, London, 1924, p. 65.
3 W G Grace, 'Forty Years of Cricket', *Cricket,* 30 October 1890.
4 William C. Murdoch, *Cricket,* Routledge, Manchester, 1893, p. 75.
5 *Daily Telegraph* (Sydney), 22 April 1925.
6 A copy of the Spofforth cartoon appeared in the Queensland journal, *Figaro,* in 1884.
7 W A Bettesworth, *Chats on the Cricket Field,* Merritt and Hatcher, London, 1910, p. 444.
8 *Wisden,* 1927, pp. 299-302.
9 Lord Hawke, *Recollections and Reminiscences,* p. 65.

10 *The Times,* 26 July 1928.

11 The details of this analysis are provided in Spofforth's Career Statistics (appendix).

12 The circumference of the ball was reduced on 4 May 1927 to between 8 and 13/16s to 9" (22.4 to 22.9 cm) whereas the ball had previously measured 9 to 9 1/4" (22.9 to 23.5 cm). The height of the wicket was increased on 6 May 1931 from not less than 27" (68.6 cm) to not more than 28" (71.1 cm). The bowling crease was widened to 8' 8" (2.6 m) on 7 May 1902.

13 Murdoch, *Cricket,* p.79.

14 'Country Vicar' (Rev. R L Hodgson), *Second Innings,* Hutchinson, London, 1933, p. 35 quoting from Neville Cardus, *Days in the Sun,* Jonathan Cape, London, 1934, pp. 149-50.

15 George Giffen, *With Bat and Ball,* Ward, Lock and Co., Melbourne, 1898, p. 167.

16 P E Reynolds, *The Australian Cricketers' Tour . . . 1878,* J W McKenzie reprint, Cambridge, 1980, p. 29.

17 Jas Scott, 'A Cricketing Miscellany', p. 59.

6 The Making of a Hero

1 After acting as an agent for the Conservative Party, 1857-70, Markham helped the Conservative Party cope with the 1870 extension of the franchise by forming Working Men's Conservative Associations. The 'Spy' cartoon, published in *Vanity Fair* on 20 March 1880, was captioned: 'He invented the Working Man'.

2 S N Hogg, 'Biographical Sketches', Mitchell Library MSS 712/4.

3 *Sydney Mail,* 22 September 1877.

4 Ibid., 2 February 1878.

5 *Sydney Morning Herald,* 30 May 1878.

6 Spofforth, 'Australian Cricket and Cricketers', *New Review,* Vol. 10 (1894), p. 626.

7 Ibid., p. 627.

8 P E Reynolds, *The Australian Cricketers'* Tour . . . *1878,* J W McKenzie reprint, Cambridge, 1980, p. 38.

9 It is not clear, from Spofforth's various versions of this story, whether this event occurred in 1878 or 1880 since the tourists played a Rochdale XVIII on both occasions.

10 Another possible reason, cited in Stanley Cohen's, *New South Wales Cricketers' Guide and Annual, 1877-78*, p. 75, was that 'Lillywhite's team paid our men £20 each (in 1876-77) to go to Melbourne for their benefit'.

11 Quoted in the *Sydney Mail*, 9 November 1878.

12 *John Lillywhite's Cricketers' Companion*, 1879 (Green Lillywhite), John Lillywhite, London, p. 52.

13 *Conway's Annual 1877-78*, Ferguson & Moore, Melbourne, 1879, p. 285.

14 Ibid., p. 286.

15 *The Age*, 20 March 1877.

7 An Eccentric and Wayward Demon

1 *Sydney Mail*, 22 and 29 November 1879.

2 Ibid., 6, 20 and 27 December 1879, 10 January 1880.

3 R F Holder, *The Bank of New South Wales: A History*, Angus & Robertson, Sydney, 1970, Vol. I, pp. 407-08.

4 A correspondent who wrote to Boyle and Scott, quoted in the *Sydney Mail*, 4 September 1880.

5 Quoted in *The Bulletin*, 18 September 1880.

6 *Sydney Mail*, 27 November and 25 December 1880.

7 T W Reese, *New Zealand Cricket 1841-1914*, Simpson & Williams, Christchurch, 1927, p. 81. Reese pointed out that the bowling figures for the tour are not complete as the bowling analysis for the second innings of the match against Nelson is not known.

8 *The Bulletin*, 7 January 1882.

9 Quoted in ibid., 7 January 1882.

10 *Sydney Mail*, 18 February 1882.

8 Ashes Test Triumph

1 *Daily Telegraph* (London), quoted in *The Bulletin*, 15 July 1882.

2 Charles Frederick Pardon, *The Australians in England, A Complete Record of the Cricket Tour of 1882*, J W McKenzie reprint, Cambridge, 1982, p. 17.

3 Quoted in *The Bulletin*, 12 August 1882.

4 Quoted in the *Sydney Mail*, 28 October 1882.

5 Pardon, *The Australians in England . . . 1882*.

6 *Bell's Life* (London) quoted in the *Sydney Mail*, 28 October 1882.

7 The Spofforth spirit, which was manifested in this Test, is

still remembered: a *Guardian* headline of 11 July 1986 declared: 'Spofforth Spirit as Carrick Turns Middlesex to Defeat'.

8 Spofforth, 'Two Historic Matches', *Cricketer*, 28 May 1921, pp. 7-8.
9 Spofforth, 'Australian Cricket and Cricketers', *New Review*, Vol. 10 (1894), pp. 633-34 and 'Two Historic Matches', The *Cricketer*, 28 May 1921.
10 Quoted in the *Sydney Mail*, 28 October 1882.
11 *Sportsman*, 30 August 1882.
12 Spofforth, 'Australian Cricket and Cricketers', p. 634.
13 K S Inglis, 'Test Matches 1877-1900', in R. Cashman and M. McKernan, eds, *Sport in History: The Making of Modern Sporting History*, University of Queensland Press, St Lucia, 1979, p. 157.
14 Pardon, *Australians in England . . . 1882*, p. 144.
15 Neville Cardus, *A Cricketer's Book*, Grant Richards, London, 1922, chapter 1.
16 John Masefield, *So Long to Learn: Chapters of an Autobiography*, Heinemann, Melbourne, 1952, pp. 56-61.
17 '85 to Win' appears to have been written some time between 1952 and 1956. Masefield noted in his autobiography that he intended to write such a poem.
18 *Sydney Mail*, 25 November 1882.
19 Ibid., 25 November and 2 December 1882.
20 Quoted in *Cricket*, 16 February 1883.
21 Philip Derriman, *The Top 100 and the 1st XI*, Fairfax Library, Sydney, 1987, p. 253.

9 The Demon Accused of Cheating

1 *Sydney Mail*, 23 December 1882.
2 Ibid., 13 January 1883.
3 Quoted in the *Sydney Mail*, 3 February 1883.
4 Newspaper clipping supplied by Philip Derriman.
5 Charles W Alcock, ed., *James Lillywhite's Cricketers' Annual*, 1884 (Red Lillywhite), James Lillywhite, Frowd & Co., London, p. 8.
6 Quoted in the *Sydney Mail*, 5 May 1883.
7 Another report suggests that the captains had a choice of batting on one of several pitches in the square. In the second innings Bligh preferred to bat on the pitch occupied by England in the first innings since the other

pitch had been occupied by the Australians after the rain and must have been more damaged. It appears, from Leslie's comments, that the Australians batted on the pitch chosen by the Englishmen for their final innings.

8 Quoted in *Cricket*, 16 February 1883.
9 *Sydney Mail*, 17 March 1883.
10 Ibid., 5 May 1883.
11 Ibid., 24 March 1883.
12 Ibid., 12 January 1884.

10 The Finest Tour

1 An *Age* report quoted in the *Sydney Mail*, 10 May 1884.
2 See Spofforth's Career Statistics.
3 Given that Spofforth mostly bowled to one slip and a point, with the possible addition of a long slip (short third man), it is not clear why he bowled to six men 'in slips'. It cannot be assumed that he suddenly discovered how to swing the ball and to bowl an outswinger. The more likely explanation is that by bowling faster he might have got more bounce out of the wicket, thereby causing the batsman to cock up the ball in the direction of slips.
4 Charles Frederick Pardon, *Australians in England: A Complete Record of the Cricket Tour of 1884*, J W McKenzie reprint, London, 1984, p. 70.
5 *Sydney Mail*, 27 September 1884.
6 Quoted in *The Bulletin*, 22 November 1884.
7 Quoted in ibid., 20 September 1884.
8 *Sydney Mail*, 1 November 1884.
9 Quoted in ibid., 1 November 1884.
10 Ibid.

11 Spofforth the Strike-Breaker

1 Although the seven Notts players received £20, those players who did not support this demand were paid £21.
2 *South Australian Register*, 13 December 1884.
3 The four-day match aggregated a crowd of c. 16,500. A Sydney Test (3–7 March 1882) with a comparable crowd (15,018) had a gate of £876 1s. 9d., although entry prices to the stand were slightly less at Sydney.
4 It is likely that this bill was made up of the £900 allocated to the players and other expenses. If this

assumption is correct, paying the players represented three-quarters of the match expenditure.

5 *Australasian*, 20 December 1884.

6 *Sydney Mail*, 27 December 1884.

7 Ibid., 3 January 1885; *Cricket*, 26 February 1885.

8 *Australasian*, 10 January 1885.

9 Minutes of the NSWCA, 19 January 1885.

10 For a fine account of the parochialism of the various colonial associations and the cricket crisis of the 1880s see David Montefiore, "Cricket in the Doldrums": The Stuggle between Private and Public Control of Australian Cricket in the 1880s', unpublished BA Honours thesis, University of New South Wales, 1989.

11 *Sydney Mail*, 17 and 24 January 1885.

12 *The Times*, 26 July 1928.

13 This and the above quotations are taken from *Shaw and Shrewsbury's Team in Australia 1884–5*, J W McKenzie reprint, Nottingham, 1985.

14 Ibid., p. 157.

15 *Sydney Mail*, 2 May 1885.

16 *Shaw and Shrewsbury's Team*, p. 26.

17 *Sydney Mail*, 25 July 1885.

18 The four Tests in 1882–83 drew 169,729 spectators, whereas the five Tests of 1884–85 attracted only 94,134 patrons.

12 The End of an International Career

1 Quoted in National Australia Bank records.

2 *Sydney Mail*, 21 November 1885.

3 It appears that a residential qualification of six months operated by this season.

4 *Sydney Mail*, 21 November and 12 December 1885.

5 *Scores and Biographies*, XIV, 518-19.

6 *Australasian*, 12 June 1926.

7 Ibid.

8 *Sydney Mail*, 27 February and 19 June 1886.

9 *The Bulletin* of 25 September 1882 referred to Bonnor as 'quiet' and 'unassuming' but other reports refer to his sharp retorts and boasting.

10 Quoted in *Cricket*, 6 May 1886.

11 Ibid., 25 November 1886.

12 *Wisden*, 1927, p. 299.

13 In the match against the Gentlemen Spofforth took 2-30 off 29.3 overs. It appears that on this occasion he did not have to complete the over after he injured his hand.

14 Quoted in *Cricket,* 17 June 1886.

15 'An Interview with Mr. Spofforth' was republished in *Cricket,* 23 September 1886.

16 The census of 1861 listed eight children at the Cadman home at Ardwick (Manchester), ranging from Elizabeth (15) to Phillis (1). There were two more additions to the family by 1871. While the census may not have listed all the Cadmans, it does suggest that there were probably less than twenty-one or twenty-two.

17 These included Joseph, Phillis, their eight children, a visitor and eight servants.

18 Benny Green, ed., *Wisden Anthology 1864-1900,* Queen Anne Press, London, 1979, p. 696.

19 Quoted in the *Sydney Mail,* 13 November 1886.

20 T W Reese, *New Zealand Cricket 1841-1914,* Simpson & Williams, Christchurch, 1927, pp. 83-84.

21 These matches are not defined as Tests because only the 1886 Australians were considered for the Australian XI. This classification is inconsistent with previous definitions of Tests: the match between the 1884 Australians and the eighth English team was the First Test of the 1884-85 season.

22 *Sydney Mail,* 15 January 1887.

23 'Felix' in the *Australasian* quoted in *Cricket,* 21 and 28 April 1887.

24 Quoted in *Cricket,* 14 April 1887.

25 *Sydney Mail,* 5 and 19 November 1887.

26 Robert Trumble, *The Golden Age of Cricket: A Memorial Book of Hugh Trumble,* the author, Melbourne, 1968, p. 49.

27 Spofforth's grandchildren remember that Phillis did not like living in Australia though they do not remember the precise reasons.

28 None of his sons appears to have been interested in taking over the business: the eight listed shareholders in 1892 included Joseph and his wife, Emma, Amy and Edith Cadman, and one son, Arthur W Cadman, a London surgeon.

29 *Australasian,* 9 June 1888; *Leader,* 9 June 1888.

30 *Cricket,* 12 July 1888.

13 The Return to England

1 *Sydney Mail,* 17 November 1888.

2 John Shawcroft, *A History of Derbyshire County Cricket Club 1870-1970,* The club, Derby, 1970, p. 38.

3 *Derby Mercury,* 12 and 19 June 1889.

4 Shawcroft, *History of Derbyshire County Cricket Club,* p. 39.

5 It appears that there was a close association between the two companies from 1899, if not before, with Ridgways as the dominant partner but with Star Tea Company maintaining its separate identity. The arrangement did not amount to a takeover because Star Tea Company, with Fred Spofforth still at the helm, reversed the situation in 1922 with Star Tea Company becoming the dominant partner.

6 Ridgways had been incorporated on 7 November 1896 with a capital of £380,000.

7 Fred R Spofforth, Managing Director of Star Tea Company to The Imperial and Foreign Corporation, Ltd., 29 November 1922, Stock Exchange Records, Guildhall Library, London.

8 Correspondence between Murdoch and the 1893 Manager, Victor Cohen, suggested that Murdoch would have liked to join the 1893 Australians.

9 *Cricket,* 29 November 1900; *Scores and Biographies,* Vol. XV, pp. 125-26.

10 David Frith, 'My Dear Victorious Stod': A Biography of A E Stoddart, The author, 1970, p. 68; F R D'O Monro, *The History of the Hampstead Cricket Club,* Home & Van Thal, London, 1949, p. 58.

11 Frith, 'My Dear Victorious Stod', p. 68; Monro, *History of Hampstead Cricket Club,* p. 55.

12 Monro, *History of Hampstead Cricket Club,* pp. 183-84.

14 A Time for Reflection

1 In 1894, for instance, Spofforth took 220 wickets for 1,181 off 606 overs at an average of 5.9; whereas in 1899 he returned only 18 wickets for 199 off 82 overs at an average of 11.05.

2 Jack Pollard, *Australian Cricket: The Game and the Players*, Hodder & Stoughton, Lane Cove, 1982, p. 676.
3 Letter to the Editor, 3 March 1951. The newspaper is unknown. The clipping is in the family files of John Youle.
4 Frith, '*My Dear Victorious Stod*', p. 178.
5 Monro, *History of Hampstead Cricket Club*, p. 97.
6 Ibid., pp. 101-02.
7 *Cricket*, quoted in Monro, *History of Hampstead Cricket Club*, p. 95.
8 George W Beldam and Charles B Fry, *Great Bowlers and Fielders: Their Methods at a Glance*, Macmillan, London, 1907.

15 Life After Cricket

1 *Sydney Morning Herald*, 14 February 1933.
2 *Surbiton Times*, 11 June 1926.
3 *Wisden*, 1913, p. 234.
4 Jas Scott, 'A Cricketing Miscellany', unpublished manuscript, NSWCA Library, p. 65.
5 Chris Cunneen, 'Elevating and Recording the People's Pastimes: Sydney Sporting Journalism 1886-1939'; R. Cashman and M. McKernan, eds, *Sport: Money, Morality and the Media*, New South Wales University Press, Kensington, 1981, pp. 162-76.
6 Edited by Lord Hawke, Lord Harris and Sir Home Gordon.
7 Ibid., pp. 130-31.
8 An undated war-time newspaper clipping in the possession of John Youle.
9 *Wisden*, 1927, p. 299.
10 Ibid.
11 While this method of comparison is of some value, Derriman would be the first to admit that it is not perfect. It has the fault of favouring strong bowlers in a weak attack at the expense of those who were part of a very strong attack.
12 A C Maclaren, 'Some Great Australian Bowlers', *Cricketer Winter Annual*, 1921-22, p. 10.
13 *The Times*, 26 July 1928.
14 C B Fry, 'The Australian Bowlers in England'.

Spofforth's Career Statistics

Prepared
by Ric Finlay

F. R. Spofforth at point

First class batting

Season	Matches	Innings	Not Out	Runs	Highest score	Average	50	Catches
1874-75	2	3	0	36	21	12.00	0	4
1875-76	2	3	0	3	3	1.00	0	0
1876-77	2	4	0	29	17	7.25	0	1
1878(Eng)	15	25	1	304	56	12.67	1	7
1878(USA)	1	2	0	8	4	4.00	0	2
1878-79	2	3	0	39	39	13.00	0	3
1879-80	2	4	1	6	4*	2.00	0	3
1880	5	7	1	115	44	19.17	0	6
1880-81	2	4	1	33	25*	11.00	0	1
1881-82	2	2	1	11	8	11.00	0	0
1882	30	41	11	263	37	8.77	0	17
1882-83	6	9	2	88	31	12.57	0	3
1883-84	1	2	0	43	29	21.50	0	0
1884	32	47	6	469	54	11.44	1	16
1884-85	4	7	0	96	50	13.71	1	2
1885-86	2	3	1	11	11	5.50	0	1
1886	20	28	7	166	37*	7.90	0	8
1886-87	5	10	1	55	25	6.11	0	4
1887-88	2	4	2	15	6	7.50	0	0
1888	1	2	0	2	2	1.00	0	1
1890	4	6	3	54	21	18.00	0	1
1892	3	5	0	30	17	6.00	0	1
1893	1	2	1	20	20*	20.00	0	0
1894	2	3	2	5	4*	5.00	0	0
1895	2	3	0	15	11	5.00	0	1
1896	3	4	0	10	7	2.50	0	1
1897	2	3	0	2	1	0.67	0	0
Total	155	236	41	1,928	56	9.89	3	83

* not out

First class bowling

Season	Overs	Balls	Runs	Wkts	Average	5 wkts in an innings	10 wkts in an innings	Best bowling
1874-75	97.1	389	158	8	19.75	0	0	3/56
1875-76	58	232	111	12	9.25	1	0	5/50
1876-77	79	316	190	5	38.00	0	0	3/67
1878(Eng)	658.1	2,633	1,068	97	11.01	10	5	9/53
1878(USA)	42.3	171	75	6	12.50	1	0	5/24
1878-79	104	416	203	18	11.28	3	1	7/62
1879-80	87.3	351	206	11	18.73	1	0	5/28
1880	207	828	336	40	8.40	6	3	8/61
1880-81	148.3	595	266	15	17.73	2	1	7/55
1881-82	181	724	344	8	43.00	1	0	6/122
1882	1,470	5,880	2,079	157	13.24	16	5	9/51
1882-83	339.2	1,358	597	23	25.96	1	1	7/44
1883-84	57.3	231	111	5	22.20	0	0	4/101
1884	1,572	6,288	2,654	207	12.82	22	10	8/62
1884-85	303.4	1,216	469	25	18.76	3	1	6/90
1885-86	184.3	739	274	18	15.22	2	1	5/43
1886	932.3	3,731	1,527	89	17.16	7	2	9/18
1886-87	198.1	793	331	14	23.64	1	0	6/47
1887-88	60	240	117	4	29.25	0	0	3/67
1888	69	276	124	11	11.27	1	1	7/67
1890	172.1	861	365	17	21.47	1	0	6/70
1892	107	535	286	9	31.78	0	0	4/75
1893	22.1	111	95	5	19.00	0	0	4/49
1894	58	290	155	6	25.83	0	0	4/93
1895	43	215	112	7	16.00	0	0	4/39
1896	127.2	637	256	28	9.14	4	1	8/74
1897	96	480	251	8	31.37	1	0	5/80
Total	5,089.2	30,536	12,760	853	14.96	84	32	9/18

Test batting

All Tests

Season	M	I	No	Runs	HS	Aver	50	Ca
1876-77	1	2	0	17	17	8.50	0	1
1878-79	1	1	0	39	39	39.00	0	3
1881-82	1	1	1	3	3*	-	0	0
1882	1	2	1	4	4*	4.00	0	1
1882-83	4	6	2	31	14*	7.75	0	0
1884	3	4	0	28	13	7.00	0	0
1884-85	3	5	0	55	50	11.00	1	2
1886	3	6	2	33	20*	8.25	0	1
1886-87	1	2	0	7	5	3.50	0	3
Total	18	29	6	217	50	9.43	1	11

In Australia

Season	M	I	NO	Runs	HS	Aver	50	Ca
1876-77	1	2	0	17	17	8.50	0	1
1878-79	1	1	0	39	39	39.00	0	3
1881-82	1	1	1	3	3*	-	0	0
1882-83	4	6	2	31	14*	7.75	0	0
1884-85	3	5	0	55	50	11.00	1	2
1886-87	1	2	0	7	5	3.50	0	3
Total	11	17	3	152	50	10.86	1	9

In England

Season	M	I	No	Runs	HS	Aver	50	Ca
1882	1	2	1	4	4*	4.00	0	1
1884	3	4	0	28	13*	7.00	0	0
1886	3	6	2	33	20*	8.25	0	1
Total	7	12	3	65	20*	7.22	0	2

Test bowling

ALL TESTS

Season	Ov	Balls	Runs	Wkts	Aver	5i	10m	BB
1876-77	44	176	111	4	27.75	0	0	3/67
1878-79	60	240	110	13	8.46	2	1	7/62
1880	66	264	128	1	128.00	0	0	1/92
1882	64.3	259	90	14	6.43	2	1	7/44
1882-83	244.1	977	408	18	22.67	1	1	7/44
1884	192.1	769	301	10	30.10	0	0	4/42
1884-85	194.1	777	306	19	16.11	2	1	6/90
1886	168.3	675	260	14	18.57	0	0	4/65
1886-87	12	48	17	1	17.00	0	0	1/17
Total	697.3	4,185	1,731	94	18.41	7	4	7/44

IN AUSTRALIA

Season	Ov	Balls	Runs	Wkts	Aver	5i	10m	BB
1876-77	44	176	111	4	27.75	0	0	3/67
1878-79	60	240	110	13	8.46	2	1	7/62
1881-82	66	264	128	1	128.00	0	0	1/92
1882-83	244.1	977	408	18	22.67	1	1	7/44
1884-85	194.1	777	306	19	16.11	2	1	6/90
1886-87	12	48	17	1	17.00	0	0	1/17
Total	413.4	2,482	1,080	56	19.29	5	3	7/44

IN ENGLAND

Season	Ov	Balls	Runs	Wkts	Aver	5i	10m	BB
1882	64.3	259	90	14	6.43	2	1	7/44
1884	192.1	769	301	10	30.10	0	0	4/42
1886	168.3	675	260	14	18.57	0	0	4/65
Total	283.5	1,703	651	38	17.13	2	1	7/44

Test bowling by innings

	First Innings	Second Innings
Balls	2,745	1,140
Maidens	270	146
Runs	1,136	595
Wickets	51	43
Runs per 100 balls	41.38	52.19
Balls per wicket (strike rate)	53.82	26.51
Runs per wicket	22.27	13.84

Test bowling by ground

	Ov	M	Runs	Wkts	Aver
MCG	322	109	598	24	24.92
SCG	298.2	122	482	32	15.06
Oval	159	78	250	20	12.50
OT	155.2	62	216	12	18.00
Lord's	111.1	45	185	6	30.83

Analysis of 38 catches taken off Spofforth's Test bowling

Wicket keeper	7	Long stop	2
Bowler	5	Short leg	2
Point	4	Third man	2
Mid off	4	Cover point	1
Short mid on	3	Long off	1
Slips	3	Mid on	1
Long on	2	Short mid off	1

Bowling dismissals, Test by Test

SPOFFORTH'S
CAREER
STATISTICS

1876-77 MCG

A Shaw st Blackham b Spofforth	1		
G Ulyett b Spofforth	52		
T Emmett c Kendall b Spofforth	48		
J Selby		b Spofforth	2
29-6-67-3		15-3-44-1	

1878-79 MCG

G Ulyett b Spofforth	0	b Spofforth	14
AN Hornby b Spofforth	2	b Spofforth	4
VPFA Royle b Spofforth	3		
FA MacKinnon b Spofforth	0	b Spofforth	5
T Emmett c Horan b Spofforth	0		
L Hone c Blackham b Spofforth	7	b Spofforth	6
Lord Harris		c Horan b Spofforth	36
CA Absolom		c and b Spofforth	6
SS Schultz		c and b Spofforth	20
25-9-48-6		35-16-62-7	

1881-82 MCG

J Selby b Spofforth	7		
51-14-92-1		15-3-36-0	

1882 Kennington Oval

RG Barlow c AC Bannerman b Spofforth	11	b Spofforth	0
WG Grace b Spofforth	4		
G Ulyett st Blackham b Spofforth	26	c Blackham b Spofforth	11
Hon A Lyttelton c Blackham b Spofforth	2	b Spofforth	12
CT Studd b Spofforth	0		
AN Hornby b Spofforth	2	b Spofforth	9
E Peate c Boyle b Spofforth	0		
AP Lucas		b Spofforth	5
JM Read		b Spofforth	0
AG Steel		c and b Spofforth	0
36.3-18-46-7		28-15-44-7	

1882-83 MCG

CT Studd b Spofforth	0		
RG Barlow		b Spofforth	28
Hon IFW Bligh		b Spofforth	3
EFS Tylecote		b Spofforth	38
28-11-56-1		41-15-65-3	

1882-83 MCG

34-11-57-0	

1882-83 SCG

RG Barlow c Murdoch b Spofforth	38		
CFH Leslie b Spofforth	0	b Spofforth	8
W Barnes c Blackham b Spofforth	2	lbw b Spofforth	3

264

W Bates c McDonnell b Spofforth   17

CT Studd   b Spofforth   25

AG Steel   lbw b Spofforth   6

EFS Tylecote   c Bonnor b Spofforth   0

GB Studd   c Garrett b Spofforth   8

F Morley   b Spofforth   0

51-19-73-4   41.1-23-44-7

1882-83 SCG

W Barnes b Spofforth   2

AG Steel   b Spofforth   21

WW Read   b Spofforth   7

21-8-56-1   28-6-57-2

1884 Old Trafford

G Ulyett b Spofforth   5

AG Steel c Midwinter b Spofforth   15

TC O'Brien b Spofforth   0   c AC Bannerman b Spofforth   20

E Peate b Spofforth   2

R Pilling   b Spofforth   3

32-10-42-4   41-17-52-2

1884 Lord's

Lord Harris b Spofforth   4

S Christopherson c Bonnor b Spofforth   17

55.1-19-112-2

1884 Kennington Oval

W Barnes c Midwinter b Spofforth   19

Hon A Lyttelton b Spofforth   8

58-31-81-2   6-2-14-0

1884-85 SCG

A Shrewbury c and b Spofforth   18   b Spofforth   24

G Ulyett b Spofforth   2

W Barnes st Jarvis b Spofforth   0

W Flowers c Jarvis b Spofforth   24   c Evans b Spofforth   56

WH Scotton   b Spofforth   2

W Bates   c Jarvis b Spofforth   31

J Briggs   b Spofforth   1

JM Read   b Spofforth   56

48-23-54-4   48.1-22-90-6

1884-85 SCG

J Briggs c Palmer b Spofforth   3

J Hunter b Spofforth   13

A Shrewsbury   c Bonnor b Spofforth   16

WH Scotton   c Jones b Spofforth   0

W Barnes   c AC Bannerman b Spofforth   20

JM Read   c AC Bannerman b Spofforth   6

R Peel   c and b Spofforth   0   *265*

29-10-61-2   20-8-30-5

1884-85 MCG

G Ulyett b Spofforth	1
W Flowers b Spofforth	16
49-21-71-2	

1886 Old Trafford

WG Grace c Bonnor b Spofforth	8		
A Shrewsbury b Spofforth	31		
G Ulyett b Spofforth	17		
J Briggs c Garrett b Spofforth	1		
WW Read		c Jones b Spofforth	9
RG Barlow		c Palmer b Spofforth	30
53-22-82-4		29.2-13-40-2	

1886 Lord's

AG Steel lbw b Spofforth	5
RG Barlow c Palmer b Spofforth	12
G Ulyett b Spofforth	19
EFS Tylecote b Spofforth	0
56-26-73-4	

1886 Kennington Oval

WG Grace c Blackham b Spofforth	170
WW Read c Jones b Spofforth	94
J Briggs c Trumble b Spofforth	53
GA Lohmann b Spofforth	7
30.1-12-65-4	

1886-87 SCG

J Briggs		b Spofforth	33
		12-3-17-1	

Index

T. Allen